Scotland Ya

'p

Scotland Yard Casebook

The Making of the CID 1865–1935

JOAN LOCK

ROBERT HALE · LONDON

© Joan Lock 1993
First published in Great Britain 1993

ISBN 0 7090 4660 X

Robert Hale Limited
Clerkenwell House
Clerkenwell Green
London EC1R 0HT

Photoset in North Wales by
Derek Doyle & Associates, Mold, Clwyd.
Printed in Great Britain by
St Edmundsbury Press Ltd, Bury St Edmunds, Suffolk.
Bound by WBC Bookbinders Ltd, Bridgend, Mid-Glamorgan.

Contents

Illustrations

Between pages 80 and 81

Between pages 152 and 153

PICTURE CREDITS

Metropolitan Police: 1, 3, 4, 5, 6, 9, 11, 12, 13, 14, 15, 23. West Mercia Constabulary: 2. *Police Review*: 16.

Acknowledgements

Grateful thanks to Richard Sharpe and Ken Stone of the Metropolitan Police Museum for their tireless assistance and intelligent interest. Also to Mary Clucas, Librarian, Metropolitan Police Library; Robin Gillis, Metropolitan Police Archivist; Mrs Lydia Warner, Curator, West Mercia Police Museum; the staff at the Guildhall Library; The Institute of Historical Research, University of London; The British Library (Newspaper and Reference); Greater London History Library, the Public Record Office and the following public libraries: Alnwick, Finsbury, Islington Central, Shrewsbury and Westminster. Private individuals to whom I owe a particular debt are John Bunker, Arthur Fanning, Peter Lovesey, Keith Skinner and June Thomson. Finally, a thank you to my husband Bob for his help in checking the typescript and with the photographs, and patience when research material seemed about to overwhelm us.

Crown copyright material from Public Record Office files (MEPO3/79/80/87/92/93/102/104/123) is reproduced with the permission of the Controller of Her Majesty's Stationery Office. Extracts from *Hambrook of the Yard* by Walter Hambrook, are reproduced by permission of Robert Hale Ltd; *A Woman at Scotland Yard*, by Lilian Wyles, by permission of Faber & Faber Ltd; *On Top of the Underworld,* by Charles E. Leach, by permission of Little Brown & Co Ltd; *Rogues and Others* by Charles Arrow, by permission of Duckworth; and *Detective Days*, by permission of Cassell & Co Ltd and the estate of the author, Frederick Porter Wensley. Tom Divall's reminiscences are from *Scoundrels and Scallywags*, Ernest Benn, an imprint of A & C Black (Publishers) Ltd, and Maurice Moser's from *Stories from Scotland Yard* published by George Routledge & Sons Ltd.

Part I

FIRST CHANGES

1   Cry Wolf

The scene which greeted burly Detective Inspector Thomson just before Christmas 1864 was one of dreadful poverty. Not only had Ernest Southey and his common-law wife, Mrs White, been without heating, food and adequate clothing for some time but they faced the immediate prospect of losing the roof over their heads.

The detective had been sent down to see them at their Putney lodgings as the result of a letter Southey had written to the Foreign Secretary, Earl Russell, claiming he had information he wished to impart. Obviously, there was a suspicion that the man might be a crackpot with dangerous delusions. Indeed, continued privations 'and want of the ordinary necessaries of life' had, Thomson noted, brought the couple to the borders of insanity. But, in his opinion, Earl Russell could relax, for the only people they seemed likely to harm were themselves.

The 29-year-old Inspector James Jacob Thomson was an educated man by police standards at the time, and the report he submitted to his Commissioner, Sir Richard Mayne, was eloquent on the couple's 'direst misery'. Consequently, as with *A Christmas Carol*, written by Charles Dickens twenty-one years earlier, this Yuletide tale had a happy ending – at least temporarily. It must have gladdened the heart of the kindly Thomson and, to some degree made up for missing out on his own festive celebrations when, on Christmas Day, he handed Ernest Southey a gift from Earl Russell – one sovereign. Mr Southey, the detective reported back, was deeply grateful. And so he might be. The weekly wage of most police constables at the time was exactly that amount.

It transpired that Southey, who was from a respectable family and 'had the appearance of a well-educated person', had not so much information to impart but a grievance he wanted aired. He had fallen on hard times but his life had picked up after going to

13

live in Brighton and becoming a 'billiard player'. Billiards was a game popular with the upper classes and, through his expertise, Southey had not only made the acquaintance of several eminent people but also a great deal of money, playing for high stakes. On one occasion, so he claimed, he had a wager with the Honourable Dudley Ward which should have netted him £1,172 but alas, Southey alleged, Dudley Ward proved to be honourable in title only. He merely handed Southey a memo of the debt, promising to pay up the following day, then left the country.

Meanwhile, the billiard player had met Mrs White, a well-educated woman with four children, three boys and a girl, who, after leaving her husband, had attempted to support them by running a school. In this she failed, so, to feed her offspring, she had, Thomson reported, 'deviated from the path of virtue'. Nonetheless, like Southey, she possessed many testimonials to her character and her manner was 'becoming'.

Following his setback with the Hon. Dudley Ward, Southey's fortunes had faded fast. The boys were sent back to their father who ran a school in Holborn. Southey and Mrs White, unable to afford a divorce for her, set up as man and wife at a variety of lodgings. At one point they went to Worcester where Mrs White was sent to see the wealthy Lord Dudley, brother of their alleged debtor, but he refused to acknowledge any responsibility and ejected her. She summonsed him for assault, but the case was thrown out by local magistrates after Lord Dudley had publicly referred to the lady as a prostitute.

Now, smarting even more, and having exhausted the charity of friends and relatives, the couple were lodging in Putney but owed seven weeks' rent and were asking that the Earl Russell (popular with the people due to his championing of parliamentary reform and better known as Lord John Russell) act as an intermediary for them with Lord Dudley. 'Should assistance be refused,' reported Inspector Thomson, 'they have resolved to poison themselves and have written a narrative to the coroner to be read by him at the inquest on their bodies.'

On 30 December, Southey turned up at Scotland Yard where he saw the ageing and exhausted Commissioner, Sir Richard Mayne. He also wrote another long letter to Earl Russell, telling his tale and informing him that the dread means to escape their ruined and hopeless existence had already been purchased. The 72-year-old foreign secretary was one of Queen Victoria's 'two terrible old men' (the other being her Prime Minister, Lord Palmerston). Russell now exercised the same principles he employed with regard to the American Civil War and that long-running territory dispute, the Schleswig-Holstein Question – those of non-intervention. And there the matter rested. For the moment.

That year of 1864 had been one of the better ones for the Metropolitan Police, despite an increase in crime due to the cessation of transportation. The detective branch, particularly, had shone after 33-year-old Inspector Richard Tanner had dashed across the Atlantic to waylay and arrest the first railway murderer, Franz Muller, who was crossing on a slower ship.

Launched in 1842, thirteen years after the birth of the Metropolitan Police, the detective branch operated from Scotland Yard (although by now there were a few detectives out on the divisions). As well as being called in to handle difficult cases, the Scotland Yard men also went out thief catching – at the races or other social gatherings which attracted both crowds and those who preyed upon them. They remained, however, remarkably few in number. At the outset only eight had been appointed – six sergeants and two inspectors. By 1865 there were eleven – two more sergeants and one more inspector. The popularity of this select group, like that of the rest of the force, waxed and waned in line with their efficiency (or, rather, their perceived efficiency) or lack of same.

The detectives were famous not only because their names were invariably mentioned whenever their cases were reported in the newspapers (and most cases were reported in remarkable detail), but also due to the fact that the detective branch had been taken up by Charles Dickens. In 1850, he had invited several of them to his *Household Words* office, plied them with brandy and cigars and later retold, with obvious admiration and approval, their tales of pursuit and capture. They were upright men who nonetheless gave 'the impression of habitually leading lives of strong mental excitement', he told his readers. The last of Dickens' detectives, former labourer, Inspector Jonathan Whicher, said to be the most brilliant of them all, had in fact only just retired suffering from 'mental depression arising from congestion of the brain'.

Inspector Thomson was typical of the second-generation detectives, taken on as much for his education and linguistic abilities as for any thief-taking skills. Born in Turkey of a Scottish businessman father and an Italian mother of some social standing, he had been brought up to speak English, French, Italian and

Greek. His first employment had been concerned with the new science of electricity, his second, as an assistant secretary to an Indian prince. In 1855 the prince had returned to Calcutta so the following year, 'partly from choice, partly from necessity', Thomson joined the Metropolitan Police as a constable. He didn't stay long, however, leaving the following year to join the Devon Constabulary and later transferring to Hampshire.

In 1862, Sir Richard Mayne had asked him back, allowing him direct entry into the coveted ranks of the detective branch as a sergeant, and he was fast proceeding up the ladder. His knowledge of foreign languages was invaluable to a department increasingly involved in complicated extradition matters and cross-channel crime. Not only that, many of their more serious cases emanated from the simmering ranks of London's European refugees, who were forever fighting among themselves or with the natives, in between giving language lessons and plotting revolutions. (Plotters in an 1857 assassination attempt on the French Emperor had their bombs made in Birmingham and tested them in Putney until the neighbours complained.)

Ernest Southey re-entered the life of Sir Richard Mayne in April 1865, following the conclusion of the long and, for the police, disastrous, Saffron Hill Affair (of which more later). Southey had written to the Hon. Dudley Ward, who was staying in Paris, and the nobleman passed the letter on to the commissioner with the comment, 'I do not consider Mr E.W. Southey is in his right mind, or ought to be at large.'

Sir Richard scribbled the pith of his reply on the back of an envelope saying that Southey's conduct had been enquired into by police who found there were no grounds for proceedings against him either for any legal offences 'or confinement as a lunatic'.

Furthermore, although clearly the work of a man obsessed, Southey's letter was mild compared to many written by the deluded which tend to be full of wild writing, multiple exclamation marks and giant capitalizations. Most importantly, he was consistent in his claims. True, he did put forward the extraordinary premise that Lord Dudley owed his life to him because he (Southey) had had a revolver in his pocket at the time Mrs White had taken the nobleman to court for assault. He carried it for the purpose of putting an end to his own life – but that given the unfair outcome of the case he could have used it on Lord Dudley – but did not do so. The outcome of the whole business would be a matter of life and death to many he insisted. In that, he was also to remain consistent.

In mid May, Southey began writing and calling upon prominent persons such as Waterloo veteran, the Duke of Richmond, and the Tory MP and writer, Sir Edward Bulmer Lytton. Both were concerned enough to contact the commissioner. To the duke he made 'dark insinuations about some dreadful deed which he said might be averted' and to Lytton he sent in 'a long incoherent paper ... which began about shooting a nobleman and ended with his resolution to murder all his own family – of 8 persons'. Mayne placated them as he had the Hon. Dudley Ward.

Astoundingly, Southey even found his way into the presence of the second of Queen Victoria's 'terrible old men' (but people's favourite), the 81-year-old Prime Minister, Lord Palmerston. Southey had again sent in a paper. Early in his career Palmerston had survived an assassination attempt by an insane lieutenant, but this event seemed to have taught him and his staff very little about the need for security precautions. 'I thought it wise to ask your messenger some questions,' wrote Palmerston, to Sir Richard Mayne, 'for the papers had been sent up to me while I was dressing for dinner with a statement that they had been sent to me by you. But when the person who brought them came into the room he proved to be Mr Southey.'

However, Palmerston found Southey, 'very gentlemanly and quiet mannered but evidentially deranged'. Sir Richard should send for him to find out who the nobleman was whose life Southey threatened. 'Mr Southey said the nobleman is a friend of mine, who acts from impulse and makes many enemies.' The Prime Minister also felt proper measures should be made to put Southey's family under protection.

As advised, Sir Richard saw Southey (who had many times called on him but usually been refused admittance) and gave him a strong warning about all these threats. He informed the Prime Minister that he was satisfied that it was not desirable to take proceedings but hoped he (the Prime Minister) would not see Southey again if he called. Shortly after, an Inspector Moran of A Division reported having to turn Ernest Southey away from the peers entrance of the House of Lords where he had been trying to hand letters to the Duke of Richmond and the Earl of Westmoreland.

Following these incidents, Southey again dropped out of sight. Such people, not quite sane, perhaps, but not quite insane either, full of plots and threats, have always been a constant police problem. Too many, and mostly too harmless, to be locked away, but a niggling worry nonetheless. Perhaps one of Mayne's detectives or even an ordinary constable, accustomed to meeting such people daily, would have been better able to discern the level of Southey's desperation. Possibly Mayne felt in his heart that Southey might have a genuine grievance. Certainly, he had not deviated from his line of complaint at any time, whereas many of the mentally disturbed seem to have armies of enemies and oceans of obsessions.

In any case, the increasingly autocratic commissioner, at sixty-nine almost worn out by a lifetime's often unappreciated toil, forming and sustaining his force, had many more things to worry about than just one persistent nutter among many. Children throwing snowballs or bowling hoops to the annoyance of pedestrians, for example. He was becoming something of a figure of fun and exasperation due, partly, to his increasing tendency to concern himself with all such matters, though these were not always as trivial as they seemed. The children's hoops, for example, were large and made of iron. But one of his problems was his inability to delegate – even the approving of detective's expenses and the direct control of their cases.

It was, perhaps, fortunate for him that he was away in Portsmouth when the dreadful news came in. On 10 August 1865, Superintendent Searle of E Division reported that a triple murder had been committed at the Star Coffee House, 21 Red Lion Street, Holborn. The victims were three little boys aged ten, eight, and six years, who had been found dead in bed – apparently poisoned. Two nights previously, a man, about thirty-five years old, had brought them to the coffee house and stayed there with them. On the second night, however, he had merely seen them to bed, promising to return the following morning. He did not appear and neither did the boys for their breakfast. When their rooms were unlocked they were found dead but, 'very placid as if they had not struggled'. The youngest, reported Superintendent Searle, had a penny between his groins 'no doubt given him by his murderer'.

At first, the police had no clue as to the identity of either the victims or the murderer. They circulated the man's description: five foot seven inches, with dark complexion and hair, dark grey eyes, no whiskers but a beard of several days growth. He had been wearing dark clothes 'much worn', a buttoned-up waistcoat and a 'scarf, black and shabby (no pin)'. They also initiated enquiries at coffee and lodging houses, and boats leaving for America – a favourite bolthole.

Detective Inspector Tanner was sent post-haste from the Yard by cab and was busy with the grisly business of taking a description of the boys when a 64-year-old Mr Saltwood White appeared and saved him the trouble. They were his sons, he said, or at least he was 'the reputed father'. His second and much younger wife had left him several years earlier to go off with her paramour, Ernest Southey, 'a Billiard Marker'. The boys had later been returned to him but his school hadn't been doing too well lately, so, when Southey offered to take them off his hands so that they could go to a new life in Australia with their mother, he had consented. They had been handed over to Southey two days earlier, just around the corner – by White's eldest son from his first large family because he couldn't bring himself to do it.

Unfortunately for the boys, Mrs White had left Southey six weeks earlier, taking her daughter, Annie, with her, an event which, Tanner learned, had badly affected him. When last seen, he had been 'in great distress of mind'. Tanner hastened back to the Yard to fetch Detective Inspector Williamson who could identify Southey and give further descriptive details. They arranged for the printing of £100 Reward notices. Superintendent Searle admitted to Assistant Commissioner Captain Hayes, that they had no clue as to Southey's whereabouts, but added, 'I fancy he cannot get away, every precaution has been taken to guard against his doing so.'

Alas, a man who had so easily tricked his way into the unguarded presence of the country's leading statesman was to find no difficulty in leaving London. Consequently, when Tanner filed an update detective officer's special report the following day, he was obliged to add a melancholy postscript: 'A telegram has just been received stating that "Southey" is in custody at Ramsgate having murdered Mrs White and the little girl alluded to.'

Tanner caught the first available train to Ramsgate where he discovered that, as well as altering his appearance with the aid of a false beard and moustache, Southey had drastically altered his *modus operandi*. No gentle poison for the females but sudden and violent death at close range with bullets to the head from a new, five-barrelled, revolver.

There was to be one final twist to this terrible tale. The Yard received a report that a few weeks earlier, a woman by the name of

White whose husband was a schoolmaster in Holborn, had left a little girl in the care of a Mrs Petty at 2 Cornelia Cottages, Lavender Road, Battersea – before leaving for Australia.

It was Inspector Thomson, in at the start of the affair six months earlier, to whom the final surprise was first revealed. He hurried over the river to Battersea where he saw Mrs Petty and Annie Elizabeth White, 'an exceedingly intelligent little girl of about 7 years of age'. Her mother, Mrs White, had indeed left for Melbourne more than two weeks earlier, sending lots of loving messages to her daughter promising an early reunion. Southey had turned up ten days later, enquired of the whereabouts of Mrs White, and tried to take Annie Elizabeth away with him. Fortunately, he was resisted on both counts by Mrs Petty and went away 'saying something very dreadful would shortly happen'.

Who, then, were the dead woman and child at Ramsgate? They were his real wife, Mary Forward (Forward being Southey's real name), and 8-year-old daughter Emily, whom he had left several years earlier to go off with Mrs White.

The Ramsgate coroner refused to release the prisoner to Scotland Yard and he was committed for trial for the murder of his wife and daughter only – despite many costly messages by electric telegraph back and forth between a beleaguered Tanner and the Yard. 'One of police to be at the trial and, if acquitted, apprehend Southey', noted Mayne on the papers. The privilege went to Tanner, who had no need to fulfil those instructions. Southey was found guilty of the murder of his wife and child and was duly hanged at Maidstone gaol shortly before midday on 11 January 1866. By then, Palmerston was dead, Earl Russell was Prime Minister again, Lord Dudley had a new bride, and war was once again looming over the Schleswig-Holstein Question.

> A rather curious incident occurred at the moment of execution [*The Times* reported]. At the very instant the snow, which was falling in large flakes, had arrested the minute hand of the clock, and the execution consequently took place before the appointed hour had struck. By rather curious coincidence the town clock outside the courthouse, in the High-street, also stopped at the same time, and from the same cause.

The Saffron Hill Affair, played out between the Yard's initial contacts with Southey and his final descent into madness and murder, began with a pub brawl between English and Italian workmen on Boxing Night, 1864. During the affray, at the Golden

Anchor in Saffron Hill, general dealer, Michael Harrington, received terrible knife wounds to his abdomen from which he later died. On his death bed he identified his assailant as glass-silverer Serafini Pelizzoni. The identification was confirmed by several eyewitnesses who had seen the incident at close quarters in a room unusually well-lit for the time, illuminated as it was by gaslight. A straightforward affair. No need even to call in the detectives. Violent pub brawls were commonplace, particularly in Clerkenwell's Saffron Hill, considered one of the worst areas in London. (Oliver Twist, who followed the Artful Dodger down Saffron Hill to reach Fagin's den, thought he had never seen a dirtier nor more wretched place). On 3 February 1865, Pelizzoni, was found guilty of the murder and duly sentenced to death. An open and shut case.

But Italian/English businessman, Henry Negretti (co-founder of the optical firm, Negretti and Zambra), did not see it that way. Some disturbing rumours had been circulating among Clerkenwell's Italian community to the effect that police had arrested the wrong man and Negretti began a campaign to throw doubt on the verdict. More than that, he tracked down the alleged right man, the accused's cousin, Gregorio Mogni, in Birmingham and prevailed upon him to confess.

A weird train of events was thus set in motion. Pelizzoni was granted a stay of execution which enabled him to give evidence at the trial of Mogni, who was found guilty of manslaughter of the same victim and sentenced to five years penal servitude (he had pleaded self-defence). This resulted not in an acquittal for Pelizzoni, only a continuing stay of execution. Two other men had been knifed that night and as both factions agreed that there had been only one knifeman, it followed that he must have committed all three acts. The police, convinced that they had arrested the right man in the first place, now charged Pelizzoni with the attempted murder of one of the other victims, the potboy, Alfred Rebbeck. He had been stabbed in the side but, after giving *his* dying declaration and identification of Pelizzoni, had recovered.

Among accusations that the police had been withholding evidence was a claim that the third stabbed man (injured only in the hand) had, at one point, expressed some doubts about Pelizzoni being the attacker. In the event, the accused (who had requested a mixed jury but settled for British only after being told that no foreigners had been called for service but he could have one if he was prepared to wait) was found not guilty of the attempted murder and released.

Not surprisingly, this succession of events caused a sensation. The outcome of what was now popularly known as The Saffron Hill Affair shared the leader columns on an equal basis with the latest news from America – the fall of Richmond, the confederate capital, after the long siege. This, together with the surrender of General Lee just before the start of the trial and the assassination of President Lincoln as it progressed, heralded the end of the American Civil War.

The leader writers tried to be diplomatically even-handed about the Civil War but there was no hiding the fact that we were inclined to be pro-South. One leader excused us in this by saying that we always tended to side with the underdog. Similarly, it was claimed, this explained the British jury's final treatment of Pelizzoni. There was, however, a general rounding on the police, whose behaviour had been consistently attacked by the defence, in spite of the judge having stated that he saw no evidence of deliberate police wrong-doing in any of the proceedings. Only *The Times* came up with what, at this distance, looks like a healthy scepticism. As that paper pointed out, it was clear that one side was lying, hugely. The question was, which one? It was by no means certain. Indeed, it was perfectly possible that the Italian community had merely thought up a clever ruse to save one of its own – there had been similar doubts in the case of a German, Carl Franz, accused of murder a couple of years earlier.

But the most interesting aspect of the case from the point of view of this book is that the landlord of the Golden Anchor was Frederick Shaw, previously a Metropolitan Police detective. Shaw was held to have been in dispute with the Italians over unpaid bills and was said to have injured their pride by having them ejected. It had been admitted that in the opening stages of the fracas he was slapped in the face by an Italian. (One contemporary anonymous letter to Scotland Yard even claimed that Shaw's wife had previously been Pelizzoni's fiancée – but when the Italian was visiting his homeland Shaw had stepped in, married the girl, left the police, and taken over the pub which had been run by her parents. But I have been unable, thus far, to find proof of this.) But, certainly, one recurring premise was that, on the fatal night, it had been ex-detective Shaw, not Harrington, who had been the intended victim.

2 'Quite a Road Murder'

The first policemen to walk Shropshire's leafy lanes were known as Paddy Mayne's Grasshoppers. This quaint title evolved because their Chief Constable, Captain Dawson Mayne RN (the younger brother of Sir Richard Mayne), was an Irishman, their uniforms were of rifle-green and the local feeling was that they were always popping up where they were least expected.

Like most of Britain in the mid nineteenth century, beautiful Shropshire was riven with unrest, due to high unemployment and subsequent poverty, and further aggravated by resentment over the lack of county and borough representation in Parliament. Election riots were commonplace, occurring even in such rustic places as Church Stretton and the quaint, half-timbered, Much Wenlock. Gangs of navvies in the area, building the ever-expanding railways, added to the turbulence – particularly on pay nights. Nonetheless, the Shropshire County Police Committee begrudged every penny spent on its tiny force and was proud that their county police rate, at less than a penny in the pound, was the lowest in the land.

They got their come-uppance in 1858, when the Home Office refused them the grant, which had become due under the provisions of a new county and borough police bill, because the force was 'greatly lacking in numbers'. The committee hurriedly took on another twenty-six men but declined to act on the suggestion that they employ a detective officer to handle the more serious crimes, despite the fact that their detection rate was one of the lowest in the country. They could, the committee declared, always borrow a detective, if necessary, from London or elsewhere.

Consequently, at 10 a.m. on Sunday, 21 January 1866, Detective Inspector Richard Tanner left London *en route* for Wolverhampton to give assistance, in attempting to unravel the mystery of the murder of Edward Edwards at Duddlewick, near Bridgnorth. Paddy Mayne had retired in 1859 and his successor, another Irishman, had given up after five years. Now in charge was Lieutenant-Colonel Edward Burgoyne Cureton, veteran of the Crimean and Kaffir Wars which had been as nothing to the 1865 riot in Market Drayton – at least for unequal odds. There, twenty unarmed policemen had faced a stone-throwing mob of five hundred and the military had had to be called in. After fifteen months Cureton, too, had had enough, and, by the time he asked for the services of a London detective, he was already serving out his notice.

There was no point in Tanner coming to him at Shrewsbury, he informed Sir Richard Mayne, as it would be a long way around, 'and I cannot give him more information than he would receive at Bridgnorth'. It would be best if the detective inspector got a train to Wolverhampton, then took a trap for the remaining 14 miles.

Cureton professed himself delighted that he was being sent 'an officer of such high repute', but this Shropshire case must have given the inspector a nasty feeling of *déjà vu*. There were so many similarities to the Kent case at the village of Road in Wiltshire six years earlier, which had cost the reputation of his famous colleague, Detective Inspector Jonathan Whicher. (Whicher had immediately suspected that Constance Kent, the daughter of the house, had murdered her young half-brother and had arrested her, but she had quickly been set free amid vitriolic condemnation of the detective from both press and public which had blighted his remaining career. In April, 1865, Constance Kent came forward to confess but, by then, Whicher had retired.) One thing the experience had taught Tanner was that the local policemen would not be quite so thrilled by his arrival as their chief claimed to be.

The venue of the Shropshire murder had a name that might have sprung from a children's book, Duddlewick, but the murder which occurred there was a particularly terrible one. The victim was 18-year-old Edward Edwards, an orphan living with his uncle, Mr John Meredith, a farmer and miller. Duddlewick is a hamlet about 8 miles from Bridgnorth, which remains today, peaceful, sylvan, and remote. On the morning of Sunday, 14 January, at about 8 a.m., the boy had gone down to his uncle's mill, set two hundred yards below the farm, to feed some pigs and a horse. He was not seen again until 4 p.m. when a search party found him in the mill, unconscious, and with twenty dreadful wounds to the head, one of them causing a piece of bone to be driven into the protruding brain. There were numerous defensive injuries to the hands. The weapons used to inflict these wounds were probably a heavy stick and a sharp-edged blacksmith's punch found at the scene and it was evident by the horrific, bloodsoaked scene that the boy had put up tremendous resistance. He died the following morning without regaining consciousness.

The suspicions of the Shropshire Constabulary focused quite quickly on a farm labourer by the name of James Childe. He had been in the Duddlewick area, without money, on the Saturday before the murder, but had arrived at a Bridgnorth public house, not short of money, on the following day. Robbery was thought to be a motive because the uncle claimed he had not yet received the mill's weekly takings. Moreover, Childe's white linen 'slop', or smock, was bloodstained and, on being quizzed about this by the observant landlord, he claimed he had been in a fight. The following day Childe went off to buy some moleskin trousers, getting rid of those he had been wearing. When other customers began discussing the crime which was causing such a sensation locally, Childe upped and left, expressing no interest, saying he was off on the road to the Black Country to look for work. The landlord told the police at Bridgnorth of his suspicions and a Sergeant Cox, 'wearing private clothes', set off in hot pursuit.

The plain-clothed sergeant found that his quarry had stopped for a drink at every public house *en route* to Wolverhampton where, in yet another public house, he arrested Childe on the Tuesday morning. The suspect, however, had an alibi. When he was brought before the magistrates at Cleobury Mortimer, witnesses came forward to say that, throughout the morning in question, Childe had been sleeping off the drink in a pub barn 8½ miles from the mill. Much to the disappointment of the public, the police lost interest in Childe. One could hardly blame them, they had their hands full trying to enforce the stringent new livestock movement regulations brought in to help stem the spread of a cattle plague raging through the country. Despite having such a small police force to operate them, Shropshire had brought in the most stringent regulations in the country, after Berkshire.

As so often happened when Yard men were called out to assist other forces, by the time Detective Inspector Tanner reached the scene the trail was cold, the story had been much gone over and elaborated on and the alibis were, by now, engraved in stone. This was particularly the case when the crime took place in a tight-knit community where everyone knew everyone else – as in the Kent case – and now that of Edward Edwards. Another familiar problem was the size and complexity of the victim's household. This one was not so large as many of the day, certainly not that of the Kents but, typically, included servants and variously related children. All the household, again typically, relied on the master of the house for their livelihood and well-being.

In this instance, there were living in the house: 21-year-old Mary Meredith, cousin of the deceased and niece of the householder John Meredith; servant, Elizabeth Harris, aged 25; her brother, Samuel Harris, aged 14, who worked as 'cowboy', and 18-year-old Timothy Fletcher who was learning the miller's trade and assisted Edward Edwards at the mill. Not resident, but on the scene much of the time were various farm workers (always referred to as servants and they, in turn, referred to their employer as 'my master'). These included John Corfield, who lived close by, and William Barker, whose wife, Eliza, came in to do Mr Meredith's washing – as in the Kent case, the laundry was to be subject to scrutiny. Tanner wrote later in his case report:

> At the commencement of the enquiry I endeavoured to ascertain what motive could exist for any person to murder the deceased, and I could find none. He was a poor boy (an orphan) solely dependent on his uncle John Meredith since seven years old. Was dressed in cord trousers and old clothes and not likely to attract the attention of any tramp, or stranger as being worth robbing. He was not entitled to any property, neither was it known that the deceased had quarrelled with any person as would be likely to commit such a crime. Duddlewick is a very small village and a stranger would almost sure to have been observed on the morning in question, but none was seen.

The detective inspector was a lively man, and a favourite of Sir Richard Mayne. One feels that he may have raised a rare smile from the old commissioner when he had the temerity to claim expenses not only for refreshment for the cabbie, who took him about on the day the bodies of the first Southey victims had been discovered, but for his horse as well. When challenged about this, Tanner wrote unequivocally, 'The driver required refreshment and so did the horse, being engaged 11 hours, and he did this to oblige us, as he could have finished the hiring at any time which would have seriously inconvenienced us.'

Tanner now turned his attentions to the Meredith household which soon yielded a very likely suspect: John Meredith, the boy's uncle who, Tanner surmised, had probably done the deed in a fit of passion after losing his self control. He came to this conclusion, he wrote to Sir Richard Mayne:

... from his manner when I spoke to him on the case, and his conduct throughout on the day of the murder which I found to be as follows: He got up about 9 o'clock, had his breakfast, and went out, returning in about ½ an hour. On his return, Mary Meredith enquired of him if 'Ted', meaning deceased, was coming home to his breakfast. He replied 'I don't know, I have been down to the mill but I cannot see anything of him, give me my coat and vest, and a cup of ale, I shall go to church.'

Now, the uncle knew well that the deceased should have brought his books from the mill to the house on that morning as was the custom every Sunday morning for the purpose of settling, before going to church, yet not seeing him he went to church exhibiting no anxiety about deceased. And did he go to the mill as he said he had? If he did, he must have seen deceased, because one thing is certain the deceased was found locked in the mill, the key put in its usual place, viz over the mill door. Then what is the conduct of the uncle when he returns from church at 1 p.m? The servant Elizabeth Harris expresses uneasiness about deceased his not having been home to his breakfast, and now not come home to his dinner, a circumstance that was not known before; the uncle then leaves, was gone about ½ hour, returns, said he had been to the mill could see nothing of deceased and adds this (in my opinion) extraordinary remark, 'but as the wind is blowing high he might have fell into the brook but we may as well have dinner and then, I will get William Dorrell (meaning neighbour) to go with me, and see if we can track his footsteps'.

This conduct seemed strange, Tanner went on, because if he really thought his nephew had fallen in the brook, surely the most natural thing to do was to go to look in the brook *before* having dinner but, even more extraordinary, was the fact that the uncle *never goes to look in the mill* ... but he appears to have diverted Dorrell's attention from the mill to the brook, even saying, when Dorrell suggested looking in the mill, 'but he carries the key'.

In fact, the key was found in its usual place over the mill door, by Sam the 14-year-old servant. Even then, Meredith's behaviour was suspect, thought Tanner, *'for instead of immediately proceeding to the mill he asks for and has a cup of ale, and smokes his pipe for nearly an hour* and then went and found the deceased insensible and nearly dead'.

Tanner had ascertained that there had been a lot of friction between the boy and his uncle due to the careless way the lad did the books. This had led to frequent quarrels.

My theory of the case is that on the Sunday morning in question the uncle who is passionate, went to the mill, saw some further neglect in the books, probably struck him with a stick which was found broken alongside the deceased then finding perhaps that he had gone too far (as the deceased was also known to be very passionate, might have threatened proceedings) then he lost all control of himself and murdered the lad.

The difficulty was – to prove it. There was a great deal of blood on the middle and lower floors of the mill, on the murder weapons, on the mill account book, and, most probably, on the clothes of the murderer. (There were even bloody fingerprints on the mill stairs but, of course, these were no good to anyone.) Tanner must have come to his conclusions quite rapidly – doubtless aided by local suspicions – because on the day after his arrival the Chief Constable was writing to Sir Richard that the London detective had recommended that Meredith's clothes should be sent to the capital 'for analysis' and sending Sergeant Cox off to deliver them.

When Cox arrived at the Yard Inspector Thomson begged to mention the name of a Dr Letheby of the London Hospital for the analysis but Mayne consulted an expert friend who, while acknowledging that Letheby was no doubt highly qualified, recommended Professor Alfred Swaine Taylor in preference to any other medical authority. Taylor was the most famous forensic scientist of his day but his reputation had suffered some severe setbacks most notably in the Smethhurst case of 1859 when his mistakes while testing for arsenic caused the suspect, ultimately, to be granted a free pardon.

Forces beyond Taylor's control were already influencing the outcome of his report. For example, the clothes had not been obtained from the suspect until five days after the murder and in a quite casual manner allowing Meredith to offer only what he had been wearing that day. Fortunately, Sergeants Cox and Christie had independently picked up a pair of bloodstained trousers from by his bedside. 'There were upwards of twenty spots of blood upon the right leg of the trousers,' Sergeant Christie told the reconvened inquest jury.

Meredith claimed that the staining had occurred when he was helping to carry the dying boy from the mill to the house. The sergeants also retrieved a second overcoat from a peg in the lobby which appeared to have a lot of blood spots on it.

'I was examining them with a glass,' said Sergeant Christie, 'when Mr John Meredith said, "You can't surely detect blood after it's washed?" The coat appeared to have been sponged.'

'We can,' Sergeant Cox had told him.

A shirt had also been sent to London for analysis. When the servant, Elizabeth Harris, had claimed not to know whether her master had worn it that day, Mary Meredith had stepped forward to assure police he had.

At least, the resumed inquest was not being held in Meredith's farm where its proceedings had begun, but just down the road at the Cock Inn, in the nearest village, Stottesden. Tanner asked that very little evidence be taken on this occasion and that the inquest be soon adjourned. He was supported in this by the local magistrates but the coroner refused to comply. (The early detective police had experience of being caught in the power struggle between London magistrates and coroners. But even the most persistent thorn in their flesh, the coroner, Thomas Wakley MP, had realized how much aid and comfort, not to say, vital information as to the police case so far, a guilty man could glean from an inquest hearing and had tried to limit damage done by witnesses' utterances.) This Duddlewick case had already been much chewed over at the Childe hearings but this did not influence the coroner's decision.

Although Tanner was present at the inquest hearing, the *Shrewsbury Chronicle* advised its readers, 'he took no part in the proceedings'. The evidence was produced by Shropshire's Superintendent McWilliam. Also keeping a watching brief, on behalf of Mr John Meredith, was solicitor, Mr R.O. Backhouse, who had actually changed sides. 'In the first place I appeared for the police,' he admitted to the coroner. 'Since then, however, in consequence of what has been rumoured abroad, I told the police that if a certain course were pursued, I should appear on behalf of Mr Meredith and the family.' And very useful to Mr Meredith his inside knowledge must have been.

Mr Backhouse proceeded to question evidence, virtually cross-examine witnesses and even correct the coroner, telling him in one instance that a witness had already answered a question but, in any case, 'a boy like that is not likely to observe time accurately'. He even tried to put words into witnesses' mouths,

'Don't you think that stick belongs to a stranger?' he asked mill servant, Timothy Fletcher, who had already said he did not recognize it. Finally, he introduced another possible suspect – a boy named Thomas Childe (Childe was a common local surname) who had left Meredith's employ because he was suffering from a skin disease. Meanwhile, police struggled on, unrepresented, although the coroner (actually 'Deputy Coroner' A.P. Trow, which might have been part of the problem) did deign to ask them at one point whether they had any questions. They whispered one to him which enquired whether any stranger had been seen about that morning.

The situation almost exactly mirrored that which had defeated Inspector Whicher in the Kent case, except that it had been in a magistrates court where the unrepresented police, and particularly the London detective, had been put at such an unfair disadvantage when a gentleman of the law hijacked the proceedings. At least, Tanner was not made to look a villain as Whicher had been, but there is no doubt he saw the danger signs.

Backhouse did not get it all his own way. The mill servant, Timothy Fletcher, deposed that the deceased and his uncle were talking loudly about 'Mr Hyde's grysts' at the mill on the evening previous to the murder and that the boy's face had been flushed. Barker agreed with Backhouse that Edward's face would have been flushed if he had been lifting bags, 'but he was talking to Mr Meredith when I saw him'.

Three days later, Inspector Tanner was writing disconsolately to Sir Richard in a manner reminiscent of Whicher's beleaguered messages from Road:

> ... tomorrow I lay before the bench of maigistrates a report of the particulars obtained, and no doubt they will grant a warrant for the apprehension of the person I suspect. I feel convinced I am on the right track, but the Coroner, as usual, has so thwarted me, and the magistrates, that I am afraid the witnesses for the prosecution (who are all personal friends of Stephenson) I suspect have been tampered with. A full report will be made but I am now very much pressed for time.

The magistrates did, indeed, issue a warrant for the arrest of Meredith although Tanner who seems to have been determined to be negative about the outcome, warned them that although he was convinced of the miller's guilt there was little hope of conviction. There may have been a touch of self-justification there.

'Detective Tanner regrets that he was not sent for earlier,' announced the *Shrewsbury Chronicle* when describing the arrest and first hearing. 'There was a desire on the part of the Shropshire police to arrest Mr Meredith a week ago, but the magistracy, through the Chief Constable, having sent to Sir Richard Mayne for a detective, was determined to postpone this step until such an officer had been upon the spot.' The newspaper then went on to demonstrate just what Tanner was up against by going all over the police case again and ending up giving Meredith a splendid character reference.

Against the supposition that Mr Meredith is guilty of this fearful crime is the fact which is well known in the district in which he lives, that he is of a kind, hospitable, and charitable disposition, ever-ready in purse and person to prove a good Samaritan to his needy neighbours. Of the deceased he was extremely fond, and had cherished him from the age of six, since which time he had been to him as his son, and we are assured that in the spirit of that affection Mr Meredith, who is a man of considerable property, has in his will left to his nephew the mill in which he was so cruelly murdered. It is easy to conceive that, though Detective Tanner recommended the arrest of Mr Meredith, yet that he does not express confidence that the evidence at present forthcoming is sufficient to prove in an assize court that Mr Meredith took the life of his nephew. Mystery, he believes, will long hang over this even as it hung over the Road murder.

The Scotland Yard man decided that this was a good moment to make his exit, leaving the further prosecution of the case in the hands of Superintendent McWilliam and the Shropshire County Police. 'The magistrates and also Col. Cureton all consider the prisoner to be guilty,' he advised Sir Richard, 'but see the difficulty of getting any evidence.'

Sergeant Cox did his best at the next magistrate's court hearing and caused a sensation by pointing out that the bloodstains on Meredith's trousers 'corresponded' with those on the mill walls and that others who carried the body had no stains of blood whatever on them. The defence counsel, Mr C.R. Kennedy, a well-known barrister (though one in bad odour due to a sex scandal), declared the evidence to be of so weak and shadowy a character that he was sure the magistrates would think another hearing unnecessary. They agreed, and discharged the prisoner.

Subsequently, the *Shrewsbury Chronicle*, possibly now

becoming aware of the error of its partisan ways, noted after the inquest resumed again that:

> The police authorities present seemed to be labouring under a great disadvantage, and were evidently not a little disappointed at being unassisted by a legal gentleman to represent the county. As we understand the assistance described was not forthcoming because the civil authorities of Shropshire believe that they have no fund out of which to provide such help to their police force during preliminary inquiries before magistrates, or at inquests.

Back to money again.

Superintendent McWilliam now asked for an inquest adjournment because, he said, if the inquest were terminated they would have nowhere to present the additional evidence they were in the process of acquiring and nowhere for Professor Taylor to give evidence. For, surprisingly enough, although the magistrates had had Taylor's analytical report, the professor himself had not been called to the stand. The problem, once again, seems to have been funds – who was going to pay his expenses? He would only be required if the case against Meredith went to trial, it had been decided.

Meredith's solicitor, Mr Backhouse, vigorously opposed the idea of another adjournment but the coroner, who also appears to have suddenly become more aware of his duty, was in favour of granting one. He consulted his jury who said they objected to spending yet another market day in the court – it would have been different if Professor Taylor had been there with something fresh, the foreman pointed out. A non-market day date was fixed, and as the room was being cleared, the coroner said, 'It is quite a Road murder.' He then gave instructions to Sergeant Cox to take *all* Mr Meredith's garments, including his recently discovered leather-leggings and the sheet used for carrying the boy, to Professor Taylor in London.

When Taylor finally appeared at the resumed inquest on Friday, 23 March, 1866, police were at last assisted by a solicitor, Mr J.J. Peele, while Mr Kennedy again looked on for Meredith. Mr Trow, newly wary, reminded Mr Kennedy that only he, the coroner, could cross-examine. Mr Kennedy agreed that technically this was so but pointed out that in Birmingham it was not unusual in important cases and where information was likely to be elicited, for the coroners to allow … This time, however, Mr Trow was not intimidated by suggestions about what went on in more sophisticated places and insisted on reserving the right for himself. Questions could be put *through* him, he pointed out.

Taylor's reports told of finding fresh bloodstains on the first trousers and shirt, none on the first overcoat, but one on the second coat – by means of chemical and microscopic examination. He was pleased to tell the jury that he had sent portions of the clothing to a qualified gentleman in the North of England, 'who was kept ignorant of the matter now under investigation' and he had come to the same conclusions.

Were the blood stains animal or human, asked the coroner? Ah, there was the rub. There was no way of telling confessed Taylor, 'in the present state of science'. The blood of a rabbit or a hare was particularly like that of a human, Taylor had to admit.

A new witness, a journeyman miller who had done some work for Meredith since the murder (he may have been a police plant, certainly Meredith suspected he was) deposed that he had noticed that the farmer always grasped the stairs with his left hand as he was climbing them, his hand going to exactly the same spot as where the bloody fingermarks were found. He also described how Meredith, who had claimed Edward had been 'an artful young dog' who would have resisted as long as he was able to rise, had given him a graphic account of how the boy might have defended himself against the blows rained on him.

Edward's half brother, a Bridgnorth butcher, recalled an even more chilling account of the way the boy's uncle had talked him through the murder. 'Here it commenced ... they had a deuce of a fight here ... He knocked him down here, and then he knocked him against here; here is blood and hair, you see ... He caught hold of the chains (for lifting flour bags) ... Here he laid on him with a stick to make him loose causing the marks on his hands ... ' and so on. First honed on policemen the tale had now obviously become Meredith's party piece.

Nonetheless, the jury brought in a verdict of murder by persons unknown, and the case was over. Not a sparkling performance by Tanner although he got a commendation out of it after Cureton assured Sir Richard that the officer had done his best to clear up the mystery – 'and gave every satisfaction to the magistrates by his reports and advice'. More to the point, he had avoided being burned at the stake like Whicher.

3 *And the Queen Cried*

Shortly after Detective Inspector Tanner returned to London, Queen Victoria opened Parliament for the first time since the death of Prince Albert five years earlier. PC Harvey James Lee, who was deputed to walk alongside her carriage, later recalled that the Queen was in tears during most of the journey from Buckingham Palace. 'She had become very unpopular and as we passed down The Mall there were hisses' (the *People*, 1926).

The Liberal government, whose bill she was to present (although not actually read), did not survive for long. The new Prime Minister, Lord John Russell, who had introduced the first Parliamentary Reform Bill in 1831 and had attempted to extend the franchise in 1852, now tried again, on behalf of the boroughs and counties, but was defeated. His government resigned, he retired, and the Reform League decided to hold a huge public demonstration in Hyde Park. The Home Secretary promptly banned it, the League went ahead, trouble-making mobs joined in and battle ensued. The military had to be called out and the blame for the ensuing 'Bloody Sunday' was, of course, put squarely on Mayne and the police – despite the fact that it was they who had suffered the most terrible injuries.

The year 1866 also saw Prussia declare war on Austria over the Schleswig-Holstein question and an attempt on the life of Tsar Alexander II which resulted in the resumption of reactionary policies. All was not gloom, however. The US Senate and Chamber passed the Civil Rights Bill (Negroes) and the Queensberry Rules were drawn up to curtail brutality in boxing. What was to prove not so good, from the point of view of the Metropolitan Police, was the fact that, in that same year, a Scotsman, Sergeant John Meiklejohn, was seconded to the detective branch.

Several days before PC Lee had accompanied the Queen on her

miserable journey to Parliament, he and his colleagues began searching premises on her route for 'Fenian and other Irish agitators' who might be about to commit one of their 'outrages'. Problems with them had increased as arms and expertise gained by Irish Americans began filtering over here with the ending of the US Civil War. 'Fenian' activities were about to escalate but, fortunately for the British Police, so was their flow of information from highly-placed informers.

Early the following year, Fenians failed in their attempt to raid the arsenal at Chester Castle and, soon after, one of their leaders was arrested in Manchester. His compatriots rescued him, murdering a policeman in the process. By September 1867 the effects of the Irish unrest were being felt in London. A military bandsman was shot as he strolled home through Bloomsbury Square after a concert and one of the motives mooted was that his attackers thought him to be a Fenian informer being guarded by plain clothes detectives.

Detective Inspector Thomson arrested a Fenian sympathizer for the murder but the case fell through when it was demonstrated in court that the bullet extracted from the bandsman's wound would not go through the barrel of the suspect's pistol, even though it had fitted in the chamber. Thomson fared better when he succeeded in arresting the second most-wanted Fenian leader, Captain Burke, and his aide, Casey, while *they* were out walking in Bloomsbury. This arrest did wonders for the reputation of Inspector Thomson and the Metropolitan Police but their luck ran out when an attempt to rescue Thomson's prisoners from Clerkenwell Prison with the aid of explosives led to the death of several members of the public. Mayne, who had been warned of the rescue scheme, was much vilified for his failure to prevent the explosion, and offered to resign. The Home Office castigated him but declined to accept. A year later, on Boxing Day 1868, Mayne died and his burden passed temporarily into the hands of Colonel Labalmondiere, one of his two assistant commissioners, to whom little work of importance had previously been delegated.

Following the Clerkenwell outrage, the department was swamped with rumours of more planned bombings, which it dared not ignore. Fortunately, there were few murder cases needing their attention that year. Among those which did take place, were a stabbing in a common lodging house in Deptford from which the suspect immediately fled leaving no trace, and a wife-beating murder in Spitalfields, which was handled by the local uniform branch. The latter was so brutal that the magistrate strongly recommended that police be given legal aid.

By contrast, the following year, 1869, got off to a bloody start and the momentum was maintained throughout. Almost all the violence centred on the East End of London, the scene of great deprivation following a slump brought about by over-speculation. The curtain raiser occurred on a Saturday night in February when five men threw an employee of the Imperial Gas Works, one Samuel Grockett, into the Regent's Canal, close by the Cat and Mutton Bridge in Hackney. When fished out, he was dead.

Reward bills were issued but Detective Sergeant Mulvaney, who was told to look into the matter after it had featured in the newspapers, held out little hope of catching the culprits, despite the existence of several witnesses. None could remember what the suspects looked like or how they were dressed, or even whether they were young or old.

'This is attributable to the fact that they were all more or less under the influence of drink at the time,' reported Mulvaney when backing up the local uniformed inspector's report. 'The neighbourhood is a very low one, and on Saturday night particularly a great deal of drunkenness exists. There is also no doubt that the deceased man had been drinking freely.' (PC Lee was to recall what an ordeal chucking out time (midnight) had been for constables after the Saturday night drinking orgies in these districts.)

Witnesses were able to remember what the suspect looked like in another case – but then he was an Irish American and, according to the *Illustrated Police News* (15.10.1867), they were easy to spot due 'to the peculiarity of their walk and their attire'. This particular specimen, who was suspected of having beaten a Greek sailor to death, also had a very fat neck to help identify him, but the police appear to have had little luck here either, despite the offer of a £100 reward for information.

In between these cases two others occurred which proved curiously similar in several respects. For a start, both occurred in Poplar, a district thought to have been named after the tree which flourished on some of its marshy land. Poplar's boundaries encompassed the Isle of Dogs, that curious loop of land formed by the meandering of the Thames, and nearby Blackwall. Here were the huge East India, West India, and several other smaller Docks.

Most of the 50,000 inhabitants were dockers or those in dock-related trades such as ships' chandling, ropemaking, shipbuilding, or the transporting of goods into Central London down the recently completed East India Dock and Commercial Roads. Henry Mayhew in *Mayhew's London* (1861) wrote:

> The docks of London are to a superficial observer the very focus of metropolitan wealth. The cranes creak with the mass of riches. In the warehouse are stored goods that are, as it were, ingots of untold gold. Above and below ground you see piles of treasure that the eye cannot compass. The wealth appears as boundless as the sea it has traversed ... and yet you have but to visit the hovels grouped round about all this amazing excess of riches to witness the same amazing excess of poverty.

Poplar had been hit hardest of all by the slump. Unemployment was rife and wealthy city men and clergy were currently forming committees to assist emigration of the unemployed to New Zealand and British North America (Canada) where their skills were needed. Emigration had long been considered one of the best ways to aid the poor and one often employed by Charles Dickens. In 1869 emigration numbers were the largest since 1854 and it was the first year in which the English and Scots outnumbered the Irish.

The bulk of inhabitants lived in Poplar New Town which straddled the top of the loop of the Isle of Dogs. A few lived a little further south in the short streets sandwiched between the high-walled docks and a ribbon of tall, Thameside taverns and lodging houses. It was in this curious isolated island of tiny terraced houses that the first of the terrible crimes took place. Superintendent Worels of K Division on 8 February 1869 wrote:

> I beg to report that at about 9.10 p.m. 7th instant information was received at Poplar Station that the police were required at No 2 Russell Place, Prestons Road, Poplar, as something serious had occurred. Inspector Smith accompanied the messenger to the above house, and on entering found a female lying on the floor in the kitchen, and a man across her legs, both having their throats cut and, although warm, apparently dead. A surgeon was immediately sent for, who, on examining the bodies, pronounced life extinct. A large spring-backed knife was found on the floor covered with blood, marks of blood on several doors, and also bloody water in a bowl in the wash-house as of some person having washed their hands. Search was made through the house (6 rooms) by the Inspector and friends of the deceased but nothing is missed.

It transpired that there was very little mystery about these killings. The victims were an 86-year-old blind man named Peter Pearson, the owner of 2 Russell Place and several other houses nearby; and his 26 year-old granddaughter, Sarah Ann Cooper. Three other persons lived in the house, the Superintendent explained: Eliza Taffe (the old man's daughter, and Sarah Ann's mother), her husband George Taffe, and Sarah's husband, John William Cooper.

On the evening of the crime, Eliza Taffe had gone out at about 5.30 p.m., to visit her sister who lived in the East India Dock Road. Her husband had followed soon after, leaving the three other occupants; the grandfather, granddaughter Sarah Ann, and her husband. When Eliza returned she had been unable to gain entry – until her brother-in-law and a neighbour climbed over the rear wall and forced the back door. Inside, they found the bodies of the grandad and young wife but no sign of the young husband, John Cooper.

Cooper was a 26-year-old, unemployed marine engineer who bore, declared Worels, 'an indifferent character'. His height was 5 foot 6 inches, his hair and whiskers were brown – the latter worn around his chin – his complexion florid but, most importantly, he had lost his left thumb. This, according to *The Times* (together with the fact that Cooper was well-known), would make him easily identifiable. An album 'containing photographic portraits' had been found on the premises, *The Times* revealed, but two photographs of Cooper and his brother were missing. 'It is supposed that Cooper tore them out of the book to prevent copies being multiplied'. Police obviously acquired a very small one from somewhere for it remains today, in the case file, at the Public Record office. As for the motive, even *The Times* had to confess this was a mystery but they had learned that Cooper had, 'lived on very bad terms with his wife and family'.

'Every exertion to be used to apprehend the murderer. Let one or two of the Detective Force be employed,' instructed Assistant Commissioner Captain Harris in the margin of Superintendent Worels' report. 'Inspector Thomson and Sgt Meiklejohn to enquire,' added Detective Chief Inspector Williamson.

At first it did indeed seem that the missing thumb would prove a great aid to capture. Almost at once, a railway policeman at Farringdon Station came up with a man of similar description to Cooper, whose left thumb was missing and who, like Cooper,

wore a blue cap with a French peak. On the night after the murder
this man had enquired about trains to Chippenham in Wiltshire
and had gone on to Paddington to board one of them. The
Wiltshire police, who were instructed to telegraph should any
trace be found of Cooper, drew a blank. Just as this negative reply
was received, a man turned up at Rochester Row Police Station
saying that in Aldershot that day a grocer had told him that a man
answering the description had asked him for relief. The man had a
thumb missing but the grocer couldn't say which one. Aldershot is
en route for Chippenham.

Two days later, a PC at Emsworth, a coastal village directly
south of Aldershot, reported that a man similar to the suspect had
stayed at the Locomotive Inn after trying to get a ship at nearby
Portsmouth and had said he would now head along the coast to
Brighton. Thomson was sent down but failed to find the man and,
in any case, thought that due to the shortness of time 'and his
having little or no money I do not think he is Cooper'.

During Inspector Thomson's absence, police at Loughborough
in Leicestershire arrested a one-thumbed tramp named Gittins and
awaited more description and advice. A couple of expensive
telegraphs to and from the Yard's Detective Inspector Clark failed
to sort the matter out so a detective was sent down with an
undertaker named Gooch who knew the suspect. The tramp was
not Cooper, Gooch declared, but Thomson, who had returned to
the Yard by now, was not entirely happy and telegraphed the local
superintendent:

ARE YOU SATISFIED THAT GITTINS IS NOT COOPER?
HAVE YOU CAREFULLY EXAMINED HIS CLOTHES?
GOOCH THE WITNESS SENT DOWN YESTERDAY IS
RELATED TO COOPER, WOULD IT BE DESIRABLE TO
SEND YOU AN INDEPENDENT WITNESS TO INSPECT
GITTINS?

The superintendent replied somewhat tetchily that there were
no marks on Gittins' clothes and, not surprisingly, that he always
preferred an independent witness. It's not clear what happened
next but the Loughborough connection petered out.

This case was unusual in that for much of the time Thomson
stayed put at the Yard, keeping in touch with the men on the spot,
Superintendent Worels and Inspector Smith, by the expanding
'Electric Telegraph' system. This was not as extravagant as it

seemed, for the Metropolitan Police had at last commenced linking their chief divisional stations by an internal telegraph system and its use was to revolutionize their work. Smith still had to get his messages the couple of miles from Poplar to Arbour Square Police Station but this was a great deal faster than the route paper system or sending messages by train. (The route paper system involved the passing of messages from division to division in all directions until all of the Metropolitan Police Area had been informed.)

Of particular notice in researching these Victorian cases is the number of · Thames- and Channel-orientated pursuits from London. Detectives were for ever rushing down river to, or contacting police at, Greenwich, Chatham, Gravesend, Dover and Ramsgate – in their attempts to prevent suspects escaping these shores. In this case, not only was Cooper likely to use these places to board ships to sign on as crew or to cross the Channel as a passenger, but he had many relatives, strung out at various points down the river and on the coast, who might give him succour or be able to provide information. Already, an uncle in Chatham had revealed that his nephew had always been a great source of trouble to all the family since boyhood. A detective was sent down to investigate further. Meanwhile, Sergeant Meiklejohn was pacing the streets of Southampton in company with a man who knew Cooper – in case the fugitive tried to get a ship there.

The newspapers, when they could tear themselves away from the subject of the Siamese twins who were in London, having fallen on bad times since their negro slaves had been given their freedom, were eager for every snippet of information. Clearly they had some prime sources. When the *Morning Advertiser* reported that the murderer was thought to be held at Loughborough and that Thomson had gone up to identify him, Captain Harris wrote beside the cutting, 'Is there any foundation for this statement?'

After Dover Police had reported that a man, 'deficient of his left thumb', had been trying to sign on a Rotterdam steamer bound for Africa and, having failed, attempted to get a ticket on a crossing to Calais, the facts were soon reported in the *Morning Post* and other papers. 'Chief Inspector,' wrote Colonel Labalmondiere to Williamson, 'How did this information get minuted in the papers?' Inspector Thomson confessed his guilt, claiming he thought the more publicity the better but the deputy commissioner was unconvinced. 'I think that quite as much harm is done as good (if not more) by the minutiae of such paragraphs, and at any rate should not be done without the Commissioner's permission which in future is to be obtained before the communication to the Press of any information.' Another shackle for the ankles of the detectives clicked on by a man who had never spent a day as an active police officer on the streets.

Nineteen years earlier, when recounting experiences to Charles Dickens, Inspector Whicher had described how he tracked down a criminal by noting the postmarks of letters delivered to and from the house of the criminal's wife – with the connivance of post office officials. Thomson received similar assistance from the Poplar postmaster whom he asked to keep watch on letters addressed to Cooper's relatives – including Gooch whom, obviously, Thomson did not trust.

'It has been ascertained from quiet enquiries made that Gooch has friends at Chadwell Heath adjoining Romford', he noted in the margin of a report informing him that Gooch had received a letter with a Romford postmark. When Cooper's mother received two letters from Hastings, quiet enquiries revealed that they came from a hospital where another son had recently been a patient but that he was now home 'in a dying state'.

Meanwhile the one-thumbed continued to surface all over southern England – low standards of industrial safety may well have made them more commonplace. The governor of Maidstone gaol had a one-thumbed bacon-stealer in his custody whom he thought might be Cooper but turned out to be a well-known old lag. Police at Steeple Claydon in Buckinghamshire came up with another possible, in a man who had been reported begging at farmhouses in the parishes of Chetwode and Preston Bissett. Following his trail, they had discovered that the man, 'stated at every place that he called at that he had lost a thumb and some of them saw that it was a fact, and it appeared to be a very recent injury'. Clearly the nutters were beginning to emerge from the woodwork.

Then came the writing on the wall – the toilet wall at London Bridge Railway Station to be exact. It read (reported Superintendent Worels):

My name is John Cooper the murderer No 2 Russel Place if you will look in the East India Dock you will find I have been sleeping in the inside of one of the iron tanks but this night I am going to drown myself and put an end to all my sorrows.

I hope my mother is quite well.
John Cooper   Murderer   Poplar.

'It might,' added Worels, 'be identified as Cooper's writing though it *may be nothing more than a mischievous act of someone.*' Nonetheless, he had had the writing preserved. Later, Thomson reported that the writing had been compared to that in a letter by Cooper but that 'it does not at all correspond'. It had also been discovered by the local police, that all the tanks at the dock were full of water. Then, several days later, albeit further up river at Wapping, a lighterman was navigating his way into the London Dock when, by Shadwell Dockstairs, he spied a floating body – it was Cooper.

On the same day that police received the news that Cooper was now lying at Shadwell 'dead house', a communication was *en route* to them from solicitors representing the landlord of 2 Russell Street, Poplar. It complained that the reward bills put out in the hope of catching Cooper had stated that the murder had taken place at that address (when it was actually Russell *Place*, a short distance away,) and that this put a stigma upon the house which the owner was currently attempting to sell. They would hold the authorities responsible if the bills were not altered at once.

Inspector Thomson, who was already employed on the *second* Poplar double murder with Sergeant Davey, was again taken to task but he was scarcely cowed: 'I beg to report that the original from which the £100 reward bills were printed was prepared at my dictation and inadvertently the word "street" was used in lieu of "place".'

He had been as careful as possible in framing the document for the printer, he insisted, but being unfamiliar with the locality, 'and from a desire to prevent further loss of time in issuing these bills, this mistake unfortunately happened. I beg leave to submit that these errors happen occasionally, and that it is difficult, when many enquiries have to be made &c &c to be as guarded and precise as to be accurate in every word'.

Thomson's multilingual abilities possibly gave him such confidence – he knew his skills were needed. Telegrams were sent to each division, instructing that the bills be taken down immediately. But the reward offered soon brought another problem. Ed Rowling, the lighterman who found Cooper's body applied to the newly appointed Commissioner, Colonel Sir

Edmund Henderson, saying he was a poor man and, although the reward had doubtless been meant for the recovery of a man's living body, 'still sir, what *there was of him*, I found, the finding of which *stopd a great expense* the country was at in searching for him.'

The pragmatic Thomson thought Rowling had a point. The finding had quelled the public alarm then existing and had spared no little expense. 'Had the body drifted into the Channel,' said Thomson, 'the murder would have remained a reproach to the whole of the police.' He recommended a £5 or £10 gratuity be paid. A report from the Thames Division Superintendent was to throw a different if more ghoulish light on the subject. It was true, the superintendent agreed, that Rowling had found the body, but he was unable to tow it in because he had no dinghy attached to his lighter, so he had passed it on to another lighterman, Maynard. ' ... Maynard, on being called away, again passed the body – to Dove, a waterman, who towed it to the landing stairs, and went to find the parish beadle to procure a "shell".' (By shell, they mean a light coffin.)

The three men had attended the inquest but only Rowling had given evidence. A dispute had arisen between them over who deserved a reward so the coroner had given them ten shillings to be equally divided between them. Henderson and the coroner decided no further payment should be made but meanwhile, Dove had gone over their heads to the Home Secretary who had given him £5. When the Home Office received a similar application from Rowling, they asked the police (whose workload far exceeded that of the drones at the Home Office), to institute an enquiry. (Sir Robert Anderson, later to become chief of the CID, noted when working at the Home Office that most of the very short (a nominal 11 a.m.-5 p.m.) day was spent gossiping, reading newspapers, lunching, playing games and ragging.) Henderson merely passed back the reports already made.

Next, in line was Gooch, the undertaker, who made a claim (on black-edged paper) for 10s.6d. a day for his two days at Loughborough. Captain Harris thought this amount exorbitant, and wrote, 'Pay him 10/-'. But Gooch's father and employer refused to accept it, saying that as manager of the firm, that was only what his son would have earned. Harris capitulated immediately, possibly illustrating why he had not been made deputy commissioner when Mayne died, and Gooch got his £1. 1s.

It may seem ludicrous that the chiefs of the world's most famous police force would bother themselves with such trivialities, but such was the system which had grown up with Mayne. He, working from ten in the morning often into the night, kept almost everything under his direct control.

The day before Cooper's body was eventually found, Superintendent Worels begged to report Poplar's second double murder. The similarities with the first were quite startling.

When a man named George Robert Still had been unable to get a reply to his repeated knockings on the door of his sister-in-law, who lived behind the tobacconist's shop she managed in Poplar High Street, he was obliged to gain entrance by a back window. Once inside, he found the naked body of his 23-year-old niece, Ann Brown, draped across a bed, her throat cut. A constable found the second body, that of 50-year-old Mary Brown, the girl's mother. A leather knife sheath was adhering to her dress, and on the back kitchen mantelpiece, there was a part-smoked cigar. The fact that in both murder cases the throats had been cut was not surprising. In those days of open razors and the carrying of large sheath knives as tools of trade it was a commonplace method.

The efficient Worels, although tactfully requesting the assistance of a detective, already had the job half done. 'Suspicion,' he reported, 'is at present attached to a man named John William Bradshaw [an unemployed engineer,] who formerly lodged with the deceased but left about five weeks since, and removed to No 8 Archibald Street, Bromley [Bromley-by-Bow, just north of Poplar] at which place he has committed suicide by cutting his throat about 8 a.m. on the 3rd inst., previous to which he had burnt a quantity of papers with writing thereon. He was seen passing the shop kept by the murdered woman about noon on the 2nd inst.'

The police surgeon thought the women had been dead at least twenty-four hours, which meant Bradshaw could have done the deed. (Mrs Brown was separated from her husband and had a magistrates protection order against him, but he had been gone for twenty years.) At the inquest, K Division's Inspector Madigan produced Bradshaw's bloodstained clothes. Some of the blood had been dry and some moist when the man's body was found. 'He inferred from this,' reported *The Times*, 'that the blood had come from two different sources at different times.'

The witnesses, gathered by Thomson and the local police,

painted an interesting picture of the relationship between the Browns and Bradshaw. Harriet Emberson, with whom Bradshaw had lived since leaving Poplar and who had expected to marry him that very Tuesday, said he had spoken of the women in very high terms saying they were very honest people. But she had also heard him speak of them disrespectfully and, at times, of Mrs Brown with an oath. What's more there had been violence between them – from Mrs Brown against him. Bradshaw had been playing the piano and reading the newspaper at the same time, Harriet Emberson recalled him telling her, ' ... Mrs Brown bawled out at him, and told him to make less noise, and because he would not desist she took up a piece of coral which he had brought home from one of his voyages, and broke it upon his head. He had suffered very much from the blow and did not often know what he was doing.'

Bradshaw's own brother evened the score somewhat by letting it be known that he had been, 'a man of violent and irritable temper', owned a gun, and that not only had their mother died in a lunatic asylum but there was insanity on the father's side as well. Mrs Brown's own brother also spoke up for her, while admitting he had not seen her since the day of Sir Richard Mayne's funeral. (The date was not given in the report so, presumably, the event had been one of some note.) Mrs Brown had told him that Bradshaw (who had been living with them as a lodger for about six years) had insulted her. He surmised by what she said, that Bradshaw had made overtures which she had successfully resisted (maybe this was when the coral was really brought into play).

After the inquest jury had concurred that Bradshaw had done the double deed they heaped great praise upon the police 'for their service in elucidating the facts of the case and thus enabling them to arrive at a satisfactory verdict'.

4   The Cat and the Canary

The energetic, new commissioner, Colonel Edmund Henderson, was an ex-army officer with experience not only in the leading of men but also the confining the worst of them. The latter had been gained from his work as Comptroller of the convict settlement in Western Australia and as a Director of Prisons in the UK. Henderson soon realized that not only did the force require more constables but those already serving were underpaid, ill-housed, and led lives restricted unnecessarily by petty regulations. He made rapid improvements in the police stations and section houses, where conditions were primitive, and granted permission for policemen to grow beards and moustaches, and to wear their own clothes whilst off duty.

He was in a good position to increase the numbers of detectives. Following the Clerkenwell explosion débâcle, a departmental committee on the workings of the branch had recommended not only an increase in the establishment at Scotland Yard but also the introduction of a substantial detective presence on divisions. With Home Office consent (always required by the Metropolitan Police), the number of detectives at Scotland Yard was increased to 27 and a complement of no less than 180 was authorized for the divisions. Each division was to have its own detective sergeant and from four to fourteen detective constables – according to local needs.

There were changes, too, in the command structure of the detective branch. For the first time they were to have their own superintendent supported by two additional chief inspectors and nine more sergeants. The complement at Scotland Yard (as published in *Police Orders*, 15 May, 1869) now looked like this:

1 superintendent at £300 p.a.
3 chief inspectors at £250 p.a. each

3 inspectors at £200 p.a. each
6 sergeants (first class) at £150 p.a. each
13 sergeants (2nd class) at £110 p.a. each

The new plain clothes allowance for all ranks was to be £10 a year and travelling expenses at 15 shillings a day for the superintendents and chief inspectors, 13 shillings for the inspectors and 10 shillings for the sergeants. 'These allowances to include everything except locomotive expenses.'

The new superintendent was Adolphus Frederick Williamson, the man already in charge as chief inspector. Several descriptions of the man have been left by his colleagues and they add up to him being honest, sensible, kind, charming, good-tempered, hard-working and popular with – even loved by – his subordinates. He was also reckoned to be a good detective who disliked his men using disguise or thieves' slang, and an able leader, inspiring confidence even in the most timid.

'Williamson was full of dry humour,' claims Chief Inspector Littlechild in his *Reminiscences*, 'which frequently came out in the anecdotes which he enjoyed telling. On Sunday mornings, when the gatherings at the office were in the nature of a friendly conference, when the work which would not wait till the morrow had been got through, then he would come among us, and many a pleasant hour can be recalled of these Sunday mornings.' He appears to have had a well-rounded life outside the force as well, enjoying the sport of sculling and finding pleasure in growing roses in the garden of his home in Smith Square – which he shared with his wife Emma, five children and two servants.

There was little reason for him to be unhappy. His admission to the detective department in 1852, after only two years service, was probably aided by the fact that his Scottish father was one of the founding superintendents of the force. The boy had been brought up above Hammersmith Police Station, from where he attended the local grammar school. But 'Dolly' (from 'Adolphus') Williamson also helped himself by, for example, studying French in the evenings while his young section house colleagues were out at the London theatres enjoying themselves – and often earning extra money by doing duty there. Surprisingly, his studying did nothing to affect his popularity, probably because he still took part in, and often led, any high jinks in which his group became involved. But, being ambitious, he managed to retain (according to Timothy Cavanagh, who had known him since childhood and was the man in charge of the Scotland Yard section house when Williamson lived there at the beginning of his career) 'a knack of keeping out of trouble, when some of the others easily got "spotted" ' (from *Scotland Yard, Past and Present*). It was a trait which, in later years, was to stand him in good stead.

By the time he gave evidence to the Home Office departmental committee on detectives in 1868, Williamson was a well-respected chief inspector – in charge of his department as far as Mayne would allow. A glimpse of apparent deliberate gathering of approval for himself may be seen in his report to Mayne's successor, Colonel Henderson, who had asked him for his thoughts on what could be done to improve the detective department. Williamson presented many of the committee's conclusions, almost as though they were newly-minted by himself, merely adding that 'some such suggestions such as the above were submitted to the Home Office by the late Commissioner'.

Not that the life of the newly appointed superintendent was all sunshine. Just as the downfall of his mentor, Inspector Whicher, was said to have upset him, it must also have been a source of some regret that his father did not live to see him rise to the top. The older Williamson died of bronchitis only three years after 'Dolly' became a detective sergeant.

Superintendent Williamson's right hand man in the detective department was 51-year-old, Chief Inspector George Clarke. A groom before joining the Metropolitan Police thirty years earlier, he was still only a sergeant when, in 1864, he accompanied the much younger Inspector Tanner to New York in pursuit of Muller, the railway murderer. Clarke did eventually achieve the rank of inspector (in 1867, after twenty-seven years service – only to be pushed up another rank two years later with the 1869 changes) but it is not clear what caused the earlier hold-up. Possibly the fact that he married early and assumed family responsibilities while still quite young meant that he was not able to devote as much time to the job as did his colleagues. But Clarke's long experience made him invaluable to Williamson. He was considered to be an expert on betting frauds and 'poisoning cases' and discreet enough ('My most confidential and trusted assistant', as Williamson described him at the Turf Fraud Trial) to be much employed on 'delicate governmental affairs'.

Inspectors Thomson and Clarke filled two of the chief

inspectors' posts and Sergeants William Palmer and Nathaniel Druscovich were promoted to become two of the three inspectors. The third, already in that rank, was Richard Tanner.

William Palmer, who, by then, had fourteen years' service, appears to have been a reliable plodder who made his way steadily up the ladder while drawing little attention to himself. By contrast, the rise of Nathaniel Druscovich had been a rapid and spectacular one. Of Polish extraction, he was, according to Williamson, 'an anxious, zealous and energetic officer'. He looked good, too, with his imperial beard and smart turn-out. Not only that, he was fluent in French and Italian and no doubt it was this ability which had helped draw him into a very curious case during his fourth year of his service, in 1865.

The *Sûreté* had asked for Yard assistance in a case concerning a Frenchman by the name of Vital Douat whose wife claimed that he had died while on a visit to Plaistow in the east end of London and had papers to prove it. Considering that Douat was a declared bankrupt – falsely it was suspected – his life insurance company, with whom he had only recently taken out a substantial policy, suspected his demise convenient to say the least. 26-year-old Sergeant Nathaniel Druscovich, was handed the enquiry. Although he failed to trace the doctor whose (almost illegible) signature was on the death certificate, he did not give up but went on to examine the Channel ferry passenger list for Douat's alleged journey to England. There was no mention of him, so Druscovich promptly set about tracing the other passengers on the list, finding all of them bar one, a Mr Roberto Bernardi – who had taken lodgings in Plaistow but was no longer to be found there.

Further efforts, revealed that 'Bernardi' had moved on to stay in a hotel in the Strand where he had become friendly with a waiter, telling him he was a traveller in wines (Douat was a wine merchant). What is more, under the guise of an elaborate practical joke he had persuaded the waiter to write and sign a cause-of-death note of 'a friend'. The young Druscovich also tracked down Douat's undertaker and discovered that he had never actually seen the body, but had merely sent an empty coffin to a Signor Rubini. The Frenchman had belonged to an extremely rigorous religious sect, Rubini had explained, which forbade anyone except one of its elders to touch the body – therefore they themselves would lay it out and place it in the coffin.

Two possible scenarios were now emerging. Either Douat had

committed murder and put the corpse of his victim in the coffin in his place or, more likely, the coffin was empty. When an exhumation order was put into effect, the second assumption was proved to be correct. Druscovich continued to pursue 'Bernardi' but the trail ended, as so many did in those days, at the Liverpool docks where passenger ships left for America. (Douat was caught later when he returned to Europe and Druscovich went to France to give evidence which helped convict him of fraud.)

By such efforts early in his career, Druscovich was soon winning praise not only from a grateful burglary victim for his vigilance, but for his efficiency and the great service he had rendered by his knowledge of languages during the visit of Garibaldi, the Italian revolutionary general. Early in 1869, Judge Baron Bramwell praised Druscovich publicly for tracking down a gang of foreign burglars and, later, a judge at Cork Assizes was to say he had never heard evidence given better than that by Druscovich and his colleagues in a loan office swindle case. 'They performed with an intelligence and ability which struck me very much.'

Six more of the Yard's sergeants were promoted in 1869 – by a rise in class (the rank ascended from fourth to first class). These included John Meiklejohn, who rose from a third to a second-class sergeant, and the 32-year-old, Somerset-born, John Shore, an able man of very limited education, who now became a first-class sergeant. Within months Shore was pushed upwards again to inspector, replacing the talented Richard Tanner who left through ill-health in July 1869.

All of these changes meant, that at a time when the iron grip of Sir Richard Mayne had finally been lifted from the department, its men were being shot up the ranks – some of them possibly prematurely. But, as Williamson and the departmental committee had pointed out, good promotion prospects within the department were essential to attract and keep the best men. Men such as James Jacob Thomson, who, only months after being promoted to detective chief inspector, became superintendent of E division – thus following a pattern established when the very first leader of the branch, Inspector Nicholas Pearce, had become superintendent of E Division after only two years in charge of the detective department. (Mayne had fought to keep Inspector Pearce in the detective department by trying to get the Home Office to agree to give him the same pay as a divisional superintendent but was told that a detective inspector's duties were not nearly so onerous, and his rewards, for successful prosecutions, far greater.)

Among the nine *new* sergeants brought into the branch at this time were George Hepburn Greenham, a marine engineer born in Trieste; John William Reimars, a tall, 40-year-old German saddler; James Pay, an ex-grocer born in Dunkirk, and ex-cavalry man and language teacher, Charles Louis Christopher Constantine Von Tornow. Von Tornow was a German, born in Heligoland, who became a naturalized British subject soon *after* joining the Metropolitan Police in 1868. Men like these were largely wanted for their proficiency in foreign languages (and, possibly, good education) and for this they were probably given preferential selection or even, as in the case of Greenham, direct entry into the detective branch without any prior police service.

The detectives operated out of a two-storey building in the centre of Great Scotland Yard. At 10 a.m. the officer-in-charge – usually Williamson or Clarke – would arrive along with the two clerks, the sergeants, and any inspectors not engaged elsewhere. 'Elsewhere' covered a multitude of possibilities: race meeting duty, appearance at courts, annual leave, or meetings with informants. (The term, 'meeting informants' has always covered a multitude of sins for detectives who sometimes make use of the fact that it is necessary to keep the identity of their 'source' secret.) The work was handed out in 'dockets', and one detective recalled having six to eight dockets on the go at one time – for different parts of London and elsewhere. The intended whereabouts of the detectives would be noted in a diary kept by the clerk but, of course, given their rank and duties, they were necessarily afforded a fair degree of freedom.

At around 6 p.m., those who were able returned to the office to write out their reports and consult Williamson. He had the knack of getting to the nub of the matter, swiftly picking out the important points from a mass of paperwork – not easy when everything is handwritten in varying degrees of legibility. He was also courageous and ready with his advice. 'I never knew his counsel to be wrong,' claimed ex-Inspector Andrew Lansdowne in his book *A Life's Reminiscences of Scotland Yard*, although he also admitted that Williamson could be obstinate, unenthusiastic, and slow to grasp a new idea – 'doubting its efficacy, seeing its disadvantages rather than its advantages'.

The single men in the branch did not have far to come to work.

They lived on top of the job – at a section house in a Georgian terrace known as Palace Place which was within Great Scotland Yard itself. It housed about twenty men and had a tiny parlour where, if they were free, most of them would gather for a chat before going off to do evening theatre duty and chat about it afterwards, or have a game of Loo (a card game).

Many of the married men did not have much further to come, a number of them living in the area just beyond Westminster Abbey. (For example, Tanner lived in North Street, leading into Smith Square, Williamson lived in the Square itself, Clarke, in Great College Street, and Greenham and Pay, in Cambridge Street, Pimlico.) Obviously such close proximity to the Yard was essential, given their duties and the limited transport of the times, but prices of such centrally placed accommodation were high and the cost proved difficult to bear, particularly since most of them had large families typical of the time. Even Chief Inspector Clarke, who paid rent of £36 a year (a seventh of his salary) was said to live frugally and to take in a lodger to help him make ends meet.

Other changes brought about at this time were improvements in the previously mentioned route paper system of circulating information to and from Scotland Yard and the marked increase in the number of stations connected to their divisional headquarters by the electric telegraph. To ease administration and communication problems, the Metropolitan Police area was also divided into four districts, each headed by a district superintendent. Registers of Habitual Criminals were introduced both locally and centrally.

The Times of 29 October 1870, pondered on the interesting items to be gleaned from the superintendents' reports included in the Commissioners Annual Report, 'The transfer of the examination of men recommended for promotion from the Board of Superintendents to the Civil Service Commissioners, is described as working very satisfactorily; an intelligent sergeant states that the examination is in every respect fair, and that a timid man soon feels confident in the presence of the examiner.'

They were bemused, however, by the idea that policemen actually had hobbies and enjoyed social activities. 'A station house has a serious look to most persons, but we learn here that there is more than meets the eye. We are told of smoking rooms, billiard tables, of "readings", and concerts, of bands and glee clubs, besides the more sedate educational class.'

Not all the changes were successful. Jealousy from the divisional superintendents at the usurping of their authority by district superintendents, whose duties were ill-defined, caused the latter to find themselves with little to do. The granting of a day off each week to every member of the force resulted in a reduction of one thousand of men available for police duties at any one time, which rather ate into the increases which Henderson had brought about. This experiment had been a bit of a disappointment, the commissioner admitted, because it had also meant that the duties of higher ranking officers had had to be handed over to inexperienced or less capable substitutes, resulting in constant complaints from the public, while constables merely became unsettled by the constant interruption of their duties. Therefore, he declared, he was thinking of reducing days off to two a month, one of these being a Sunday. Annual leave, was to remain at four weeks for superintendents, two for inspectors, ten days for sergeants and seven for constables. The enlarged detective branch, however, was deemed a success, having made no less than 2,416 arrests, with many commendations, a conviction rate of 63.4 per cent and no complaints.

To say that dead babies were thick on the ground during the years 1869/70 might be something of an exaggeration – but not too much of one. 'Child dropping' of stillborn babies, or those who had died soon after birth due to suffocation or neglect, was commonplace in poor areas. Pathetic parcels containing the tiny corpses were discovered (often by inquisitive small boys) in gardens, fields, hedges, and on dung heaps and the backs of carts and cabs.

It was not a new problem but one exacerbated by the economic situation. Working-class unmarried mothers still had to earn their own living so not only were they unable to look after the baby themselves but they could not cope with the expense of an extra mouth to feed. Others dared not, for shame, keep their baby with them. But lack of proper birth control and a high incidence of prostitution meant the babies kept coming which, in turn, assisted abortionists and proprietors of dubious 'lying-in' establishments to flourish. It was from the latter that many of the newborn dead were thought to come. However, increasingly, during 1869/70, the bodies of babies from six to ten weeks old were also found and the suspicion arose that many of these came from the newly termed 'baby farms'.

A baby farm was merely a private nursery operating without controls and staffed (if so formal a term may be used), by untrained women. Many of their advertisements to be found in newspapers purported to be from childless women who offered to 'entirely adopt' a baby (a term which has echoes of Dotheboy's Hall 'no vacations') for a lump sum of from £5 to £15, while others charged five shillings a week for upkeep. Again it was the poor and the desperate who tended to be the customers.

Not surprisingly, the lifespan of these deserted mites was inclined to be unusually short, even for those times. Poor feeding and drugging with laudanum to stop them crying would weaken them, while utter squalor and overcrowding (sometimes ten babies to a room) encouraged the spread of the many infections lethal to babies. The suspicion that they were sometimes deliberately starved and neglected to death was given voice by influential coroners such as Dr Lankester of Westminster who (as recounted by the *Islington Gazette*, 1869) somewhat ingeniously, enquired of an Islington servant girl who had been given no financial support by her baby's married father, 'I suppose you never offered to make a present to Miss Brooks [the baby farmer] if the child died?' The girl admitted the child was a burden to her but denied ever wishing it dead – but then she would say that, wouldn't she?

The reason baby farmers 'dropped' babies was to prevent drawing attention to themselves and the fact that they may not have called medical attention to a dying child in order to save the price of the burial, and to be able to cash in on the baby's clothes by pawning them. They, too, came from the ranks of the poor and desperate.

Another reason for the increase in child murders (for that was often the inquest verdict on the unidentified little corpses) was, according to Dr Lankester, 'the apathy of the police, and irregularities in the law'. Indeed, one inquest juryman even accused the police of waiting for a reward to be offered before making any enquiries. Suddenly, in June 1870, the matter came to a head, as these things are wont to do, when, in the space of a few weeks no less than sixteen dead babies were found in parcels scattered around Camberwell.

Two years earlier, Druscovich and Meiklejohn had been put on the track of a notorious Soho abortionist said to have boasted of having 'murdered' 555 infants during the previous twelve months but, although press attentions pressured her to move to the

Railway Hotel in Woking while retaining her Soho base only as 'a place of introduction', the detectives were unable to obtain sufficient evidence to prosecute her. This was due, claimed Druscovich, to 'her extreme caution and the fact that the law held both parties to the act responsible'. The woman herself solved the problem in November 1869 by dying. Despite their experience, it was not clever Williamson or Druscovich who were eventually to shine in this field but two uniformed officers, Sergeant Relf and Constable Tyers, who answered a baby farming advertisement in *Lloyd's Weekly Newspaper* and so gained access to the baby farm run by Mrs Waters of Brixton. The name Waters had been found on one of the Camberwell baby wrappings.

In the kitchen Sergeant Relf found five dreadfully emaciated babies huddled together under a dirty blanket and in a foul condition, and five others, better kept, out in the yard. The latter had not been taken in for a lump sum transaction but were being supported by weekly payments so it paid to keep them alive. Relf arrested Mrs Waters and her sister Sarah Ellis and took the children off to a workhouse where, gradually, they all died (the conditions there were not exactly conducive to long-life, either). The two women were charged with murder and, as the case progressed, baby farming became the hot topic and Sergeant Relf the hero of the hour. Pressured by the Reverend Thorpe, vicar of Christ Church, Camberwell, who ran a high-profile campaign, and Dr Lankester and the *Islington Gazette*, who, between them, saw that all local cases got maximum publicity as they had been doing for the past year at least, the Metropolitan Police were obliged to take more aggressive action.

Inspector Druscovich and Sergeant Meiklejohn were put on the job of following up the cases which had been brought to police attention, and also following in Relf's footsteps by answering baby farming advertisements and reporting the results.

'Quiet enquiries' (a favourite term used by Druscovich) established that one Mrs Hall of Coldharbour Lane, who accommodated young ladies during their confinement, 'and it is believed that occasionally, by a certain process, succeeds in bringing the children into the world stillborn'; currently had several such young ladies in her care. However, the detectives discovered that Superintendent Gernon and Relf and Tyers had beaten them to it in this case, so Druscovich 'begged to be permitted to withdraw ... as two persons endeavouring to obtain evidence against the same party and at the same time would in all probability frustrate their common object'.

A lying-in establishment in College Street, Islington, looked promising and Druscovich suggested that the local detectives keep observation. They did so, for three weeks, but to no avail. Later, it was decided that what was needed was a quick dose of Relf and Tyers who were brought across the river to be lodged in College Street. But they found nothing suspicious, primarily because 'they know they are being watched and are careful since the recent baby farming convictions'. And well they might be cautious for, by this time, Waters had been found guilty and hanged and her sister given two years' hard labour. The woman, Hall, had also been prosecuted.

Some felt that Waters had been merely a scapegoat, pounced upon in a typically British fit of moral indignation, and that she was merely poor and ignorant. She had gone bravely to the gallows, still protesting she had never meant to kill anyone. Relf was awarded £20 for his efforts and won the praise of the prosecuting counsel, the judge, and much of the Press. There were suggestions that Relf should be employed full time on catching baby farmers and given additional rewards, although one medical man (writing to the *Morning Advertiser*) cast doubt on the wisdom of paying policemen extra 'for making all this mirage about lime-water and narcotics that they do not understand'. (He was referring to the fact that the children were alleged to have been given drugs to keep them quiet.)

The commotion did, however, bring about the formation of a Parliamentary Select Committee on the Protection of Infant Life, with Sergeant Relf and Superintendent Gernon as prominent witnesses. While it was sitting another, rather odd baby case was in progress – again on L Division – but this time in a more well-to-do residential area. The first the commissioner heard about it was when a short, sharp blast of press criticism was aimed at the evidence given at an inquest on the death of a baby by one of the new divisional detectives. What was exercising the *Morning Advertiser* and the *Standard* in April, 1872, was that Divisional Detective Sergeant Mullard appeared to be suggesting that Agnes Norman, the baby's nurse, was not only in some way responsible for the tragedy but other similar occurrences as well. He was making accusations against a poor, undefended woman – guilt feelings about the treatment of Waters may have been at work here. The inquest found the child had died from suffocation, accidentally caused. 'Either the nursemaid has been made a mark of the most unfair and foul suspicion,' said the *Standard*, 'or a mystery exists which should be probed to its very depths.'

Inspector James Pay, old in service but still quite new in the department, was given the job of probing or making 'careful inquiry'. He did a thorough job, tracing back the career of 16-year-old Agnes Norman for two-and-a-half years and indeed discovered that, as Sergeant Mullard had claimed, the mortality rates of her charges did seem high even by standards then current.

The infant mortality rate for children under one year was 15 to 16 per cent. If bottle-fed, the rate went up to 40 per cent and higher among the poor living in insanitary conditions.

Back in January 1869, Agnes had been looking after the four children of the Milner family at 19 Park Road, Kennington. Soon after her arrival there the arm of 10-month-old Thomas was found severely bruised and the eldest boy, 8-year-old Alfred, told his father that the nursemaid had let the baby fall off the table and had given him a halfpenny not to tell. Within a short time baby Thomas was dead. He had been a reasonably healthy child but the previous week had suffered convulsions while teething. The inquest jury, in its wisdom, brought in a verdict of 'Natural Death (fit of dentition)'. Two weeks later, Agnes was left in charge of the remaining three Milner children (from ten in the morning until ten at night) and, when the parents returned, the delicate, 3-year-old Amelia, had died. Dr Nott was called and, as in the first case, refused to issue a death certificate, but this time no inquest was held – despite the fact that the baby's brother, Alfred, had disclosed that Agnes had put Amelia in the wardrobe at one point and (again) had given him a halfpenny not to tell.

A couple of months later saw Agnes in the service of the Gardeners of Stockwell Road, when a Mrs Taylor, a friend of the family, came to call, bringing along her 5-month-old baby boy. She left him in the nursery with dogsbody Agnes for a couple of hours but when she returned to collect him the baby was dead. At the inquest, where Agnes gave evidence, as she had at that of Thomas Milner, a verdict of 'Natural Death due to spasms of glottis' was returned. Two-and-a-half weeks later, the previously weak and sickly baby of the house, 1-year-old James Alexander Gardener, was also dead. A fact which failed to surprise Dr Pocock, who had also been called to the previous death. He happily provided a certificate to say the baby died of convulsions. But an even stranger element was now emerging as Pay later noted in his report: 'During the six weeks that Agnes Norman was in the service of Mr Gardener 3 dogs, a cat, a parrot, 12 canaries and linnets, and some goldfish, died very mysteriously.'

Agnes then entered the service of Mr Brown of Temple Street, St George's Road, where the grandson of the house, 10-year-old Charles Parfitt, complained of waking up, suffocating, to find Agnes with her hands over his mouth and throat. When he had screamed, he alleged, she gave him a sweet not to tell. Agnes denied this vehemently but was asked to leave. Pay wrote:

> She was in service at Mr Brown's a fortnight, during which time the cat, a canary, a linnet, and some goldfish, died, and the parrot was thought to be dying. Mr Judd, a bird fancier, was called in to see it, and he was of the opinion that its neck had been pinched, it being swollen at the time.

In her next post, all the animals died but no children. Finally, came the case which had caused the initial commotion. On 15 April 1871, Agnes Norman entered the service of Mr and Mrs Beer of 58 Newington Butts, where the tempo of events reached a crescendo. Only two days after her arrival (and, it must be said, after being left in charge of the three Beer children for nine hours – from 3 p.m. until half-past midnight) the previously strong and healthy, 14-month-old Jessie Jane Beer was found dead of suffocation. She was the fifth baby to die while in the care of Agnes Norman. The cat and the canary were also by then deceased – 'mysteriously' as Pay once again put it.

The problem was, of course, that a great many babies died mysteriously as, indeed, a number still do. Pay reported that Alfred's mother thought him capable of giving a clear account of baby Amelia's being placed in the cupboard but his father thought him too excitable and refused to allow him to be examined. The inspector was given access to 10-year-old Charles Parfitt, who seemed to him a very timid boy, ' ... it was with difficulty that I could get answers to questions from him, and his friends think that he would be easily puzzled by cross questions, and almost made to say anything'.

However, the lower lip of the last baby to die, Jessie Beer, had marks of upper teeth upon it and the doctor who carried out the post mortem felt these could not have been caused by the child herself lying on anything – pressure must have been brought to bear. Moreover, a servant acquaintance of Agnes revealed that, previous to the child's death, Agnes had told her Jessie had fits (which was untrue), afterwards claimed the death was caused by these fits (also, apparently, untrue) and confessed to being afraid to enter the room when the parents found the body, 'in case they might say I had done something to it'.

Williamson thought there was sufficient evidence to arrest Agnes Norman for the murder of Jessie Beer and, since it was a case of considerable importance which required the evidence of witnesses to be very carefully brought out, the police *must* have legal aid. They got it, but, due to the disagreement of the medical witnesses as to whether the death could have been accidental, the judge stopped the case. However, Agnes Norman was found guilty of the attempted murder of the timid Charles Parfitt and sentenced to ten years penal servitude. The five other charges against her were not proceeded with.

Babies, it must have seemed, were not even safe in their own homes. But at least those who were 'put out to nurse' began to receive some protection from the new Infant Life Protection Act of 1872. This brought in registration and control of child minders by local authorities which helped, but did not entirely solve, the problem. Indeed, a further six baby farmers were hanged after 1872: Jessie King (1889), Amelia Dyer (1896), Ada Chard Williams (1900), Annie Walters and Amelia Sach (1903), and Leslie (*sic*) James (1907). Reverend Thorpe continued to bring suspected cases to police notice and, it appears, Sergeant Relf remained something of a reproach to the detective department. As far on as 1877 an assistant commissioner was adding a note to a baby-farming allegation file which read: 'Supt. Williamson – This matter should be carefully enquired into. It may be placed in the hands of Sergeant Relf in conjunction with one of your officers if necessary.'

In fact Relf was, by then, an inspector.

5   Extradition

On the way up the career ladder, Williamson had gained valuable extradition experience and came to be regarded as something of an expert in the field. Among his cases had been the sensational arrest and trial of Dr Bernard, who, while in exile in London, had planned an attempt on the life of Napoleon III in Paris, and whose prosecution required a special act of Parliament. Another was the strange case of the Baron de Vidil, extradited from Paris in 1861 for the attempted murder of his own son.

Increasingly, a great deal of the work of the detective branch seemed to lead across the English Channel and beyond. Not that that appeared to disturb Williamson unduly. When George Greenham, one of the new sergeants, was sent out on a seemingly fruitless search for a smuggler, Williamson told him to have a nice little trip to Dover and Calais, enjoy the fresh air, and return invigorated in health, adding 'spare no expense in tracing the man if you see any chance of success'. This was said with one of Williamson's 'usual happy smiles'.

Of course, the process was two-way. In 1874, for example, the detective branch caught fourteen foreign criminals and returned them to their own countries to stand trial. Not many, thought the *Daily Telegraph*, considering that England had been called a *refugium peccatorum*, and London, the common sewer of Paris and Rome. The newspaper was commenting dryly on the commissioner's annual report but nonetheless compared its innocent frankness very favourably with the complete lack of information the French people received about the extremely shady goings on of their police.

One detective even went as far as Australia to deliver a prisoner and give evidence. The case was extraordinary. One Saturday night in December 1869, 47-year-old George Dyer, 'a person of diminutive stature', called into Hunter Street Police Station in

Bloomsbury to confess to a murder he had committed at a gold digging in the Australian outback thirteen years earlier. He had first gone to Melbourne in 1853, he told the inspector in charge, but, after his wife had died in 1855 he had sent his three children home to England before setting off to become a gold digger on the banks of the River Loddon, north-west of Melbourne.

Following the Californian gold strike in 1848, gold was sought for, and found, in New South Wales, three years later. Gold mania took hold and the Government of Victoria, wanting to get in on the act, offered £200 to anyone finding gold in the 300 kilometres around Melbourne. An arc of such sites was discovered and a similar manic rush ensued. First came other Australians followed by a flood of Europeans and Americans. Conditions on the sites were primitive, competition grew ever more tough and, subsequently, crime more violent. Two years after his arrival, Dyer had found himself in need of a mate and invited an English sailor, George Wilson, to help him work his claim. He explained to Superintendent Thomson at Bow Street where the surprised Hunter Street inspector had taken him:

> We got on very well together for nearly a month, when a quarrel arose between us in my tent as to the quantity of gold realised. It led to mutual recriminations, and he drew his knife upon me, and to defend myself, I took up a spade and cut him down with it. He dropped down dead in a moment. I cut his head clean open. He was killed immediately. Fearing discovery, I took the body and threw it into a well 30 or 40 feet deep. The quarrel began after we left off work, and it was about ten o'clock at night when I killed him. There was another tent on the hill, 100 or 150 yards off. Some Cornish people occupied it, but I cannot recollect their names. It was light at the time. The well was a few yards from the tent, and I dragged the body and threw it in. It was quite warm. I returned to the tent and went to bed. We were both perfectly sober – in fact I have never kept any spirits in the tent. Next day I went to work alone, and when asked by a Cornish party as to what had become of my mate, George, I said that he had gone to Inglewood Rush – a new digging.

No-one else enquired about Wilson, but Dyer took the precaution of moving to a digging a couple of miles away which he worked for another four years without any luck. Returning to Melbourne he went on to New Zealand for a while before coming back to England in 1868. Now he lived in Islington, with a new wife of only two months but, he claimed, the events of that night still preyed on his mind and he had had no peace since.

When Dyer appeared before Mr Vaughan, the magistrate, at Bow Street the following Monday, he obviously had had second thoughts and already had a defending solicitor who said there was a man in the court room who had been in Australia at the time alluded to and he had no recollection of such a murder. That was very likely, Mr Vaughan pointed out, as no one was aware that it had happened. Police countered with a witness who had been chief of police in Melbourne and who declared that such murders had been common at the time.

Although he had declared himself sober and of sound mind when he made his confession, during the long wait for exchange of communications with the police in Victoria, Dyer changed his mind and claimed he had been out of his mind when he entered Hunter Street Police Station. Alas, for him, such a body as he described had been discovered some years earlier, near where he claimed to have put it, and a reward of £100 had been offered for information. Other details were similar – although there appeared to have been more than one blow to the victim's head caused by a pick-axe rather than a shovel. Nonetheless, the Victoria police were satisfied there was a case to answer and sent a detective to collect Dyer. He was duly extradited almost exactly six calendar months after his confession – not bad, given the distances entailed.

Such far-flung expeditions were, obviously, a lot less common than cross-channel dashes such as that following the Park Lane Murder in April 1872. Mme Maria Caroline Besson Riel was the 42-year-old mistress of Lord Lucan, the general who had ordered the Charge of the Light Brigade. On Sunday, 7 April 1870, Mme Riel's maid went to the top of the house to continue her duties, leaving her mistress in a room below – preparing for a morning walk in Hyde Park. When Mme Riel's daughter Julie, returned from a trip to Paris early the following day, the maid told her that she had not seen her mother since that time. Although somewhat curious about this, she was a simple girl who spoke no French and, since Mme Riel and her cook spoke little English, she was accustomed to being left rather in the dark as to what was going on. Mme Riel was not to be found at Lord Lucan's, and a thorough search of the house by the two women also proved fruitless – until they came to the pantry, which was locked. Inside, they found the battered body of Mme Riel.

'The features were much distorted,' reported Superintendent Dunlap of C Division, 'the hands clenched and deeply scratched, and the nails broken. The whole appearance of the body,' he continued, 'is that of having been subjected to great violence.' Furthermore, the victim had a rope around her neck which had obviously been pulled very tightly. In the surgeon's opinion the death had occurred at least fifteen hours earlier.

Another member of the Park Lane household had been missing since 8 p.m. the previous evening – the French cook, 28-year-old Mme Marguerite Diblanc. Also missing, were some Bank of England notes and several French bonds. Divisional Detective Sergeant Butcher was the first plain clothes man on the scene but Detective Inspector Pay of Scotland Yard soon took over. He set about tracing the dark-haired, sturdily built French cook who had last been seen wearing a green, French, merino wool dress; dark, waterproof cloak and brown bonnet.

Warning telegrams (including the 'submarine' made possible by the undersea cabling under the Channel and across the Atlantic) were sent out to many ports resulting in various possible sightings being reported. At one point, information suggested that Marguerite Diblanc had been in Hull and was now making her way across country to Liverpool and thence to America. But, by far, the most promising lead came from a cabbie who revealed that, on the Sunday night, he had driven a woman who answered the cook's description, from Park Lane to Victoria Station. Once there, she had headed for the London, Chatham and Dover Railway terminus, and it was that company's interpreter who informed the police that, at 8.20 p.m. on the evening in question, such a woman had enquired about the next train to Paris. Because she 'had the appearance of a servant' he had presumed she required a seat on one of the cheap, service trains, and told her that she was out of luck – the last one had left two hours earlier. But she had assured him that the first-class-only express, leaving in fifteen minutes, would do her nicely. The interpreter escorted her to the ticket office, where she paid her fare with a Bank of England note, then saw her on to the train. The company was not only able to tell Druscovich her ticket number but also that, as the Calais portion of the ticket had been duly collected, she had actually arrived there.

A telegram sent to the Paris police, was followed, post-haste, by Chief Inspector Druscovich and Inspector Pay. They, too, left Victoria Station on the evening train, arriving in Paris the following morning. They went straight to the British Embassy to obtain a letter of introduction, which they took to the Prefect of Police. He, in turn, put two police officers at their disposal: Inspectors Raviart and Hinschberger.

Inspector Pay had come armed with the address of an acquaintance of the missing cook, a Mme Guerin of 192 Rue St Denis, with whom she had lodged during the Commune revolt of the previous year (a bloody uprising following the long siege of Paris in the Franco-Prussian war). That had been a dangerous time for all Parisians and friendships formed then were likely to be strong ones. (*The Times* had already informed its readers that Mme Diblanc had been one of the rebel communists, who had developed a 'taste for the horrible'. She had boasted of the deeds she had committed during that terrible time, they declared, and added that she had come to London to escape retribution.)

The officers discovered that Mme Diblanc had also been friendly with a Mme Bouillon, the concierge, who hailed from her village. Bouillon admitted receiving a letter from Marguerite, written two days before the murder, advising her not to write as she was coming to Paris. But 'subsequently written', on the second page, was the news that Mme Diblanc would not see her friend again – as she was off to America. Warning telegrams were fired off to any ports not already covered: Brest, Le Havre, St Nazaire, Bordeaux and Cherbourg. 'I must beg of you to keep this information to yourself,' Druscovich wrote, somewhat peremptorily, to Superintendent Williamson in a letter dashed off from the hotel that evening, 'so as to prevent it getting into the newspapers as the French papers copy everything connected with this case.'

The British papers were also champing at the bit. *The Times* commented on the fact that the police had not made an arrest yet, and added tightly, 'They profess to be in possession of information which they are unwilling to disclose.'

The London detectives must have been exhausted by now but, their first day in Paris was not yet over. They returned to the Bouillon residence to speak to the husband, by now, home from work. He admitted that, in fact, Marguerite Diblanc had *slept* in their home after her arrival on the Monday night, but had left the following morning without saying where she was going. Druscovich felt that M. Bouillon seemed annoyed with his wife for not having told the whole truth. He also divulged the name of Diblanc's sweetheart who worked for the Omnibus Company of Paris. They went off in search of him but without success.

At 5 a.m. the following morning the French Police raided the Bouillon home. Druscovich claimed that they took this step because he had told them that, despite M. Bouillon's frankness, he was still not happy that the couple were telling all they knew (but this was a subsequent comment and may have been a bit of face-saving). The search revealed Mme Diblanc's green dress, eight Bank of England notes, some gold, and a ring set (in Druscovich's opinion) with imitation diamonds and emeralds. The couple were arrested, the husband now declaring he would rather die than give any more information.

'But I think,' confided Druscovich to Williamson in the next evening's letter, 'we have other means at our disposal, upon which enquiry may be made and perhaps with some chance of success.' He and Inspector Pay had not considered telegraphing their latest news for fear of it becoming public – 'secrecy now is everything now'.

His 'other means' probably referred to the useful addresses which the heavily pregnant Madame Bouillon and her family were now rapidly pulling out of the hat. To follow up these leads, the British and French officers fanned out over Paris, picking up Diblanc's trail and catching up with her 'sweetheart', but not the suspect herself.

'Nothing fresh since yesterday,' telegraphed Druscovich on Saturday, 13 April 1872, 'send me a bill offering reward by tonight's post.'

Sunday's telegram home told a different story: 'Marguerite Diblanc has been apprehended here.'

One of the addresses, gleaned as they went along, had been that of a coal merchant in the Rue de la Porte, St Denis. Here, on Inspector Hinschberger's second visit, who should he find, sitting on the doorstep, but the missing cook. He recognized her instantly, having just been shown her photograph. (Later, the coal merchant was to claim that he called the police himself.)

Once arrested, Marguerite Diblanc freely admitted her guilt explaining that Julie Riel had sacked her but insisted on giving her only a week's notice – and pay which left her in a desperate position. Then, on the Sunday morning, Madame Riel had come to the kitchen. They had quarrelled violently and, in the process, her mistress had been accidently killed. (The rope around the neck had, she claimed, only been used to drag the body to the pantry, but the doctor, who carried out the post-mortem, insisted the act must have been much more deliberate than Marguerite made out, given the damage to the woman's throat.)

Druscovich followed up his triumphant telegram with another letter to Williamson giving details of the arrest and carrying a postscript which said: 'I may mention that on neither occasion has sufficient postage been paid on your letters; on the first occasion I had to pay 90c and the last 1.50.' Clearly a man in whom pedantry tended to overcome tact.

The extradition proceedings were complicated by the fact that Mme Diblanc turned out to be not a Frenchwoman, but a Belgian. No matter, when her case finally came to trial, the fact that she was one of two passionate foreigners locked in battle actually became a strong point in her favour despite the fact that there was evidence to suggest that the murder may have been premeditated. Having it both ways, the Press also painted her as a stolid and crude peasant type but, *The Times* generously assured its readers, her features were 'not as hideous as has been pretended'. However, she was a strongly built woman, with a clear complexion, a large sensual mouth, slightly dilated nostrils, cold blue eyes and a low, broad forehead. Her hair was thick and black and her neck and shoulders powerful but, most telling, her hands 'which she tries to conceal behind the folds of her skirt, are those of a man'.

The English maid told the court that Mme Riel was very excitable, gesticulated a great deal and was often unjust, while Lord Lucan admitted that, 'Like a good many French ladies, she was a little *vive*. I don't know an English word which would describe her better. She was hasty.' A more risky defence move, one would have thought, was getting Inspector Raviart to agree that, when escorting her to Calais, [the handover point for prisoners coming this way], he had told her that, if she had been tried in France the extenuating circumstances would have been taken into account. Marguerite Diblanc was found guilty of the murder of Mme Riel, but the jury thought that premeditation was not proven and gave a strong recommendation to mercy – which was shown. A few days after being sentenced to death, she was reprieved and her sentence commuted to penal servitude for life.

In due course, Inspectors Raviart and Hinschberger received rewards of 20 pounds each, although the Yard soon got itself into a lather when they failed to come up with a receipt. Inspector Pay received ten pounds, Druscovich seven pounds ten shillings, and C Division's Inspector Hambling, third on the scene, five shillings.

The lowly, Divisional Detective Sergeant Butcher collected only three shillings and the uniformed police constable, first called, nothing.

Even while the Diblanc extradition proceedings were in progress, Detective Sergeant Greenham was being withdrawn from protection duty with the exiled Napoleon III, who now lived in Chislehurst, and was then sent to Nice in pursuit of a bank clerk who had absconded with £12,000 of his employers' money. Protection of exiled foreign royalty, of which we had an abundance, as well as that of the British variety, was another of the responsibilities of the detective branch. Often, of course, it was the exiles' own disenchanted countrymen who were out to get them, but this was not quite the situation in a bizarre case handled by Superintendent Williamson in June 1874.

Gustave Bernard Gennovich, a jeweller who lived in Store Street in Bloomsbury, claimed to be not only a native of Warsaw but a Polish prince. He felt attached to his adopted land, however, and felt that, in these dangerous times, Britain should have 'the best of arms' with which to defend herself. To this end, he had invented a new mobile cannon, and attempted to interest the War Office in this 'superior invention', but they failed to respond. Having, as he put it, corresponded quietly on the subject for some time, he then decided to try the effect of 'a louder correspondence'.

This entailed the donning of a uniform and the loading of his model cannon into a cab. He then proceeded to Portland Place where he stopped outside the house of Prince Edward of Saxe-Weimar, set up his cannon and fired it, before knocking on the door to enquire what the Prince thought of that? Not a lot, in fact, as he was not at home (although he did hear the loud report *en route* to a levee). The butler, however, was frightened out of his wits by the explosion and the sight of an excited middle-aged foreigner in military uniform. Gennovich called back a few days later, but this time, the butler gathered his wits sufficiently to call a policeman who arrested the eccentric artillery man.

The Pole had also been dashing around, trying to demonstrate his not-so-secret weapon to Disraeli, the new prime minister, and 'the Princess of Prussia at Buckingham Palace' (Queen Victoria's daughter). The offending ordnance, which was according to the *Police Guardian* 'about the size of an ordinary blunderbuss', had been brought to court as an exhibit and he offered to demonstrate its capabilities, much to the amusement of those gathered. The offer was declined.

Superintendent Williamson revealed to the Bow Street magistrate that the Pole was no stranger to him having first 'come under the cognizance of police' as far back as 1857. Five years later, in 1862, he had been found wandering in the grounds of Windsor Castle, and, shortly afterwards, he sent a photograph of himself to the Queen. Prince Edward of Saxe-Weimar, who sat on the magistrate's bench on this occasion, said he knew the prisoner by sight – simply because he kept popping up at places he attended, bowing and waving to him.

The magistrate remanded the fiery Pole for inquiries to be made into his state of mind even though there seemed little doubt about that.

The increase of the department's extradition work, brought on by treaties signed in 1870 and after, is demonstrated by the fact that in December 1874, Sir Thomas Henry, the Bow Street chief magistrate, gave Chief Inspector Druscovich a five pounds reward and Sergeants Gibbs and Greenham two pounds ten shillings each, for their attention to extradition cases generally and more especially for their very clever recapture of a prisoner named Jules Moreau wanted for forgery in France. Sergeants Reimars and Von Tornow also received two pounds ten shillings each for their diligence in executing extradition warrants.

All this foreign travel may have seemed very attractive to the uniformed constable, spending long hours pounding his beat in all weathers – for little reward and no public recognition. But the excursions were often extremely uncomfortable, tiring, stressful, and even dangerous – in one case, costing the detective his life.

Early in 1876, Detective Inspector Daniel Davey (who had worked with Thomson on the Brown mother-and-daughter murder in Poplar) was sent to Naples to extradite a criminal and, while awaiting the court's decision, fell sick with a fever. When the extradition warrant was finally granted the doctor attending Davey thought him not yet fit to travel. But, being ill among strangers in a foreign land is wretched, and the inspector insisted he was now well enough to go home. His condition worsened on the long journey by boat to Southampton but was ameliorated by the kindly attentions of his prisoner who, while acting as sick nurse, grasped the opportunity to find and destroy his own extradition warrant.

By the time they reached port, the prisoner had gained such

trust that he was allowed the dignity of disembarking without handcuffs. But as soon as the opportunity arose, he escaped, and the now weak and tottering inspector was able to make no more than a feeble attempt to recapture him before falling prostrate to the ground. After coming round, Inspector Davey wandered about Southampton desperately seeking his charge. He even went into a police station for help, but they were unable to make sense of his delirious ramblings. By 4 a.m. the next day he had somehow managed to make it home to Cambridge Street in Pimlico. His wife fetched their neighbour, Sergeant Greenham, who reports in his memoirs, how he found Davey lying on his bed, fully clothed, blue in the face and delirious. 'All I could get out of him was that he had lost his prisoner at Southampton, and that he was ruined. He moaned piteously.' (Losing a prisoner has always ranked high on the list of police 'crimes'.)

Greenham was sent down to Southampton and, with the help of the local police, combed the hotels and boarding houses where, eventually, they found the prisoner – just as he was about to leave. They disabused him of the presumption that, as his extradition warrant no longer existed, he was now safe – and rearrested him. A few days later, Inspector Davey died. According to police records, the cause of death was typhoid, but George Greenham recalls it as typhus – the two were often confused. (Greenham did not actually name the inspector but gave his exact date of death which tallies, so I have presumed it was Davey.) As for the criminal, Greenham reports that he got 'his deserts' at the Old Bailey.

Inspector Davey was not the only such loss to the department at that time. The previous year, the 45-year-old Inspector Pay had suffered a heart attack and died. Two renowned ex-detectives had also gone by then. Richard Tanner, described by a contemporary as the best detective, barring Whicher, the department had ever possessed, died of apoplexy in October 1873. In September 1874, Inspector Field, said to be the model for Dickens' Inspector Bucket in *Bleak House*, passed away at his Chelsea home. (Dickens, himself, had died in 1870.)

According to Chief Inspector Littlechild, one of the tales Williamson liked to tell his detectives was of the time he attended the funeral of 'one of the old officers' (probably Field, whose grave I found recently) at Brompton Cemetery and wandered around afterwards, looking at the inscriptions. He came across a tall, well-set-up, elderly man tending a grave and, thinking he recognized him as one of their pensioners, asked if he was once in the police force? 'No,' replied the man, 'thank God, I have never sunk as low as that yet!'

That brief encounter could be seen as prophetic. For, by then, the canker of corruption had already begun to worm its way into Williamson's select little group of trusted men.

Even while Inspector Davey's funeral arrangements were in progress, Superintendent Williamson and Chief Inspector Druscovich were organizing what was probably their biggest extradition trip so far – at least, in terms of numbers. They were off to Calais with five other officers to pick up no less than eleven prisoners of six different nationalities. These were the men from the sailship, *The Lennie*, who were accused of murder on the high seas. The previous November, six men had landed at La Rochelle in a small boat, claiming that they had been shipwrecked. But the French authorities were suspicious and sent out a man-of-war which came upon the fully-rigged, British/Canadian ship, *The Lennie*. There were seven sailors aboard but the captain, first mate and second mate were all missing. All three had been murdered. Two of the crew claimed not to have been involved and they gave evidence against the rest. The accused were mostly Greek and Italian but there was also a Turk, an Austrian, an Englishman and a Dane. To complicate matters further, all had given English names when they signed on, followed by different, false names to the French. As a result, most were charged under at least three names each.

After their trial at the Old Bailey, four men, all of them Greeks, were found guilty of the murders and hanged – and praise was heaped on the zeal, energy and intelligence of the French authorities.

It was cheaper to have a foreign crew, but such a mix – of mostly inexperienced men – was known to be explosive and the case was almost a replay of *The Flowery Land* mutiny twelve years earlier. In that instance the captain, first mate, and captain's brother, were murdered as the ship was *en route* for Singapore. The life of the second mate was spared so that he might navigate to Brazil where the crew landed, claiming to be from a foundered ship. They were soon arrested and six Spaniards, one Turk, and one Greek, were brought back to England for trial. One was acquitted, two found guilty but reprieved, and the remaining five were hanged.

6 Scandal

Judging by what emerged later, it seems likely that John Meiklejohn was corrupt even before he joined the Metropolitan Police in 1863. His transfer to the Detective Department three years later offered him just the opportunities which he had been looking for. But it was not until 1873, when he was a 35-year-old detective sergeant, that this Scotsman from Dunblane on the edge of the Highlands, took the path which was to bring about the downfall of the whole department.

In addition to handling extradition matters, keeping a lookout for Fenians and baby farmers and taking charge of the more serious murder enquiries, the Yard detectives also investigated cases of fraud, particularly those associated with horse racing. Chief Inspector Clarke was the accepted authority on the latter and had many successes, breaking up the gangs who were forever thinking up crooked new schemes to part the public from their money. Inevitably, the other detectives had a hand in these cases and, indeed, another related duty was to assist in policing race meetings where 'the swell mob' preyed upon the wealthy punters by stealing their wallets & watches or relieving the gullible of their cash in rigged gambling games. Then there were the 'duffers' who got things up to look like what they were not – from horses to 'gold' rings, and the 'shofulmen' who passed dud coins. Con men went in for 'gammoning [to talk plausibly and, in this context, deceitfully] a countryman', purporting to be able to get jobs for rustic types or selling them something which did not exist – even getting themselves up in smocks and hobnail boots for the purpose. And for good measure there were the welshing bookmakers, potential horse dopers, and even those demanding protection money from stallholders. As 'the Turf' became increasingly disreputable the need for detectives on the race courses grew. Druscovich was even excused from the Central

Criminal Court, part way through the Park Lane Murder Trial to attend Ascot race meeting. So it was little wonder that many of the detectives became familiar with the racing fraternity – and those who battened on to them, such as the swindler, William Kurr.

In 1873, Kurr, with two accomplices, set up a betting agency in Edinburgh but its methods soon came under police scrutiny. One of the partners was arrested. But, before the others could be found, Meiklejohn had tipped off Kurr in time for the latter to flee to America. Six months later, he judged things would have quietened down enough to return and he called upon the detective sergeant to reward him for services rendered. Further bribes for warnings were forthcoming as Kurr, an associate named Harry Benson, and several others, set up various betting frauds. But they were in the process of preparing a more elaborate swindle and needed bigger fish than Meiklejohn on the hook. Luck was with them. Druscovich, whose work had even been praised by Alexander III, the Czar of all the Russias (probably for tasks performed during the preliminaries for Prince Alfred's marriage to a daughter of the Czar), found himself in urgent need of £60. He had backed a bill for his brother which he could not meet. Meiklejohn, who, by then, had made enough for bribes to buy himself a house, was unable to help – but he knew a man who could – William Kurr.

Meanwhile, the work of the branch continued.

'A TRAGEDY?' is how the *World* headed its discussion of a matter 'which, strange to say, has hitherto been kept out of the columns of the newspapers. Westminster Hall is, as a rule, too busy with briefs to occupy itself with speculations on possible cases for criminal courts. But it is just now profoundly stirred by grave suspicions and is agitated by fear that a tragedy has been enacted almost within its precincts.'

Until 1882 the Law Courts were housed in Westminster Hall, now part of the House of Commons. What they were talking about in their issue of 10 May, 1876, was the curious death of a young (unnamed) barrister, the hasty and unsatisfactory inquest which had already been held, and the subsequent suspicions of his 'comrades at the Bar' who had already contacted the Home Secretary – 'with what result may shortly be seen'.

Assistant Commissioner Labalmondiere, asked Williamson to look into the matter but Chief Inspector Clarke had already been investigating, since a friend of the deceased had divulged his suspicions nine days earlier, so it was he who reported the next day. The victim had died in agony in the bedroom of his Balham home only four months after his marriage to an attractive widow. He was Charles Bravo and this was the most mysterious Bravo Case. That Charles Bravo had been poisoned was never disputed – but, by whom? As he lay dying, he could not or would not say, and Florence, his wife and her companion, Mrs Cox, claimed they were completely in the dark – but strongly suspected it was suicide due to money worries. Indeed, they seemed keen that Clarke should agree with that diagnosis.

Chief Inspector Clarke appears to have made quite painstaking and intelligent initial enquiries. His problems were both the complexity of this strange case and the ten-day gap between Charles Bravo's death and the calling in of the police – and then, only by the friend, not a doctor or coroner's officer. By the time Clarke arrived, the trail was not only cold, but any possibly poison-tainted vessels were either well-rinsed or, as in the case of some empty wine bottles, either placed in the cellar among others or sent back to the wine merchant, so that even a so-called expert on poisoning such as himself, had little to go on. It does seem that he failed to help himself in one respect. While paying great attention to the pouring and distribution of the wine on the fateful evening (thought to be the possible means of administering the poison), he was a little slow in retrieving the empty bottles remaining in the cellar and sending them for analysis.

The affair generated immense interest among both the public and the police. Superintendent Thomson of F Division, who appears to have found it difficult to keep his nose out of detective work, informed his old colleague that he had received information that Mrs Bravo and a Dr Gully, who already figured on the peripheries of the case, had had a passionate affair and that the death of her first husband, Captain Ricardo, had caused considerable comment and accusations that Gully might be involved. Ricardo's body should be exhumed, he advised. But Clarke was already on to the Gully connection, on which so much prurient attention was soon to focus. He had interviewed the man himself who had been quite frank about the liaison which, he claimed, was now over.

The Chief Inspector admitted to being unable to find any firm evidence against the doctor, the wife, or her companion, but it is evident, by the tone of his reports that he still had his suspicions.

In one such he points out that the two ladies were 'much given to drink' and as regards Mrs Bravo's feelings towards her husband, she did not appear to have had 'that sympathy and love for him that he might have expected, and she certainly shows no grief at his death'.

He had to accept that Charles Bravo must have taken the poison himself because, 'during his two days' illness, I cannot find that he expressed any surprise as to it, or asked any question how it could have been brought about'. Whether the poison had been put in his room by him, 'or secretly by some other person, I refrain from giving an opinion ... His friends are still strongly of the opinion that he did not commit suicide and aver that he had no cause to do so, but in making these enquiries, it appears to me that his marriage was not altogether a happy one, although it does not appear that he complained.'

The *Daily Telegraph* ran a campaign for the setting up of an enquiry – and a new inquest. They got both. First, a private enquiry by Treasury Solicitor, Mr A.K. Stephenson, who issued peremptory lists of numbered instructions to Chief Inspector Clarke, one of which was rather startling: '3. Make a full report of previous history of Mrs Cox so far as can be ascertained from "the Matron" whose letter (as always, the Yard had received a number of letters offering information) you showed me today. Any communication you may have with "the Matron" must be in your own discretion and not from instruction from me.'

Clarke was not that silly, however, and could also be peremptory. After supplying answers to the solicitor's other questions, he concluded his report, 'As regards Mrs Renwick [the matron] I have made no arrangements with her as she appears to me to be a dangerous woman to have anything to do with, and I can see no good to be gained by employing her.'

Just before the second inquest opened, a Major Bond, the Chief Constable of Birmingham, telegraphed to say he could inform a detective from London how to establish a criminal connection between the principal parties. Sergeant Andrews, who had been assisting in the enquiry, was sent up to the Midlands to see Major Bond. He reported back with the news that, when she was Mrs Ricardo, Florence Bravo had been discovered cuddling on a sofa with Dr Gully. Andrews was obliged to track the source of this rumour, which had been passed on from person to person, but the trail was brought to a halt in Norfolk when someone in the chain refused to divulge the name of their informant.

This whole, time-consuming exercise afforded Clarke no fresh insight – he already knew about Gully. Indeed, when a verdict of murder by a person or persons unknown was brought in by the second inquest jury, he respectfully called the commissioners's attention to the fact that despite all this extra investigation nothing had been elicited 'other than is contained in my former reports'.

No one was ever charged with being responsible for the death of Charles Bravo although there are various theories. These include the possibility that the young barrister had accidentally taken poison he had meant to give his wife, either in small doses to cure her excessive drinking or, in larger quantities, to kill her. She was wealthy, he was not.

The same month as the new Bravo inquest verdict was brought in, July 1876, Meiklejohn, Kurr and Benson dined together at the Cannon Street Hotel to discuss their plans for a really big fraud. They were to publish the *Sport*, a racing journal which would be printed in numbers sufficient only to send out to wealthy, French, betting enthusiasts. The first issue's leader declared the intention of the owner to thwart English bookmakers, who refused to take his bets because he was so successful, by getting agents abroad to place them for him – in their own name (of course) and with their own money. He would give them 5% of his winnings. The gang were going to need to be warned, if and when any complaints came in. As most of such foreign correspondence came in to Scotland Yard through the hands of Druscovich this was the time to begin hauling in their catch. Giving him to understand that they were involved in merely a technical evasion of the Betting Act, nothing criminal, they asked the chief inspector to warn them. He agreed, but refused to take any money, although it was later claimed that £25 offered was tucked into his pocket.

Clarke, whom they referred to as 'the old man' was (again, they later claimed) already in their pay and was now roped in. He was given some envelopes containing blank pieces of paper which he was to send off whenever he thought the gang needed to be informed about something. Meiklejohn, who had like-minded contacts everywhere, also arranged for a couple of Post Office officials in their pay to watch for incoming mail.

Soon, their French scheme caught the attention of the wealthy Comtesse de Goncourt who, after being elaborately hoodwinked, was persuaded to bet with her own money. First, she sent £1,000 to the address they gave her, receiving her winnings in cheques, which she was asked to hold on to for a while in order to comply with English law. This was followed by the gang deciding to allow her the wonderful opportunity of investing £30,000 in a similar scheme. Finding herself temporarily out of ready cash, she consulted her lawyer about raising funds. He realized instantly that she was being duped and promptly alerted a London solicitor, Mr Abrahams, who went to the Yard. He saw Williamson who put his trusted aide, Chief Inspector Druscovich, on to the case. Druscovich warned the gang, as did Clarke, but when the former began to grasp the real implications of the matter he went into severe shock and refused to communicate further.

Kurr dashed off to Derby to get Meiklejohn (who was now an inspector and on loan to the Midland Railway Police as their Superintendent) and told him he must come to London to speak to Druscovich – but to be careful not to arouse the suspicions of Williamson. Meiklejohn thought that was highly unlikely, and described his chief as 'a calf' – 'He will never tumble to it in a thousand years.'

Meiklejohn sought out Druscovich who, by now, was in a panic and insisting he must arrest *someone*. For a while, Kurr (against whom there was little evidence) was mooted as a suitable detainee but it came to naught. Despite refusing to co-operate further, the chief inspector did slow down one line of enquiry by writing (instead of telegraphing) to the Scottish police to tell them to watch out for French bank notes being changed through the Bank of Scotland. He was no fool and must have realized that the capture of the crooks would probably mean he was done for as well.

Eventually, even 'the calf' began to wonder why, despite the amount of information coming in, there was so little progress being made on this case. Suspicion mounted when Meiklejohn was reported as having been seen in the company of members of the gang, and Williamson himself became certain he recognized the handwriting on some suspect letters as that of Chief Inspector Palmer.

Suddenly, Benson and others were arrested in Rotterdam. Kurr sent a bogus telegram to the Dutch police, using Williamson's name, advising them that they had the wrong people. This desperate measure almost effected their release but second thoughts caused the recipients to await confirmation. Druscovich and five other officers were sent across to extradite the men.

With Druscovich out of the way, a warrant was obtained for the arrest of Kurr and handed, under conditions of great secrecy, to 30-year-old Detective Sergeant John George Littlechild, who had been in the department for six years and had himself shown some promise in fraud cases. He had already been following Kurr for some time, a task he found exhausting, as the man dashed from race meetings to prize fights, often using his smart horse and trap.

Littlechild was later to ascribe his successful career to reading the work of great writers: Dickens, Thackeray, and, most particularly, Bulwer ('the pen is mightier than the sword') Lytton. One of Lytton's characters declares, 'For a bright manhood there is no such word as *Fail*'. Littlechild, who was to claim that this whole life had been based on knowledge gained from his author's work, may have had these noble sentiments in mind when he set about his vital task. He and 'a trusty colleague' watched Kurr's Islington home throughout New Year's Day, 1877, a dreadfully chilly and tedious task. It was already dark by the time Kurr and two accomplices emerged. The detective sergeant swung into action, moving fast to arrest his quarry, 'a big, powerful fellow'. But he met some fierce resistance, later described in true *Boy's Own Paper* fashion in the *Police Review*, 1893. The men ran and the two detectives chased after them when suddenly Littlechild found himself seized around the chest by a hefty minder. Nothing daunted:

> I dealt him a fearful blow with my blackthorn and freed myself. The man we wanted ran off. We followed.
> Just as I reached him he turned at bay and thrust his hand into his hip pocket for his revolver. I seized him, and said as he was taking it out – 'Don't make a fool of yourself,' and took the weapon away; but it was an exciting moment.

After the trial and conviction of the Turf Fraud gang they began to talk. In due course Meiklejohn, Druscovich, Palmer and Clarke followed them into the dock at the Old Bailey. The evidence against Clarke proved to be flimsy – most of it based only on the statements of the convicted men. (Clarke acknowledged contact, but put a different interpretation on it.) Consequently, his defence counsel, Sir Edward Clarke, aimed merely to show how 'the old man' had been duped by them. He later admitted according to author George Dilnot in his introduction to *The Trial of the Detectives* that he had spent many hours framing the questions he would put to Williamson, regarding Clarke.

I was informed that he still had some friendly feeling towards his old colleague, and that he would not be sorry if his evidence were to assist me in my defence. But he was a man of strictest honour, and every question would certainly be truly answered, whatever the effect of the answer might be. My task, therefore, was to frame my questions that each should bring a reply in my client's favour, without provoking any qualifying phrase which would indicate the opinion of the witness on the case ... My labour was well rewarded and Superintendent Williamson did much to help me to success.

Being economical with the truth is the current term for such dissembling.

Chief Inspector Clarke was acquitted but retired soon after. The remaining accused were found guilty of conspiracy to pervert the course of justice and were each given two years hard labour.

With almost all of their senior officers either in prison or under a cloud and several of the lesser ranks quite possibly tainted, the department was in complete disarray. Quite apart from the scandal, there had been dissatisfaction with their performance for some time, particularly with regard to their handling of some of the more serious cases. As well as the Bravo case in 1876, there were, for example, the murders of Jane Clouson in 1871; Mrs Squires and her daughter in 1872, and Harriet Buswell in the same year, for all of which no convictions had been achieved, and the unsolved Paddington Station jewellery thefts of 1874/5.

Pregnant housemaid, Jane Clouson, had been found crawling on her hands and knees in an Eltham lane. Her head was smashed in so that her brain protruded, her jaw was broken and her eye hanging from its socket. Edmund Pook, her ex-master's son, was arrested and there was substantial evidence against him. But, according to J.H.H. Gaute and Robin Odell in *Murder Whereabouts*, a clever lawyer 'created a climate of confusion in which it was difficult for justice to work', some witnesses probably perjured themselves, and parts of the police case were badly prepared with Pook's alibi not being properly checked and useful clues overlooked. The result was a very confused case and an acquittal. Local people, however, remained convinced of Pook's guilt.

The elderly Mrs Squires and her middle-aged daughter, had kept a wholesale and retail print shop in Hoxton. Like Jane Clouson, they had received severe head injuries – probably inflicted with a hammer. The crime was thoroughly investigated by Chief Inspector Palmer and Sergeant Lansdowne, who even had a canal dragged in the hope of finding the weapon, but the case remained unsolved. It has to be remembered, of course, that shopkeeper murders have always posed problems – similar to notoriously difficult prostitute-killings. Both types of victim have many casual contacts for business purposes only. Added to which, there remained the problem of there being no means of making use of the many physical traces left behind by killers. In this instance, bloody thumbprints on a map, hairs grasped in the daughter's fingers, and a blood-soaked duster and apron found at the scene were of no practical value. (There was still no way to differentiate even between animal and human blood and hair.)

Harriet Buswell, the victim of the Great Coram Street murder, on Christmas Eve 1872, was a prostitute. A suspect was identified – a German pastor on a brig bound for America – but he had been picked out by witnesses going to the ship with the intention of identifying another suspect. There was other evidence against him, such as the fact that he sent several blood-stained handkerchiefs to be laundered shortly after the crime, so he was duly arrested. But his alibi (of being sick in his hotel and having been heard coughing in the night by the hotel owner) was accepted by the Bow Street magistrate and he received governmental apologies and a public subscription contributed to by Queen Victoria.

The murder of Harriet Lane by her lover, Henry Wainwright, in 1874, was solved but required no great detective skills as he was caught by an ex-employer, as he ferried bits of her rotting corpse across London. Furthermore, the man had great difficulty in convincing police of his story, and had to run after the cab containing the parcels of human flesh until he found a constable (the third he had called upon) who would take him seriously. Similarly, the murderer of Mr William Collins by his niece's boyfriend, in Pimlico in 1876, was no great mystery because others in the family who had also been attacked (Mrs Collins and the niece) survived to tell the tale. The role of the police was merely to raise the Hue and Cry, which did result in his rapid capture.

The first of the two jewellery thefts at Paddington Station took place in December 1874, when a lady's maid put a jewellery case (belonging to the Countess of Dudley, and with contents estimated at more than £20,000) down on the pavement for a moment while she turned to help her companion out of a cab. When she turned back, the case had gone. The subsequent search was hampered by the arrival at the station of the Prince of Wales, bound for Windsor by special train and the thief was never found.

The second theft, a month later, in January 1875, was of a dressing case, and its valuable contents – the property of Baron Bulow, the Russian Ambassador. Curiously, the Baron and other passengers including the Duke of Edinburgh, were, at the time, on their way to visit Lord and Lady Dudley, the previous victims, at their country seat.

And, of course, there was the failure in the most mysterious Bravo affair.

Some of the criticism was doubtless justified, some unfair. These attention-grabbing cases were, after all, only part of the wide range of work with which the department had to cope, and much of it they carried out well. Yard detectives did, however, feel hampered by the divisional detective system which, as far as they were concerned, was not working, despite its praises being sung by some divisional superintendents. They complained particularly of the lack of efficient local detectives to assist them when they arrived at the scene of a crime.

The problem was that these divisional detective constables and sergeants, many of whom were worthy, but most of whom were relatively uneducated, were left largely to their own devices. No one seemed to be in charge of them. They could work, or not, as they wished and, even if they did, there was no one of rank to direct their operations or pat them on the back if they did well. A side effect of this state of affairs was that they failed to grow in expertise. When detectives were introduced on to divisions in substantial numbers in 1869, Williamson had tried to get divisional superintendents to take more interest in the cases, or for two detective inspectors to be appointed to each of the four districts and for the whole system to come under the control of the detective branch at the Yard. Superintendents (with the obvious exception of Thomson) said they were too busy to get involved themselves, but neither did they want men on their divisions to be under the control of someone else.

The answer, suggested one of the district superintendents, A.C. Howard in 1871, was to get the men to keep diaries and submit a copy of each day's entry to the district superintendent. That had worked in his last appointment in India when he had sole charge of a district 100 miles long by 50 miles wide 'with several large towns and one city of 200,000 souls'. Williamson may well have felt that advice from a Poona Wallah was just what he didn't need,

The building at the centre of Scotland Yard which in the early 1880s housed the CID headquarters (including the Special Irish Branch)

Members of the Shropshire Constabulary in 1868. Two years earlier the Yard's Detective Inspector Tanner had been sent to aid them with their investigation of the Duddlewick mill murder

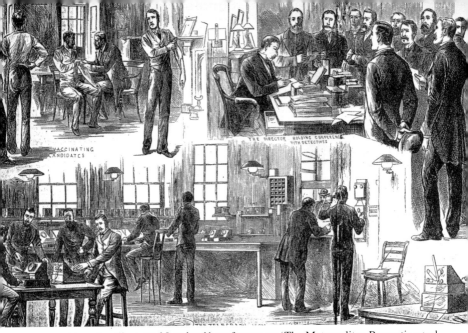

From the *Illustrated London News* feature on 'The Metropolitan Preventive and Detective Police', September 1883. Sir Howard Vincent, the first head of the new CID in 1878, is shown holding conference with the detectives. To his left is Chief Superintendent Williamson, and, far right, the uneducated, but expert thief-catcher, Chief Inspector Shore

Three of the four defendants at the Turf Fraud Trial 1877, *left to right:* Inspector John Meiklejohn and Chief Inspectors Nathaniel Druscovich and William Palmer. Druscovich is depicted as the most evil, possibly due to his foreign background, while in reality the Scotsman Meiklejohn was the most culpable

The damage caused to the CID and Special Irish Branch Offices and the Rising Sun public house opposite by a Fenian bomb placed in an adjacent urinal in 1884

'Identification' from a feature in the *Graphic* on Marlborough Street Magistrates Court, in 1887. Second from left is Detective Drew from Vine Street who was liked among the nobility due to his success at solving diamond robberies. The man to Drew's left is 'Robert the Devil', a regular offender

TWO MORE WHITECHAPEL HORRORS. WHEN WILL THE MURDERER BE CAPTURED ?

THE FIFTH VICTIM OF THE WHITECHAPEL FIEND.

FINDING THE MUTILATED BODY IN MITRE SQARE.

Reaction following the finding of two Ripper victims on the same night of 29/30 September 1888: Elizabeth Stride in Berner Street and Catherine Eddowes in Mitre Square

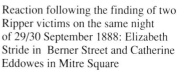

Report in a popular sensational journal on the first of the 'official' Jack the Ripper victims, Mary Ann Nichols. She was found with her throat cut and stomach wounds at Bucks Row on 31 August 1888

One of the early Bertillonage file cards, 1895. The hands are included as their shape and condition were regarded as 'extremely significant'. A well-placed mirror ensures a profile as well as frontal view of the face

A reward poster for the murderess, Marguerite Diblanc, 1872

The men who dug up the remains of Cora Crippen. Inspector Drew is on the far right

Superintendent Frank Castle Froest, the first chief of the Murder Squad who was famous for his exciting extradition adventures, poses in the Yard's photography room

Early twentieth-century detectives disguised ready for observation duty

The four men appointed as CID district chiefs in 1920, *left to right:* Superintendents Hawkins, Wensley, Carlin and Neil. They became known as The Big Four

Sergeant Lilian Wyles, who was to become one of the first policewomen in the Metropolitan Police CID

particularly as there was no record of how the 200,000 souls felt about the type of justice meted out by the diary-writing policemen of an Indian province.

He responded to Howard's suggestion by pointing out that this idea was impracticable, 'with the present stamp of men'. A number of them would, 'from their want of education, find it impossible to make a daily comprehensible report of their proceedings'. Moreover, such a demand would exclude from the detective branch many useful men. He was right, there. Good thief-catchers did not need to be educated or even particularly intelligent. Energy, enthusiasm, gut reaction, knowing their patch and their people, were often sufficient compensation. And while tact, mental agility and flexibility, combined with the ability to act quickly on conclusions drawn, might be necessary to solve the more complex cases, academics or great thinkers were certainly not required. They would a) find much of the groundwork boring and b) still be pondering on the finer esoteric points when the whole thing was over. Indeed, it had been the need to acquire more educated men to handle the numerous sensitive and mysterious 'government enquiries' and extradition cases which had allowed into the department men who were not necessarily keen enough, hungry enough, single-minded enough or trained sufficiently in the ways of the world – and which, subsequently, had contributed to landing them in such a mess. Men open to new ideas and capable of taking an overview of police methods and operations – now that was, and is, something always needed in such a conservative organization as the police.

Of course, all this became academic in itself after the scandal. Even while the men were awaiting trial a Home Office departmental committee was being summoned to enquire into 'the state, discipline and organisation of the Detective Force of the Metropolitan Police'.

Part II

THE CID

7 Femmes Fatales?

When out on enquiries divisional detectives in the Metropolitan Police were expected to walk the first three miles, only from then on could they claim travel expenses. To add insult to footsoreness, refreshment and plain clothes allowances were inadequate, and such were the problems in justifying any small, incidental expenses to the authorities that the detectives often absorbed these themselves – to the tune of several pounds a month. One detective sergeant even told the 1878 Home Office enquiry that had he known about the difficulties caused by these miserly allowances, he would never have joined, and that if he got the opportunity of a job with better remuneration he would take it. (He stayed, and was later to solve an important case, The Muswell Hill Murders, in 1895.)

These were just some of the problems revealed by those giving evidence before the commission. They included Williamson, Shore, Greenham and Littlechild; four divisional detectives, including one ex; two divisional superintendents, and several chief constables from the major cities which had detective branches of their own. Other matters highlighted were: poor pay and promotion prospects, causing suitable men to go back to the uniform branch; the appalling lack of security with regard to detectives' confidential reports and files, which seemed to allow thieves almost equal access to them; the lack of vital legal assistance in the 'getting up of cases' and, perhaps most damaging of all, the intense jealousy which existed between the divisional and Yard detectives.

The divisional men were, as a rule, found to be 'the least educated and least intelligent of men in the force'. Some had even been put into plain clothes for the simple reason that they didn't look good in uniform, and instead of devoting themselves to fighting crime, were being used as messengers and dogsbodies by the uniformed inspectors. Worse was the lack of co-operation between the two sections. The divisional men even went so far as to withhold information from the Yard officers, which might lead to an arrest, 'rather than allow the interloper, as they call him, to carry off the prize'. (The prize included not only the credit but the bulk of any reward). Clearly a better selection and supervision process was called for and (opinion was (almost) unanimous), the new department should be forged into one united branch separate from the rest of the force.

The commission, which began sitting just before the end of the Turf Fraud Trial, also had the benefit of a report on the French detective system, submitted by a young barrister, Howard Vincent. He had been to Paris to study their organization – previously assumed to be inferior to the British. One of his recommendations was that the department should be run by a civilian and, perhaps not surprisingly, the new, grandly named post of Director of Criminal Investigation, went to him. Charles Edward Howard Vincent, 29-year-old second son of the Reverend Frederick Vincent, eleventh baronet, Canon of Winchester, was, in fact, even relatively new to the practice of law, having been a soldier before being called to the bar in 1876.

Not everyone was sold on his *methodes Francaises*. The *Daily Telegraph*, while urging him to concentrate on the prevention of crime as well as investigation and, particularly, to go after the many professional receivers, claimed that this would not be as straightforward as in France because the British police did not have the benefit of the extended system of espionage by concierge. Nor did they keep dossiers on all citizens. 'Our plain sailing and less inquisitorial national character makes us averse from assuming that everybody may possibly be "wanted" for a crime some day or another.' A warning, perhaps, to Vincent not to take these Continental policing practices too far.

Quite apart from concierges and dossiers, the greater powers of the French Police were of 'incalculable assistance' to them, as Vincent himself admitted. They could keep detainees under preventive arrest for an unlimited period, 'reconstitute' crimes, and interrogate suspects repeatedly without their having recourse to legal assistance. The price of English freedom, Vincent later pointed out, was paid for by the occasional failure of our justice system.

Though deprived of the top post, Superintendent Williamson

was not punished for his failure to spot the creeping corruption in his department. Indeed, he was promoted – to Chief Superintendent – but it was noticed that the 'calf' was now 'much less confiding' with his men than before. 'The exposure of certain inspectors', reported Andrew Lansdowne in his book, 'appeared to shake Mr Williamson's faith in his men greatly.' Which, surely, was no bad thing.

Another man promoted was the ill-educated, but obviously considered honest, Inspector John Shore. He became a chief inspector, while the remainder of the branch, barring one sergeant, were placed on three months probation.

Police Orders of 6 April 1878, revealed the shape of the new department. The number of inspectors at the Yard was to be increased to 20 but, more significant, was the introduction of a detective inspector to each division (to be known as the local inspector). At last, someone was going to be effectively in charge out there – the new local inspector – under the direct control of the centralized CID. In fact, the divisional superintendents, angry at their powers being usurped, soon demanded and obtained a degree of local control even though their previous lack of interest had been one of the main reasons that the divisional detective system had been unsuccessful.

The divisional detectives, too, were placed on three month probation in order to prove themselves worthy of the new organization. It was not easy, however, to find sufficient local talent of the calibre required to replace those found wanting and to bring the divisional detectives up to their new strength of 15 inspectors, 160 sergeants and 80 constables (these last to be intermittently employed in plain clothes). However, several shrewd and trusty sergeants were found for rapid promotion to the rank of local inspector.

One Yard inspector, Edward Sayer, made it through his probation period only to die of pleurisy shortly afterwards at the age of thirty-eight. The death of one of the new divisional detectives, Sergeant Allday of G Division, eight months after the formation of the CID, was to cause a sensation. This was initiated by press reports claiming that he had been forced back on duty 'whilst in feeble health' and that he had died the same night. There was no foundation to these rumours, the *Police Guardian* assured its readers. Allday had been on the sick list for six months, had resumed against the wishes of his superior officers – possibly he was trying to hold onto his desirable detective job (now better paid than the uniform branch and with automatic seniority) – but had needed to go sick again after being on duty for just six days. Three days later, he died.

Allday, who had twenty-two years' service, was given an impressive funeral, attended by 180 men, four inspectors, one chief inspector, one superintendent and the G Division band playing 'The Dead March'. Due to the press speculation, 'more than the usual interest was manifested' by the public, reported the *Police Guardian* – before going on to admit that, in fact, several thousand members of the public had come to line the route of the funeral procession.

Of course, the national death rate was much higher at the time and police figures reflected this. The greatest threat to policemen was tuberculosis which accounted for twenty-seven of the sixty-four Metropolitan Police ('Town and Woolwich Divisions') deaths during 1878. Pneumonia, bronchitis and pleurisy saw off eight more, while scarlet fever, diphtheria and typhoid killed another five. The remaining twenty-four died from causes ranging from accidents (three, including one drowning) to tetanus, and complications following a foot abcess. One constable committed suicide by jumping out of a window.

It would be nice to claim that the new system proved to be instantly more successful than its predecessor, but this was not quite the case. Progress was, as ever, mixed.

Three of the first murder cases tackled by the new department were startlingly similar to each other. The handling of the first of this trio fell to the newly promoted, Dorset-born, local inspector at Bow Street, Francis Frederick Kerley. Kerley had won the approval and admiration of his superintendent, James Jacob Thomson, when as a sergeant in 1873, he had boarded a smallpox-stricken ship to continue his enquiries (into the Coram Street murder) after all about him (including the German consul and a German policeman) had fled.

The daring Kerley was soon joined on the case by an inspector from the Yard, the newly promoted Andrew Lansdowne, who later confessed that the most discouraging thing which could happen to a detective was 'to find himself without a clue' and pointed out that it was frequently cases such as these which captured the imagination of the public. 'I refer to mysterious murders.'

The enquiry began in the early hours of Wednesday, 12 December 1878, after the battered body of an elderly Jewish widow, Mrs Rachel Samuels, was found in the kitchen of her large house in Burton Crescent, Bloomsbury. Her lodger, described by *The Times* as 'a Bohemian musician', had realized something was wrong when he came home at around midnight to find that his supper had not been left out for him in the parlour, as was the usual practice.

Mrs Samuels was rumoured not only to have a great deal of money hidden about the place but to be excessively parsimonious. 'This impression', confided *The Times* the next day, 'was strengthened by the fact that, notwithstanding the large size of the house, she kept no regular servant.' In fact a girl came in each morning to clean and departed at 2 p.m. Mrs Samuels also had an ex-servant, Mary Donovan, who had left her service on marriage several years earlier but still visited her ex-mistress two or three times a week to do odd jobs about the place. By all accounts, the pair seemed fond of each other, despite the fact that Mary complained about the old lady working her too hard, paying her badly, and feeding her little. Relationships with her three grown sons who lived nearby, were rumoured to be strained but, like good Jewish boys, they supped with mother every Saturday evening.

All that appeared to be missing from 4 Burton Crescent was a gold wedding ring, a detachable pocket usually worn by Mrs Samuels, a few pounds rent money and a pair of new boots. Contrary to rumour, the old lady did not keep a great deal of money in the house (only £25 was found tucked away) and, despite the fact that her sons were in the trade, she was not fond of jewellery.

The detectives discovered that Mary Donovan, who liked her drink, had been on the premises on the night of the murder. She'd been seen there at 8.30 p.m. by a young woman who had gone for an interview for a job – to replace the morning girl who came in to clean. As the lodger usually returned home at 10 p.m. to find his supper ready it seemed probable that she had been killed between 8.30 p.m. and 10 p.m. Mary Donovan's landlady assured police that Mary had not returned home at all that evening and, when she did put in an appearance the following morning, she was in a very disturbed and disorderly state and was carrying a bundle under her shawl. The woman was in no doubt about this as she was looking after Mary's stepchildren (Mr Donovan being a nightwatchman at a distillery) and was not very pleased by her lengthy absence.

'Bloodstains' on Mary's shabby and dirty clothes seemed to clinch the matter and Inspector Kerley, with Inspectors Lansdowne and Fordham went to arrest her. While making the arrest, Fordham noticed that the prisoner kept her hand in her pocket. In it, he discovered a purse containing 16 pence and fifteen pawntickets. The latter merely revealed how desperately poor she was. The earliest pawnticket, dating back nine months, was for a gold wedding ring. More recent were those for a towel and pillow-case (sixpence); and a shirt (sixpence). The latest, was for a coat (14 shillings). Also in Mary's possession were some new boots which she claimed her husband had bought for her, but of which he denied knowledge. When a pawnbroker's assistant identified Mary as the Mrs Donovan who had pledged a gold wedding ring shortly after the murder there seemed to be no doubt the police had their murderer.

Shortly after Christmas, however, the police case began to fall apart. The inexperience of the detectives in the handling of 'mysterious murders' (Lansdowne being newly promoted) and the streak of recklessness in Kerley may have caused them to make their arrest too early on – but bad luck also played a part. The pawnbroker's assistant decided it had not been Mary Donovan at all who had pledged the ring. He had picked her out on an identification parade because, being a regular customer, her face was familiar. In fact, the ring had been popped by *another* regular, a Mrs *Ann* Donovan, who – as luck would have it – lived in the same street as Mary, two doors away in fact. And it was obviously her own ring, Inspector Kerley ruefully admitted, because it fitted her perfectly.

The boots in Mary's possession turned out *not* to be those missing from Burton Crescent and, although the public analyst agreed that some of the many stains on Mary's clothes and boots were blood, and recent at that, there was no way to disprove her claim that it was her own, nor, indeed, to prove it was even human – merely that it had all the known properties of human blood. Bloody fingerprints had been found on a knife at the scene but, of course, nothing could be made of them.

Williamson had already asked the Press to publicize the distinctive missing boots – which were lined with red flannel and trimmed with black fur – and had issued handbills describing them.

New evidence suggested a good motive for Mary in addition to possible resentment at and the sudden acquisition of a little ready cash. It seemed that Mary might have been about to have her nose pushed out of joint by her own sister who had been invited to live with Mrs Samuels. But nothing of particular assistance emerged apart from Mr Poland, for the prosecution, managing to prove that Mary had lied when she said she had cut the old lady's toenails that evening as they were still almost an inch long. He made a plea to the public for assistance, but had to admit to the Bow Street magistrate, Mr Flowers, that he had nothing to add to the evidence. It was only right, however, to say that the police had neglected no duty in the matter and he would now leave the result to Mr Flowers' discretion.

Frederick Flowers, son of the Reverend Field Flowers, was as kind and gentle as his name suggests (although some thought him a deal too lenient) and had the rare propensity to see things from the point of view of others. He agreed that there was no blame attached to the police, they had done their duty, but he felt no jury would convict on the merely suspicious circumstances, and discharged the accused. Given Mr Poland's negative attitude he could scarcely do otherwise although, strictly speaking, the circumstantial evidence against Mary was quite strong. Suspicious circumstances are, after all, what evidence is all about and there was little else to base a case on in those days.

Curiously, the entry in the Annual Register for 10 January 1879, quotes Mr Flowers rather differently from *The Times*, making it appear that he chastised the police for charging her at all – which seems unlikely given his mild character. As far as I know, no one else was charged with the murder.

Early one morning, a few weeks later, a coal cart driver spotted a wooden box half-submerged in the Thames, near Barnes, in West London. He hauled the box in, opened it up, and found what looked like 'a lot of cooked meat'. Some of the meat looked fresher and vaguely human. It proved to be the partial remains of a woman's body, some of them having been boiled. There was no head and none was ever found but, five days later, a foot turned up on a dung heap, just upstream at Twickenham. A local surgeon declared the remains to be those of a woman under thirty years of age.

As before, the investigating team comprised of the new local inspector, Henry Jones of T Division, and a Yard man – the stocky, ex-Wiltshire labourer, Inspector John Dowdall. It is not easy to proceed very far with a murder enquiry until the corpse has been identified and the team were unable to find any clue as to the woman's identity so the inquest brought in an open verdict. (Identification was made more difficult by the fact that London had such a large itinerant population. Lansdowne and Sayer had had a similar case five years earlier when portions of a woman's body had turned up, bit by bit, in the Thames: 'the left upper quarter of a woman' off Battersea Water Works, 'a set of lungs' under the second arch of Battersea Bridge, and so on. On that occasion a man had identified early segments as remains of his missing daughter but had changed his mind when the face and scalp were recovered.)

Two-and-a-half weeks after the finding of the box, three men presented themselves at Richmond Police Station where they proceeded to reveal their (belated) suspicions regarding a servant named Katherine Webster whose mistress, Mrs Julia Martha Thomas, appeared to be missing from her home at 2 Vine Cottages, Richmond (Richmond, Barnes and Twickenham are all on the same leafy stretch of the Thames). By this time, another surgeon had examined the remains and had raised the likely age of the victim to over fifty years and estimated her height to have been 5 feet, 2 inches. The missing woman was fifty to sixty years old and five feet, three inches tall.

Given the circumstances, their call was well overdue. One of the men, Henry Porter, was a painter and decorator who lived at Hammersmith. Eighteen days earlier, on the day before the box was found, he and his family had received a visit from an old friend whom they had not seen for several years: 29-year-old Katherine Webster. They noticed that the tall, thin, Irish woman was better dressed and more confident than they remembered her and was showing off rings, trinkets, and photographs of relatives. She explained that she was now a widow, named Mrs Thomas, and had come into some property in Richmond from an aunt. She wondered whether Porter could find her someone to help clear it out? While discussing the matter, Webster, Porter and his 15-year-old son, went to a pub for a drink. After a while, Katherine Webster left them to cross over the river to Barnes to see another old friend. When she came back, she no longer had the heavy black bag she had been carrying. The younger Porter saw her home to Richmond and, once there, she got him to help her carry a large corded, box down to Richmond bridge where she was supposedly meeting yet another friend. As the boy left her, to go for his train home, he heard a splash and when she caught up with him again at the railway station she no longer had the box.

Despite all this, Porter arranged for a local beerhouse keeper, John Church, to effect the house clearance. Evidently, Church and Katherine Webster took a shine to each other, making several convivial visits to her Richmond property to collect smaller items before returning finally with a cart to load up the larger furniture. As this was taking place, the woman who really owned the property and who lived next door, enquired what was happening – and asked the whereabouts of Mrs Thomas. These questions put Katherine into something of a panic and perplexed Church and Porter who, of course, thought *Katherine* was Mrs Thomas. They retreated in disarray.

In the pocket of one of the dresses previously removed from the premises, they discovered a letter to Mrs Thomas. On checking with the person who wrote it, Church, realizing that Katherine was *not* the real Mrs Thomas, finally went to the police – but by this time the bird had flown. The landlady next door had been a bit tardy as well. She now described to police how, on the day after Mrs Thomas had been last seen alive, she had heard sounds of frantic activity in the next-door kitchen and a strange smell emanating from the house. Under the boiler were found charred remnants of human bone and, in it, a great deal of grease.

Katherine Webster was traced to her home in Wexford. Inspectors Dowdall and Jones made the eighty-day round trip across the Irish Channel to collect her. Had anyone else been arrested? she asked them, before claiming that it was really Church who had committed the murder – she had merely come upon the scene later. Church was duly arrested and appeared alongside her at Richmond magistrates court on All Fools Day, 1879.

The female accused had no characteristics of a criminal in her face, *The Times* revealed to its readers next day, and, though not handsome, was 'not ill-looking'. Her jacket, they went on, was of a shabby cloth trimmed with imitation fur, her dress of the material and cut usually favoured by respectable servants but, while her hat was stylish, it was out of keeping with a servant's position. 'The man Church has the appearance of an artisan.' This sneering tone was resumed in another, speculative, *Times* report relating the rumours that John Church and Katherine Webster had been having some sort of dalliance while arranging for the furniture removal, and had been heard calling each other 'Jack' and 'Kate'. 'One day she took a fancy to a large pair of earrings, of a common, inartistic pattern, in a shop at Richmond ... at her examination she wore these and a satin-trimmed "beefeater" hat which was also purchased after she assumed the name of Mrs Thomas.'

It seemed that, as well as the offence she was charged with, Katherine Webster had simultaneously committed the crimes of both being poor and of trying to raise herself. The public appetite for such information was enormous. Not only were all the endless proceedings of the inquest, magistrates' court hearing and trial published in astonishing detail – almost word for word – the press felt free to speculate in a most damaging fashion. Defence counsel complained about them constantly anticipating evidence or making things up but, while the bench agreed that such a state of affairs was deplorable, they assured him they did not read the type of papers which published such things.

Katherine Webster may not have *looked* like a criminal, but she did have a criminal record listing several crimes of theft and the associated use of aliases. However, Mrs Creece, the woman who looked after Katherine's illegitimate little boy, had found her to be an affectionate and good-hearted girl who had shown great kindness to Mr Creece during a long illness. She was also very fond of her own son whom she visited every Sunday on her afternoon off – making sure she got back in time for Mrs Thomas to get to church for evening service.

A really damaging witness against Katherine Webster was another acquaintance, a straw bonnet and hat maker, Mary Durden, who claimed that the accused had told her of an inheritance from an aunt *before* Mrs Thomas died.

Katherine persisted in putting the blame on Church and claimed a previous relationship with him, but the prosecution, unable to find evidence of this, said she was merely attempting to prevent him from testifying against her, and, offering no evidence, had him dismissed from the case. (In fact, at the trial he showed up as a very strange and dubious character, claiming he could not remember quite recent past employment and whereabouts.) Kate also implicated Porter but that didn't stick either, and she, alone, was found guilty and sentenced to death. She maintained her innocence but said she was sorry now she had implicated the two men and that the person really responsible for all this was the father of her child who had deserted her and that, in consequence, she had to steal and go to prison to support the boy. (It may be pertinent that Mrs Thomas died on a Sunday evening – the day of Katherine's weekly visit to her son.)

In an attempt to postpone her execution, Katherine claimed to be pregnant again but this proved not to be true and she was hanged three weeks after sentence – following a confession. When worse for the drink, she had become aggravated by her mistress's manner, she now admitted, and had pushed her down the stairs, then strangled her.

Katherine Webster's case is usually considered in isolation (and with little sympathy) but in fact becomes more interesting in context and alongside the earlier Diblanc murder and the two other similar investigations taking place at the time. On the same day as Katherine Webster's trial began, Hannah Dobbs, another young servant, was appearing in another Old Bailey court room accused of the murder of a wealthy older woman. The availability of servants may seem enviable today but, clearly, it had its dangers to both parties. Despite competition from the latest news of the Afghan and Zulu Wars, the attention of the wealthy must have been riveted by the minutely detailed accounts in their morning papers of these two trials running side by side. One can imagine them, pausing between mouthfuls of kedgeree, to glance up from the tiny print and focus instead on their normally invisible tweeny or butler – and wonder.

This third murder in the curiously similar trio took place at 4 Euston Square – only five minutes walk from the venue of the first, that of Mrs Samuels. On 9 May 1879, a decomposed body was found in one of the coal cellars. It was eventually identified, somewhat tentatively, due to its condition, as that of a previous lodger, 66-year-old widow, Miss Matilda Hacker, who had rather mysteriously left the premises, without notice, two-and-a-half years earlier. According to the landlord and his wife, the only person privy to this leaving had been the servant who looked after the lodgers, 25-year-old Hannah Dobbs and she had been the only other adult in the house at the time of Miss Hacker's going. Again, the case was handled by a combination of a local inspector, Gatland, and a Yard man. The latter, the tall (six foot, one and a quarter inches), Prussian-born, Carl Max Hagen, had been made local inspector in the 1878 reshuffle but had rapidly been moved to Scotland Yard.

As with the other victims, Mrs Hacker was reputedly quite well-to-do but parsimonious. Hannah Dobbs was found to have been in possession of Mrs Hacker's watch (if it was dangerous to have a servant in those days, it was even more dangerous to own a watch) and other trinkets belonging to the late lodger. Like Katherine Webster, Hannah Dobbs was a convicted thief and, in fact, was in prison on a felony charge when the inquiry commenced. This time, the servants' unexpected (and ultimately fictitious) benefactor was claimed to be an uncle. Hannah said that the forced cash box found in her possession was her own, but she could not, however, explain the large stain found on the carpet in Mrs Hacker's room after the woman had left. At her trial, Hannah Dobbs then claimed that the watch had been given to her by the landlord, Mr Bastendorff, and his obvious interest in her helped muddy the waters, as did the possibility that he and his wife could have done the deed and be pushing the blame on to her. As happened so often, the size and complexity of the household at the heart of the investigation complicated police enquiries – so many tangled relationships, hidden motives, simmering passions and hatreds. The still-remaining doubts about the identification of the body and the fact that so few people knew anything about the supposed victim, further weakened the prosecution case. At the end of the second, long day, Hannah Dobbs was found not guilty.

It is quite possible that all three women were guilty. One can quite imagine the tensions in a close relationship where one woman is wealthy and leisured and the other extremely poor and overworked – by the former. Despite finding her not guilty, the jury was said to have retained grave suspicions about Hannah Dobbs. Charles Kingston (*The Bench and the Dock*) believed she must be considered one of the luckiest prisoners to stand in the dock at the Old Bailey and that her defence probably only succeeded because her counsel, Mr Frederick Mead, concentrated on the weaknesses in the prosecution case, thus influencing the judge to sum up strongly in her favour.

Another possibility is that the lone, unprotected women servants were easy targets – the witch-hunt syndrome. If that were so in this case the witch had her revenge. Following the completion of her felony sentence Hannah was made much of by the press, particularly two members of the Central News Agency. They obtained her collaboration in the writing of a pamphlet, *The Life of Hannah Dobbs*, which was distributed by one of the popular true-crime magazines, the *Illustrated Police News*. They sold a great many copies at 1d. each – not surprisingly, for her story contained some startling allegations. These included the claims that Hannah had had relations with Severin Bastendorff *before* becoming a servant in his house, that the murder of Miss Hacker, *and two others* (that of a lodger, Mr Findlay and a young boy) had been committed by the Bastendorffs and that she had been given the watch so that she would keep her mouth shut. It was only as a result of the religious teaching of the prison chaplain that she realized she must be truthful and tell all. Sounds familiar.

Not surprisingly, the publicity did Mr Bastendorff's business no good at all and he had little choice but to sue Mr Purkess, proprietor of the *Illustrated Police News*, even though the police themselves did not appear to believe Hannah's tale. He also applied for an injunction to prevent further distribution of the pertinent issues. This was his undoing. He swore in an affidavit before a judge in chambers that he had not 'known' Hannah in any sense before she became his servant. But he was dealing with bigger fish now, and Mr Purkess took out a summons for perjury and found witnesses who told of Bastendorff and Dobbs meeting when she had been cleaning windows at another establishment, back in 1875. The pair had exchanged saucy chitchat and gone on to consummate their affair in a hotel where they proved a memorable couple, he being short in stature and she being tall.

The perjury case went to trial, the prosecution declaring that they were not relying on the testimony of Hannah Dobbs as they knew this to be tainted. (A bit rich, that, considering that Purkess, who originally brought the summons, had been happy to sell her revelations.)

Bastendorff was found guilty and sentenced to twelve months hard labour.

8   The Fourth Estate

Not surprisingly, the press in general had been on the qui vive for
signs of incipient corruption in the CID as well as evidence of the
dreaded French police methods being put into practice.
Consequently, when the Titley case arose in July 1880, they had a
field day. As with so many sensational cases at the time, it
concerned sex and was the result, in essence, of the social situation
of women.

Police at Bow Street had received a tip-off that a young chemist,
by the name of Thomas Titley was unlawfully providing abortion
drugs to ladies in distress, but they had no solid evidence to back
up a charge. Local Inspector John O'Callaghan, and Detective
Sergeant Shrives set about finding some.

There were no women police, who might have been able to
make discreet enquiries without arousing suspicion, so O'Callaghan turned to Martha Diffey, the wife of a police pensioner. She
was employed as a woman searcher at Bow Street Police Station
and had helped police previously when the female touch was
needed in an enquiry. This time, she was instructed to pretend that
her daughter had been 'got into trouble' by the son of the house in
which she was a servant and was thus in desperate need of one of
Titley's special potions.

The chemist was understandably wary and asked to see either
the girl or, at least, the young man in question. As neither existed,
police produced instead a letter from the worried young man but
this strategy also failed to convince. Consequently, a Detective
Sergeant Stroud was drafted in from an outer division, got up in a
frock coat and tall hat, dubbed 'Henry Williamson' (a little in-joke
there) and sent along to play the young gentleman seducer. This
did the trick. The drugs were handed over and Titley was arrested.

There did seem, however, some truth in his protestations that he
was only trying to help out certain women (usually the women who

98

had been indulging in some extra-marital sex whilst their husbands were abroad 'and tradesmen's daughters') for he charged Sergeant Stroud only four shillings for his mixture of ergot of rye, perchloride of iron and other extracts thought to be suitably noxious to pregnant women.

There was an instant outcry about police acting as spies and *agents provocateurs*, and when Titley appeared at the Old Bailey the detectives and the hapless Martha clearly felt themselves to be on trial. They were constantly referred to as accomplices and accused of falsehood, bribery and forgery, but defence counsel, Sir Edward Clarke, took care to disassociate their leader from any such criticism, despite the fact that O'Callaghan had revealed that Howard Vincent had known about the plan and sanctioned the expenses. Sir Edward even defended the CID chief, pointing out that they were not to know how the case had been presented to Vincent. He conceded that it was a pity that Vincent had been induced to part with £25 of public funds, to help present Detective Sergeant Stroud as a man of means, but he should be sorry to say one word which was unfair to that gentleman (who just happened to be a fellow lawyer, and son of a baronet). The entire responsibility for this disgraceful and nefarious police scheme lay with Detective Inspector O'Callaghan, he insisted, and it was he who was 'the mover and concocter'. As to Mrs Diffey, she had played a most vile part in the proceedings; but it was to be hoped she was ashamed of what she had done. The jury must show that such action was (that old favourite expression) 'repugnant to any Englishman' and find Titley not guilty.

The judge, while, like everyone else, condemning the 'disgraceful' police actions, insisted that the jury divorce that matter from the question of Titley's guilt. He was found guilty but with a recommendation to mercy because of the police incitement. The judge sentenced him to eighteen months hard labour. It may have been some consolation to him that the trial of the three detectives, Shrives, Stroud, O'Callaghan, and Martha Diffey, on charges of incitement, was to take place in the same court on the following day.

They stood indicted on four counts but, not only had they not been given the usual initial magistrates' court hearing, the true bill against them had been drawn up hastily and three of the counts were found to be 'bad law' and the fourth had a substantial defect. They were released, leaving the matter open for further action later, but none was taken. This may have been a contrived exercise, for had the case been proceeded with, the depth of Howard Vincent's responsibility may have been exposed. 'I was never so pleased as when those excellent officers, Local Inspector O'Callaghan, Sergeant Shrider (*sic*) and Sergeant Stroud, stepped out of the dock,' Vincent wrote later. 'It was well understood that they were in no way whatever to blame but they were grateful to me for sticking to them so resolutely.' (He doesn't say who *was* to blame.)

Belton Cobb, writing in 1956 (in his *Critical Years at the Yard*) feels, however, that Vincent himself *was* very much to blame and chastises him in a curiously Victorian manner. 'It was unfortunate that Mr Vincent had a strong leaning towards methods which were quite unEnglish.'

Questions were asked in the House and the Home Secretary made a statement saying that the police should not, as a rule, set traps for people, but adding that in a case which had occurred *since* that of Titley the police did not have sufficient evidence *until* a woman and 'child' had died from an abortionist's attentions. A telling point.

The whole experience cannot have done much for Inspector O'Callaghan who was probably already feeling less than well. He died four years later of consumption – after only nine days sick leave.

Despite their attacks on himself and the CID, Vincent, like the Fieldings in the eighteenth century, was in favour of using the press as part of the fight against crime. He did so, particularly, in the hunt for the Balcombe Tunnel murderer. The case has been referred to as a triumph for the CID but, in one sense, it was quite the reverse – at least initially.

At 3.20 p.m. on Monday, 27 June 1881, a ticket-collector at Preston Park Railway station, on the outskirts of Brighton, opened the door of a first-class compartment on the express which had just arrived from London Bridge. Inside, he found a bloodstained young man, 'his collar gone', who claimed he had been attacked by two other men as the train had passed through the first tunnel after Croydon (Merstham). He gave his name as Arthur Lefroy and told the gathering officials that he had heard a pistol shot and almost simultaneously, was knocked unconscious. He had just come round and now needed a doctor. Suddenly, a guard spotted a chain hanging from Lefroy's shoe and, on pulling it, found a watch attached. Lefroy claimed it was his own and that he had put it there for safety.

There was no sign of his 'attackers', whom he claimed had got out further up the line, so he was taken on to Brighton where the railway station superintendent came to the conclusion that this was a bungled suicide attempt. Lefroy was taken to the police station where a Detective Inspector Howland took a statement from him which included a full description of his assailants. One was about sixty years old, of medium height, with slight grey whiskers, and wore dark clothes. The other was about forty to fifty years old, again of medium height, with a fresh complexion, dark whiskers to the side of his face, no moustache, and was dressed in a greyish suit.

Lefroy was then taken to the county hospital, where his wounds were found to be relatively minor, before being escorted back home to Wallington by a Detective Sergeant John Holmes of the railway police. *En route*, they learned that the body of a man had been found by the track in Balcombe Tunnel – which was about fifteen miles south of Merstham Tunnel, where Lefroy said he had been attacked. At Wallington Railway Station, Holmes received a telegram from Detective Inspector Howland asking him to check the number and make of Lefroy's watch, as no watch had been found on the body. Holmes waited until he got Lefroy home before doing this but, by the time he got back to Wallington Station, another telegram was awaiting him. This time, he was instructed to detain Lefroy until Howland arrived. Holmes ran back to the house but did not enter for fear, he later said, that Lefroy might dash out of the back. When reinforcements did arrive, they found that the bird had flown.

The body beside the track proved to be that of Mr Isaac Gold, a 64-year-old retired businessman and coin dealer. Every Monday, Mr Gold had gone to London to collect takings from a shop he part-owned, sometimes returning with cash, but usually banking the money – as he had done on this occasion. Before falling on to the track he had sustained a bullet wound in his neck and stab wounds to his chest. His hat and umbrella, Lefroy's collar and what was thought to be Lefroy's hat, had been found scattered along the line.

So far, the whole case was remarkably similar to the Muller railway murder seventeen years earlier, the solving of which had been such a triumph for the detective branch. In that case, too, the victim had been elderly and well-to-do, was attacked then thrown from the carriage, and watches and hats had played a large part in the evidence; although, it must be admitted, such items did appear in so many crimes at that time. Watches, because they were such high-value, easily stolen items – being pocket, not wrist – and hats, because so many people wore them and they tended to get knocked off in struggles or left behind at the scene. The major difference between the Muller and the Balcombe Tunnel case was that in the former, the police had no suspect, whilst in the latter, they had one on a plate but had let him go.

The hunt was on for Arthur Lefroy and many a young man found himself being apprehended on suspicion of being the latest railway murderer. To assist, *The Times* helpfully reported a correspondent's suggestion that Lefroy, 'being acquainted with the arts of disguise as practised in the farces and dramas of the second-class theatres, may be disguised as a female'. Meanwhile, the inquest on Mr Gold was opened – as did the baptism of fire on poor Detective Sergeant Holmes. The coroner left no doubt as to his opinion of Holmes' detection skills after he had admitted that not only had he failed to connect the body on the track with the bloodstained Lefroy but had also accepted the first watch number the suspect had given him, without checking it until later and finding it false.

'Did you not think this was all very strange?' the coroner asked.

'No', Holmes replied, 'because I do not know the number of my own watch.'

'Did you not think it curious that he should know the number and not the maker?'

'No.'

'You did not think any of this business was strange?'

'No, Sir, I did not.' He had believed Lefroy's story, the painfully honest Holmes admitted, and pointed out that the man had not attempted to escape from him.

'What if he had done?' asked Mr Brewer, who was keeping a watching brief for the London, Brighton, and South Coast Railway Company.

'It would have created a suspicion on my part', answered Holmes.

What was so embarrassing for Howard Vincent was the fact that John Holmes had declared himself to be a detective sergeant in the Metropolitan Police – attached to the railway company. Vincent was already doing his best to limit the damage by taking a special interest in the murder and issuing a statement to the press asking for their help in the hunt. The *Daily Telegraph* had even published a sketch of the fugitive 'by a gentleman who knew Lefroy and had frequent opportunities of noting his characteristics', alongside the description issued by Vincent: 'Age 22, middle height, very thin, sickly appearance, scratches on throat, wounds on head, probably clean shaved, low felt hat, black coat, teeth much discoloured.'

The *Daily Telegraph* then added that, in the interests of justice, the public should be fully informed about Lefroy's appearance and drew their own word picture of him which was not only much more telling but gave the impression (as did the sketch) that it would not be possible to miss the man.

> He is very round shouldered, and his thin overcoat hangs in awkward folds about his spare figure. His forehead and chin are both receding. He has a slight moustache, and very small dark whiskers. His jaw-bones are prominent, his cheeks sunken and sallow, and his teeth fully exposed when laughing. His upper lip is thin and drawn inwards. His eyes are grey and large. His gait is singular; he is inclined to slouch, and when not carrying a bag, his left hand is usually in his pocket. He generally carries a crutch stick.

Williamson attended the inquest on Mr Gold, which lasted several days, and the reliable Yard men, Detective Inspectors Swanson and Jarvis, were assigned to the case. Donald Sutherland Swanson hailed from Thurso, near Caithness, at the very northern tip of Scotland (as, confusingly, did a uniformed inspector, Donald Swanson, also serving on A Division). The 37-year-old, Frederick Smith Jarvis, had left the force in 1876 after nine years service but had rejoined two years later and his star was now in the ascendant.

But the continued identifying of Holmes as a Metropolitan detective sergeant irritated Vincent, causing him to make a tactical error. After the coroner had completed his summing up on the final day of the inquest, he announced that he had received a telegram from the director of the CID saying that Holmes was *not* a detective officer in the Metropolitan Police. He and twelve others, Vincent insisted, 'although still on the register of that force' were wholly attached to, and in the employment of, the General Post Office and three railway companies, – 'under whose orders they entirely and exclusively act'.

Mr Brewer commented drily that Holmes had been in the

Metropolitan Police for eleven years and for only about three months with the railway, and added that they paid Scotland Yard, not the man. In any case, they drew police from Scotland Yard 'for the purpose of getting the very best men'.

The following day, *Punch* (parodying Howard Vincent's instructions to his men) came out with some 'Police Precautionary Regulations', one of which was:

> *Guarding a Suspected Charge.* Make yourself quite comfortable about this, and don't take a narrow view of the matter. Treat your charge with every confidence, and remember he deserves it. If he wants you to come down to Folkestone, and then, jumping on board, says, 'Look here, I *should* like to have a look at Boulogne – *let him*. Be quite sure he'll come back by the next boat – or by the next but one. If he happens to have somebody else's drawing room clock in his hat, is gashed from head to foot, and has nothing at all about him beyond this to excite suspicion, treat him with gentlemanly tact. In short, manifest a generous trustfulness, and thankfully act on his suggestions. Offer a reward for him. Set the public by the ears, arrest several wrong people, and so shed lustre on the Defective Department generally.

The same day, as a result of 'information received' Lefroy was arrested by Swanson and Jarvis in a Stepney boarding house. It was found that Lefroy had cut off his whiskers and moustache but, to the delight of the press, was in possession of a false set. Opinion was divided as to whether he looked anything like his picture (which the Yard had had copied and issued). Nothing like, said some witnesses, very like, a fellow lodger told the *Daily Telegraph*.

Previous to the crime, Lefroy had travelled only in second- or third-class railway carriages but on the morning after his arrest, he was travelling first class once more when being taken to Lewes Prison by train – on the same line on which his alleged offence had been committed. The irony was not lost on the press, even though they were under the impression he was heading for East Grinstead magistrates court. The *Daily Telegraph*, possibly carried away by the impact of their illustration, went somewhat overboard in their extremely lengthy coverage of this journey even by the standards of the day.

> The weather was beautiful – perfect holiday weather – but sadly out of harmony with the grim business on hand. A light wind chased some gauzy clouds along the sky, and blew the smoke sideways

from the chimney tops across the yard of the railway station. There was neither hurry nor bustle; nor, with the exception of a little crowd of policemen drawn up inside the station to the right of the first entrance, were there any visible signs of preparation. Outward-bound holiday makers, bent Brightonwards, took their tickets unconcernedly, not dreaming that they were to be fellow-travellers of the suspected murderer. Some workmen and persons employed about the station, knowing who was expected to arrive, were on the watch for the four-wheeled cab, which presently, at a smart pace, drove into the yard. Suddenly the group of policemen displayed extraordinary activity. Keeping together, they pushed about the passengers, driving them back like chaff before the wind.

Some passengers, who failed to appreciate the necessity for this brisk treatment, became involved in altercations of the 'Do you know who I am?/I'm only doing my dooty' variety.

While this – to the police – possibly pleasant diversion was going on Inspectors Swanston (*sic*) and Jarvis had hurried their man into a first-class compartment of the Brighton train, and drawn the blinds.

Despite these drawn blinds, our trusty reporter described a great deal of what happened in the carriage. Lefroy at first talking in an unconcerned manner with his captors, gradually growing more cheerful until he could have been mistaken for 'an ordinary commonplace traveller'. Until, that is, the train steamed into the Merstham Tunnel 'when he became silent and disturbed, first holding his arms across his breast and drooping his head, next lifting his head, thrusting his neck forward, and with his right hand stretching out his under lip, and letting it contract again and again'. Noisy mobs threatened, jeered and hooted at the carriage (booing was still in its infancy) at East Croydon and Redhill Stations.

By the time the train reached Three Bridges, it was known that a change of instructions had been received from headquarters and the prisoner was to be taken to Lewes, and not East Grinstead, so that at Haywards Heath a fraught change of carriage had to be made. The *Daily Telegraph* man admitted that Lefroy being marched along the platform between two detectives:

looked a wretched object ... He evidently felt his degradation deeply. His face worked convulsively, his fingers clenched and then opened, and his arms twitched in the grasp of his captors ... Why so many persons along the line should have made a holiday of the

procession to gaol of a wretched, friendless lad accused of a
shocking murder is not easy to understand.

Quite. The report went on and on, not forgetting to add that
despite Lefroy's lack of whiskers and crumpled billy-cock hat, 'It
was not difficult to identify him by the sketch portrait in the *Daily
Telegraph.*'

In their next issue, an unrepentant *Punch* published a picture of
the bewigged lawyer, Vincent, surrounded by the paraphernalia of
fictional detection: false moustaches, handcuffs, a carnival mask
and a dark lantern, and reading one of the popular detective
novels of Emile Gaboriau whose Parisian police detective, Lecoq,
was a master of disguise. *The Pirates of Penzance* had had its
first staging four years earlier and the police sergeant's song was on
everyone's lips. The picture's caption declared that Vincent might
be the Directeur des Affaires Criminelles de la Police
Metropolitan de Londres and a Membre de la Faculté de Droit et
de la Société Générale des Prisons de Paris –

AND YET
When there's practical detection to be done,
    To be done,
This Director's lot is not a happy one.
    Happy one.

Underneath, was 'The Diary of a Modern Detective' in which,
having received one of Vincent's circulars together with a copy of
one of Gaboriau's novels, the diarist is now on the alert and
keeping a sharp look out for a man with one eye, one arm and one
leg. 'There's a task for you!' Fortunately, the suspect also has
green hair and a dark blue complexion but the detective still has to
write 'for further particulars' and, meanwhile, is studying the
novel which he finds engrossing.

The evidence against Lefroy was already strong but Swanson
and Jarvis worked hard to ensure their case was iron-clad and to
disprove Lefroy's story. Their parade of witnesses included a man
from the next carriage who swore to hearing several 'explosions' as
the train entered the Merstham Tunnel, and a woman and her
daughter who lived by the track who described seeing two men
scuffling in a carriage as the train passed their cottage. A guard
declared that Lefroy's 'attackers' could not have left the express
before Preston Park as it did not stop after Croydon. Had they
tried to do so, as it slowed to three or four miles an hour by some

signals, they would have broken their limbs. It was admitted that it was possible to get from one carriage to another via the footboard but only if the carriage windows were wide open and, even then, it was highly dangerous. There was an electric alarm, the guard revealed, but it had not been used.

It was shown that only three first-class tickets had been sold for that particular train. Two of these had gone to ladies and the third to Lefroy, who was known by sight by the ticket collector as a regular traveller – and as someone once suspected of travelling without a ticket. Mr Gold (the dead man found on the track) was also well-known – as the holder of a first-class season ticket – and when Lefroy had had difficulty opening the door of Gold's compartment, the ticket collector had assisted him. There was no way to define whose blood it was that saturated the coconut matting on the floor of the carriage, but medical witnesses were brought to say that it was more likely to be from Gold's wounds. Precise evidence on distances and express speeds was tied up with various incidents, including judging the exact moment the various articles must have been thrown on to the track (*after* the slow down at the signals). The watch, found on Lefroy, was identified as Mr Gold's and it was proved that Lefroy was desperate for money. Most damning of all was the fact that he had redeemed a pistol from a pawnbroker only two hours before the express left London Bridge.

It was all up for Percy Lefroy Mapleton, 'otherwise Arthur Lefroy' who was probably not mentally or physically fit to stand trial. He was found guilty, sentenced to death, and hanged at Lewes prison on 29 November 1881, having confessed his guilt the previous evening. The journey from Maidstone Assizes to Lewes was made in a first-class carriage.

Moonshine, a contemporary of *Punch*, also continued to attack Vincent and the CID, which it had dubbed the Criminal Instigation or Defective Department. Those against Vincent personally were sometimes as vitriolic as those suffered by Sir Richard Mayne for so many years. Witness a short note in *Moonshine* on 1 July 1882:

Theatre Royal, Scotland Yard
Day and Night. The ever-verdant piece, *Imbecility*, which has had an unprecedented run, and will, in all likelihood, continue so long as the present management retains possession. Large company. No expense spared. Mr Howard Vincent, stage manager as heretofore.

Any Information Thankfully Received precedes the drama. Several tragedies always in rehearsal.

and on 28 October of the same year:

Mr Howard Vincent is to marry a Miss Moffat. The fact has been announced and re-announced until we note it in sheer desperation. What on earth does it matter if the Chief of the Defective Department does get married? He will not change his name to Moffat. N.B. Muff it is the way it is pronounced.

In fact, the ceremony had already taken place two days earlier and before an intriguing assortment of guests including the home secretary, policemen (most of the metropolitan superintendents and some lower ranks), actors, soldiers, MPs, and members of the aristocracy, among them the Duke of Teck 'bronzed by the Egyptian sun'. But the superintendents were not to be outdone in the matter of wedding presents. Alongside the many silver objects listed in one newspaper was the superintendents 'handsome silver epergne' and the 'valuable claret jug from the CID Inspectors'.

One of Howard Vincent's most innovative moves was the introduction of his *Police Code and Manual of Criminal Law*. He was convinced that many of the mistakes made by recruits were due to ignorance and lack of theoretical knowledge. In this, he was correct. Indeed, the lack of training was remarkable considering their responsible task. Heretofore, the maximum instruction thought to be necessary for a police recruit was some first aid training and a little drill. To help solve this problem, Vincent produced his manual, which was later referred to by *The Police Review and Parade Gossip* in 1908, as 'a useful little work'. It was to be revised many times and, in fact, survived well into the twentieth century. *Punch* and *Moonshine* were quick to get hold of a copy and duly satirized its instructions in *Our Police: A Running Commentary on the New Code* by Verges Wrongscent.

Doubtless, had they seen it, either periodical would have parodied a Police Order issued on 26 February 1883, which insisted that the advertising placards put out by newsboys should be 'confined within proper limits' as, not only had their careless placement been an obstruction and danger to traffic, but was 'causing horses to start'.

In 1884, the newly married Howard Vincent, decided he had had enough and 'retired' to take up world travel. Later, he was to write a book about his travel experiences before being elected as

MP for Sheffield (his new wife was an MP's daughter). As such, he was the mover of the Police Superannuation Act 1890. Previously, a police pension had not been a right but a privilege granted.

During his relatively short reign as Director of the CID, Howard Vincent had brought about several improvements in the system. For example, quite early on he had realized that the *Police Gazette*, which since the time of John Fielding had been a means to keep police informed about wanted men and stolen property, was not all it should be. It was badly laid out, repetitive and dull. Before attempting the necessary revamp and trying to persuade the authorities that the editorial function should be transferred from the Chief Clerk at Bow Street to Scotland Yard, Vincent solicited the opinions of all senior officers in the Metropolitan Police and Chief Constables throughout the country. What did they think of the present format? Did the idea of illustrations of wanted persons and stolen property appeal? Why not feature short reports on cases of interest rather than just terse lists of suspects and property?

It was a clever way to go about getting backing as well as involving people in the change so that they were less likely to resist it when it came. Opinions he thus garnered about the existing production ranged from the polite 'it has seldom been found to be ... of any service.' (Williamson), to 'one of the most uninteresting documents a police officer can occupy his time with' (C Division superintendent), and the even blunter, 'entirely useless', from the chief inspector of the Executive Branch. That very few actually read the thing became obvious and even the Chief Clerk at Bow Street was 'unable to gainsay the reasonableness of such a course' as the removal of the editorship from his control. Everyone liked the idea of illustrations and many the suggested reports on interesting cases. His quaintly titled report, 'The Police Gazette: Its Present State & Inutility', did the trick in bringing about a brighter and more readable publication.

Chief Superintendent Williamson was said to hold the Fenian conspirators in contempt and, after an informant had told him that some of them were practising cavalry tactics in Jerry Flanagan's back kitchen in the Theobalds Road, he also found their activities somewhat comic. Nonetheless, he kept an eye on the situation and, in 1880, when the first rumblings of fresh troubles were heard, he instructed Inspector Littlechild to make a special study of the subject. From then on, all Fenian inquiries went to Littlechild and what was to develop into his Special Irish Branch.

The expected mainland hostilities commenced in 1881 with a thwarted attempt to blow up the Mansion House and a successful explosion at Salford barracks which killed a child and injured others. The whole issue took on an even darker hue when, in May 1882, Lord Frederick Cavendish, the new chief secretary for Ireland, and Thomas Burke, his permanent under secretary, were hacked to death in Phoenix Park, Dublin. The murders were committed by an extremist faction known as The Invincibles. Littlechild went to Dublin and spent five months there, 'which gave me a wonderful insight into it'. He also, he claimed in an interview with *Cassell's Saturday Journal*, ten years later, 'assisted the Dublin Police by posing as a certain character and staying in low hotels in the city'.

Only the previous year, the US President, Andrew Garfield, had been assassinated and a Fenian sympathizer had made an attempt on the life of Queen Victoria (the sixth attempt during her reign so far). This, doubtless, had helped concentrate the minds at the Yard on the subject of protection duty – for it was at this time that twelve Webley .455 'Bulldog' revolvers were purchased for that purpose.

The mainland attacks recommenced in 1883 with two bombings in Glasgow. Shortly afterwards an explosive device was found at *The Times* newspaper offices and another exploded outside the Local Government Board Office (which the Fenians probably thought was the Home Office) just off Whitehall – breaking a great deal of glass but harming no one. As before, the Yard had been forewarned of the coming campaign which was planned by Fenians in the United States. Chief among British spies there was US Civil War veteran and leading Fenian, Henri Le Caron – who was actually an Englishman, Thomas Billis Beach.

In February, 1883, a Birmingham chemical company employee noticed that a local painting and decorating shop was putting in orders for a remarkable amount of pure glycerine. So as not to alert the suspects to the subsequent police surveillance, a local policeman sent his children to play in the street and report any movements. Soon came news that a man had been seen leaving the premises – carrying a very heavy suitcase. The Yard was informed and Littlechild and his men sped to Euston Station to question those invaluable witnesses, cab drivers. One of them recalled not only the street to which he had taken the man described but, once back in the street, was able to identify the house as well. (Another version has the Birmingham Police finding the London address when they raided the bomb factory.) The suspect had just gone out but Littlechild waited in the parlour beneath for him to return. When he did so he was accompanied by the gang leader, Thomas Gallagher, and both were arrested. In their room was a suitcase containing nitro-glycerine in a 'dangerously sensitive' state. Others were arrested and, amid a great deal of publicity, four of them were sentenced to penal servitude for life.

Another tip-off sent Yorkshireman, Inspector Maurice Moser, to Liverpool where suspicious imports were expected. The ex-clerk from Bradford did take the Fenians and their 'ghastly horrible plots and deeds', seriously. However, in his *Stories from Scotland Yard* he declines to recount 'the loathsome, hateful details of the proceedings of these cowardly blackguards' – lest he aid the enemy. ' ... suffice it, that the whole of the United Kingdom was wrung to the very vitals by the doings of these hireling dastards.' He does oblige us, nonetheless, with the details of his exhausting search for suspicious substances at Liverpool – but then Moser was not one to suffer in silence. His was by no means a light task, he assures us. The wharves and quays on both sides of the Mersey 'made a considerable hole into twenty miles' and, although it was spring at the time, it was bitterly cold.

> It was a sickening, weary task this, going in and out of the different warehouses, looking over, almost casually, of course, thousands of tons of goods of every possible description, making careful notes of anything unusual, and keenly watching the hundreds of individuals who thronged this great and busy hive from morning until night, sometimes perching myself in an uncomfortable position for hours together on the top of a pile of goods for the purpose of making my observations without being seen, with oftentimes nothing but a few biscuits and a friendly pipe.

Three weeks after his arrival Inspector Moser took another look at 'quite a little mountain' of casks of cement, which had been carefully stacked on their sides. They had been there for ten days, he discovered, but when he checked up on the firm listed as recipients he found it did not exist.

On examining the barrels more closely, the Scotland Yard Inspector noticed that 't', in the roughly painted 'Boston' on the side of each barrel, was crossed in only eight instances. He opened these barrels and found in each 'a fully charged infernal machine, fitted with the usual clockwork apparatus, provided with an eleven ounce cartridge of dynamite, quite sufficient to play very considerable havoc wherever it was destined it should eventually be placed.' His lonely vigil was over.

Watch was kept, but although no one ever attempted to claim the lethal cargo, the finding was to cheer up Inspector Moser by putting him firmly into the spotlight for a while. He describes with some delight how the arrival at the Yard of these latest American devices caused something of a sensation. He was called upon to show his trophies to a great many important people – including those who feared themselves to be potential targets – such as members of the House of Lords.

Nonetheless, explosives were still getting through and several bomb incidents occurred on the underground and at railway stations late in 1883 and early 1884. Always, it was observed, they were designed to go off in twos or threes, simultaneously if possible. Truly concerted action was never achieved (indeed several bombs failed to explode or were disarmed) but the occurrences on the night of 30 May 1884 came very close.

The reported times vary a great deal. Those given are from the Home Office report to Parliament which took notice of the diversity of the accounts but placed most reliance on the timings given by Lord Cathcart.

At 9.18 p.m. a device exploded in the area in front of the kitchens at the Junior Carlton Club in St James's Square, injuring twelve employees. Fifteen seconds later, a bomb blew up on the window-sill of the morning room of the nearby home of Sir Watkin Williams-Wynn M.P. Amazingly, despite the flying glass and masonry, the only injury suffered by the party assembled within was a minor cut to a lady's hand. The servants were not so lucky. Two had been standing on the doorstep and were injured, one, as the official Home Office report noted, 'somewhat severely'.

Less than two minutes had elapsed before it became the turn of Scotland Yard. The target was the offices of the CID and the Special Irish Branch on the first floor at an easily accessible corner of the conveniently situated building in the middle of the yard. Directly below these offices, in a space carved out of the wall, there was a public urinal – a perfect site and perfect cover for anyone who might otherwise feel somewhat conspicuous placing a parcel under a CID office. Littlechild was in the habit of working late but a friend had sent him tickets for the opera which, as a keen music lover (he was a founder member of the police minstrels), he was unable to resist, so had left his office at 8 p.m. to attend. His assistants, Sergeant Robson and Kerry-born Inspector John Sweeney, worked on. Robson left soon after and, just after 9 p.m., Sweeney, too, called it a day. Twenty minutes later the bomb wrecked the office, the front of the Rising Sun public house opposite and 524 panes of glass in the police buildings alone. The explosion was so violent that a window of a building on the other side of Whitehall was broken. Afterwards, Sweeney was able to contemplate what was left of the desk at which he had been sitting, now in full public view and totally destroyed – as were a number of papers concerning the Fenian organization. The PC, who was supposedly on a look out for suspicious persons carrying suspicious parcels was cut about the face and head by bits of flying urinal (in which the dynamite had been placed) and suffered deafness. Two coachmen, waiting for fares from the Rising Sun, also received injuries, one suffering a broken arm. It was some consolation that, in both instances, their horses were relatively unscathed.

But the night was not yet over. While confusion reigned at Scotland Yard, a boy spotted a black bag, close to one of the lions at the base of Nelson's column. When taken to the Yard (surely a manic thing to do, given its confines compared with the open square), it was found to contain eight-and-a-quarter-pounds of American lignin dynamite known as Atlas powder A, a substance not licensed for importation.

Their battle with the Fenian bombers caused something of an image retrieval for the detectives, even in *Punch* and *Moonshine* – but then, national pride was involved and, due to good information, they had had some success. Shortly after the capture of Whitehead, the bomb-maker, Williamson was featured in the *Moonshine*'s, 'Days with Celebrities'. It showed the tackling of Fenianism and the tone was jingoistic. A respectful cartoon also showed 'Mr Inspector Littlechild' with one hand holding aloft a bag marked 'From America' with the contents of slabs of dynamite and a clock on the table before him, while behind his back in his other hand he held a pair of handcuffs.

In September 1883, the more conservative *Illustrated London News* were complimentary to a degree when, under the title 'The Metropolitan Preventative and Detective Police' they wrote up and illustrated the recruits examination and initiation procedure, the activities in The Telegraph Room and the Convict's Office, and the CID. They made it clear that the feature was designed to give comfort to the upper and middle classes who escaped London for the late summer and early autumn, leaving their houses empty for 'the burglary season'.

The detective organization had been improved of late years, the *Illustrated London News* assured their readers, and they described how Vincent's code laid down that if a good and recognizable description of a burglary suspect was available, a multiple telegram would be sent to every adjacent force on the route that he may have taken 'so as to block his escape'.

The article also described the work of the Convict Supervision Office, in the charge of one Chief Inspector Neame. On its shelves were albums of photographs and registers containing the details of convicted criminals. These were used by the staff to check details when a criminal came to report while on licence; by other police officers to identify an arrested man or witnesses who attempted to identify the person who did the deed. The categories of prisoners allowed to be photographed had widened since the advent of Howard Vincent (dead bodies, too, were now being photographed to aid identification). He had sensibly laid down that the photographs should be taken as near to the time of the convict's release as possible. Also, in ordinary clothes and that the face should be placed in half profile 'so that the shape of the nose may appear'. (As the owner of no mean nose himself he knew what he was talking about.) The *Illustrated London News* reporter added:

> that it is also considered desirable to make the men hold their hands up so as to be shown in their photographs; for the police are wont to scrutinise the hands very attentively, finding their shape and condition extremely significant; and the hand of any person, if properly studied, will be found to have strong character of individuality.

Some of the detectives were less convinced of the value of the photographs in the Convict Supervision Office – hands or no. According to Walter Hambrook, who joined in 1898, they were badly printed, made everyone look alike and, although taken near time of release, the convicts still had their close-cropped hair and stubbly beards (they were not allowed to shave). Consequently, not only did they look identical to each other, but (according to *Hambrook of the Yard*) they bore no resemblance to what the individual *would* look like after release. Inspector Lansdowne went so far as to say, 'I have never arrested a man from having recognised his portrait in the collection of photographs in the Convict Office. I have arrested scores by means of descriptions which have been supplied.' He did concede that the photographs were of use to officers in the Convict Supervision Office who visited prisons and saw the original print and, presumably, the man himself, before his release.

9   The Local Inspector

Since the advent of the local inspector, Scotland Yard men no longer held centre stage alone. They now had competition from one or two very keen and highly successful local inspectors, and a good example was George Abberline of H Division. George was one of the first local inspectors to be taken on in 1878. By 1883, an Old Bailey judge was having to admit that he had run out of superlatives to describe Inspector Abberline's work, having complimented him so many times, that it was hard to know 'what to say afresh'. It seems sad that today, the man is remembered chiefly for his association with a major investigative failure – the Jack the Ripper enquiry.

What Dorset-born Abberline had in his favour was fifteen years of solid and varied police experience; local knowledge – he had been on crime-ridden H Division for five years and his new work kept him there, and assistants who shared that knowledge. (He had also known tragedy in his personal life. His first wife, Martha, died of consumption only two months after their marriage. Eight years later, at the age of 32, he married again, just before becoming a local inspector.)

The arrival of local inspectors had also proved useful to Yard officers in that, at last, they had more professional local assistance when they were called in on cases – if they were called in. In addition, the new system began to provide the Yard with a steady flow of experienced, streetwise detectives, with which to leaven the ranks of the more privileged, educated linguists – some of whom had gained direct entry into the department. Several of the local inspectors soon began making a name for themselves because they were so keen. Starting from lower down life's ladder they were hungrier for success and more grateful for an interesting job.

Abberline, a former 'clocksmith', began his police career at the age of nineteen on busy N, or Islington Division, where his thief-catching skills were soon noticed. He was often put into plain clothes to nab the pickpockets in the rough Caledonian Road area, or those who preyed on the crowds attending the many public events taking place at Islington's huge and splendid, new Agricultural Hall (later Royal Agricultural Hall), built by the Smithfield Club to exhibit their cattle. He also went undercover, following Fenians, and at one point was employed in plain clothes on this work for a year. Later, he became acting inspector in Kentish Town, before moving on in 1871 to become a divisional detective sergeant on Y or Highgate Division. Two years later, he was back in uniform again, as an inspector on H or Whitechapel Division, acknowledged to be a major crime centre. Finally, in 1878, he became H Division's local inspector – a job he felt so suited him that it is said he resisted invitations to be 'promoted' to Scotland Yard.

Despite having only a small patch, in contrast to the roving commissions enjoyed by the Yard men, Abberline's job was almost as varied although, naturally, a higher proportion of minor crime came his way. Theft from cargo in the docks area was handled by Thames Police and the Port of London Authority, but the roads leading to them were the scene of much stealing of goods-in-transit. Local Inspector Abberline and his men caught several of the 'van gangs' who made off with not only the van and its contents – sugar, tea, currants, tobacco, etc. – but the horse as well. Usually, but not always, the horse and van were later turned loose.

One night, in Bethnal Green, a constable discovered an open warehouse door and, on investigation, disturbed three 'thieves' who promptly fled. Inside, he found a remarkable variety of goods: rolls of cloth, a chest of tea, a case of dyes, tubs of butter, boxes of cinnamon, some handbags, and so on. The puzzle was that no one would admit to owning the premises. Gradually, it dawned on the police that the 'warehouse' was, in fact, a stash-house for goods stolen by van robbers. Abberline mounted a complex inquiry, involving detectives from nearby G, K and M divisions and the City of London, which resulted in the conviction of eight men for theft and receiving – some of these felons being the drivers themselves of robbed vans.

Burglary, coining, fraud, embezzlement, illegal gambling, assault, fortune-telling and robbery were all part of H Division's crime cocktail, but being a man on his own patch who liked to keep his hand in, Abberline didn't only react to crime – occasionally, he found some of his own. Such as the time he spotted one Charles Burdett walking in Shoreditch, with a handsome bulldog in tow. Burdett swore it was his own animal but Abberline was unconvinced and arrested him. In the prisoner's pocket he found a piece of prepared liver, such as that used by dog-stealers to entice their prey. The dog turned out to be a prize beast – and stolen. At Burdett's house, several other dogs were found, including a toy terrier and a collie, who really belonged in elegant houses in Kensington. It was not truly as brilliant a catch as it may seem, given that Burdett was known as 'The King of the Dog Stealers', but it was, of course, one in which local knowledge played a part. (Dog stealers watched the papers for notices offering rewards for the 'lost' dogs but, if none were forthcoming, they would sell the animals. Advertisers were reluctant to call in police when they got a response, in case the thieves took fright and killed their pets.) Burdett got two years hard labour.

Two years on, the butler of the Duchess of Montrose let his employer's pet dachshund out for an early morning run in Belgravia. It failed to return and, in due course, the man who answered their anguished advertisement claimed that it just so happened that he had purchased a similar dog recently. He invited the butler down to Bethnal Green to identify it and effect its exchange for money. Abberline heard about the transaction and, upon calculation, realized that Burdett had been out of prison for two whole weeks, so began keeping a weather eye open. Eventually, his diligence was rewarded in what turned out to be a virtual replay of the original bulldog scene. One afternoon, he spotted Burdett proceeding down Commercial Street in the company of a white bull terrier which he insisted was his own but, yet again, proved not to be. Another two year sentence for the 'King'.

However, when it came to Abberline's occasional cases concerning the welfare of local children, convictions and heavy sentences were not so easy to come by. A cook-shop keeper and his wife were arrested, following complaints by neighbours that they were neglecting, starving, overworking and assaulting their 13-year-old daughter. The man received only twenty-one days inside and the magistrate thought it unsafe to convict the mother who had been accused of assault. Abberline suffered a similar lack of luck in a case of suspected murder which occurred only two months after his becoming H's Local Inspector.

Fanny Lazarus, the 19-month-old daughter of a tailor, had gone missing when playing outside her home one June evening. Two days later, her body was found lying on the doorstep of a neighbour. It was wet and covered with sand. The cause of death was found to be drowning and the obvious place of death was the nearby baths and wash-house where some repairs were taking place. Inside the locked site were found full water butts and a barrel of sand. Peter Wincey, the 62-year-old watchman, who was known to chase annoying children with a stick, had also behaved very strangely on the day the body was found.

He had appeared at the child's home and asked to see the corpse. Thinking he was 'a parish officer', the parents agreed. Wincey felt the child's hands and head, then began trembling and, putting his hands to his head said, 'Leave it all to me and I will make it all right.' He then asked to be shown the step where little Fanny was found, corrected the father saying, 'No, it was the middle step' and mentioned that the child's clothes had not been wet at the bottom (which was true). The inquest jury brought in a verdict of murder by person or persons unknown.

Abberline gathered evidence to show that the body had not been on the step shortly before it was found at 1.15 a.m. and that one of the finders had seen someone resembling the watchman disappearing in the direction of the baths. He arrested Wincey (an educated, professional man, down on his luck) who admitted to going past the spot at 1 a.m. He could give no reason for his presence there but now, he denied the statements he had made to the father, claiming he had merely called on them out of sympathy, being a parent himelf.

The magistrate found the evidence insufficient to hold the prisoner. The child, he said, could have fallen into the tub and someone, having pulled it out, could have secreted it until it could be left in the street. The matter, he said, could be re-opened if further evidence was obtained.

From time to time, Yard men and divisional detectives mounted combined operations. In one instance, Chief Inspector Shore, Inspector Moser and others, joined with Abberline to put a stop to the pubs on his division being used as betting houses. On another, Moser and Abberline became involved in one of the many Russian rouble forgery cases which had become an ongoing saga for the department.

For many years, such a flood of forged rouble notes had been reaching Russia that the imperial government were seriously concerned, often being forced to withdraw whole issues. Chief Inspector George Greenham claimed that these cases had, perhaps, been the most trying and intricate of his *Scotland Yard Experiences*. According to Greenham, the forged notes were taken into Russia by Polish Jews and used for purchasing livestock and the like from 'ignorant peasants'. When, in 1878, Williamson handed young Greenham his first such enquiry it was with the words: 'Here is a nice little case for you, that will require all of your time and energy; but don't go away with the idea you will succeed, for I am almost certain you will be disappointed.'

'Then why give it to me?' Greenham had asked, only to receive the reply 'I must give it to someone who is conversant with foreign languages.' Williamson had added that some of the best officers, 'formerly in the department' had, for the last fifteen years been endeavouring to track down these forgers, without success.

Thus challenged, Greenham studied all previous reports, decided to adopt a different approach and then realized, a month after starting, that success was assured. He doesn't quite tell us how, confiding that a full description of the enquiry would be too tedious to the reader (and he is probably right). It involved a great deal of following of suspects by himself and (he admits) others, including Inspector Littlechild. Eventually, they arrested seven Russians – one, a priest, and seized a large quantity of forged notes and some lithographic stones and presses. Greenham recalled:

> I shall never forget the expression on Mr Williamson's face when I reported to him what we had done, and showed him the spoils. He appeared very pleased with the result, and said: 'It must have been a lucky chance that enabled you to succeed in such a case the very first time, but I am afraid it will be the last.

(This is the second of, at least three quoted instances of Williamson's curiously negative attitude, but Greenham never makes it clear whether it was a natural pessimism, such as has already been noted in the man, or his humorous way of issuing a challenge. Then again, making his tasks seem unsurmountable like this could have been Greenham's way of accentuating his own triumphs – a habit not unknown in detectives.)

Williamson was wrong – three months later Greenham landed an even more skilful gang.

By the time Maurice Moser came to the Yard in 1882, he found its officers looked forward with considerable interest to Russian rouble forgeries. Firstly, because the arrests brought great kudos. Secondly, the work was 'of an interesting indirect character' and, thirdly, 'and not by any means the least important' – the Russian government had proved very liberal with its rewards. The notes were not particularly easy to forge, quite the reverse, in fact, but the gangs involved were expert, businesslike, cautious, and had great personal loyalty to their members. Catching one was not enough, it had to be the whole gang at once or nothing. Therefore, good informants were vital to the work – but they cost money.

This was so in the long and complex enquiry embarked upon by Abberline and Moser in the summer of 1883. The case involved the forking out of a great deal of money to informants – the whole amounting to about a third of the detectives' annual salaries. Had the case failed, Moser was at no small pains to point out, they would have had to absorb these costs themselves, 'Scotland Yard excusing itself under the standing order of "they have never sanctioned the expenditure". This illiberal treatment of our detective force in matters of this kind is one of the crying evils of the day.' (Clearly, not all expenses problems had been solved following the 1878 committee recommendations.)

It did not fail, but resulted in the arrest, not of a gang, but of a 'Russian Pole' (with previous convictions for similar offences), an English compositor named Henry Hill, and his wife, Mary Anne. They were found in possession of suitably watermarked paper, printing blocks, plates and a press for the manufacture of Russian roubles, plus a quantity of the finished product.

Mary Anne was found not guilty but the other two were convicted, the Russian Pole getting seven years penal servitude and the Englishman, six months hard labour. The grateful Russian government stumped up a £500 reward, but an indignant and disgruntled Moser claimed that not enough of it found its way into the right hands – his. A quarter of it automatically went to a reward fund; 'sundry allowances were stopped out of it, and the various officers, who had, perhaps, only in the most perfunctory manner been associated with the arrest and although they had not the slightest connection with the pecuniary or physical risk in the capture, were remunerated in some wonderful manner or other which neither I nor anybody else seemed able to understand or appreciate'.

Moser ended up with £150, out of which he had to deduct considerable 'not sanctioned' expenses, such as informers' fees and fares, which left him with just £60 'for all my trouble and anxiety and time'. To add insult to injury, he was denied permission, either to accept or wear, a decoration from the Russian government. Abberline, who did not write his memoirs, merely added a note to the newspaper cuttings in his scrapbook stating that he only received about one-eighth of the £500 'the remainder was given to the Police Orphanage'.

Small wonder that not many cases had been solved before the keen young Greenham got going in 1878. Of course, it is possible that some of the old detectives had found it easier to be paid for inactivity – as is perhaps hinted by Greenham's quote saying the best officers 'formerly in the department' had tried and failed in these cases.

By 1885, Abberline (together with his assistants, Sergeants Thicke and Marriott) was already well-known to the newspaper crime-column reading public, but he was to leap into greater prominence during the frantic early months of that year. It all started with more than one bang when, on 24 January, *almost* simultaneous explosions took place at Westminster Hall, the Houses of Parliament and in the White Tower at the Tower of London. Abberline was called to the last incident. On his arrival, he found the gates closed with 220 people, mostly sightseers, locked inside. (Many years later his superintendent, the keen and active Thomas Arnold, credited Abberline with the good sense to close the gates, but his own telling admits they had already been closed, by a PC on duty there, when he arrived. In his scrapbook notes he does, however, claim that it was his idea to question all those within. Contemporary newspaper reports of his evidence quarrel with this a little but, no matter, the resultant triumph was largely his.)

One young man questioned, a James George Gilbert, proved particularly hesitant in his replies to simple questions, and his halting answers were supplied in a voice overlaid by a heavy, Irish-American, accent. He was an Englishman, he claimed, who had last worked a few weeks earlier in the Liverpool Docks, but had recently spent five years in America. After further interrogation (an unfair one, by the suspect's later account, because police were not only friendly and obliging but they offered him whiskey and brandy), Gilbert admitted to using the name

Cunningham on his journey across the Atlantic. Cunningham, as Abberline possibly knew, was the name of one of the latest gang of Irish-American Fenians to be sent over on active service. Furthermore, enquiries revealed he had never worked in Liverpool docks, but had recently been back and forth across the Atlantic and had ties with a man named Burton (another of the gang) in whose trunk a detonator was found. Both men were arrested and charged.

Whilst their intelligence sources assured them they had the right men, the actual evidence was thin. As a result, there followed a period of extremely hard work and anxiety for Abberline, who was not helped by the home secretary insisting on a regular morning report which, after a frantic day, the Inspector would have to compile, often staying up until 4 a.m. or 5 a.m. The movements of Cunningham and Burton and their luggage were painstakingly pieced together by the evidence of no less than 110 witnesses. Cunningham accused the police of planting the detonator, but Abberline later insisted that, until the finding, he had never even seen a detonator in his life. The accused were found guilty and given life sentences, and the bombings ceased. Later that year, Gladstone changed his mind in favour of Home Rule, which led to hostilities being suspended.

While he was still very busy in connection with the enquiries into Cunningham and Burton, Abberline still had to cope with his regular duties as head of H Division's detectives and any crises which arose in that connection. Such as the time he was roused at 2 a.m. on a Sunday morning (presumably Abberline had had an early night because the Home Secretary would not require a report on a Sunday morning) 'to find the murderer of Howard'.

Howard had been the fiancé of Mrs Eliza Russell, the 34-year-old widow of H Division's PC John Russell who had died of injuries acquired in the execution of his duty six months earlier. After her husband's untimely death, Eliza was doubtless grateful for the attentions and monetary assistance from his friend, a 'diminutive' German baker by the name of Henry Alt. Alt was alone in this country, having left Germany five years earlier to seek his fortune in England. He was obviously very taken with the widow Russell who, with her little boy, were fellow lodgers at 107 Commercial Road. But their landlord began to feel that their situation was improper (though Eliza swore that that was not so) and asked them to leave. In any case, she could no longer afford the rent, so she took rooms in nearby Rutland Street while the 31-year-old Alt found lodgings above a beer shop in the Whitechapel Road. Alt paid her rent (in return, it was said, for her 'keeping his box' – presumably containing his valuables) and constantly proposed to her. There was some evidence that she gave him a little encouragement but eventually began to tire of his persistence.

But there was no doubt about her response to another man who came on the scene in February 1885. Eliza met farrier Charles Howard at her sister's house and there was an instant attraction. Within two weeks she had accepted his proposal of marriage whereupon Alt's attentions grew frantic. On the evening of Saturday 28 February, her faithful fiancé was escorting her home when they bumped into Alt. They did the civilized thing by going for a drink together. Afterwards, both men escorted her back to her lodgings where, on the doorstep, Alt made his final proposal of marriage. Again, Eliza refused his offer, making it plain she wished to have no more to do with him. Pointing to Charles Howard she said, 'This man is going to be my husband; are you not, George?' (George was Charles's other name.)

Those words were George's death warrant. Alt drew out a lethally sharp, double-edged knife, and stabbed George to the heart. He had previously threatened Eliza with the same knife while making the classic male threat, if-I-can't-have-you-no-one-else-will, and now he moved to make good that boast. He stabbed Eliza twelve times before turning the knife on himself. Somehow, his last efforts failed to strike so deep. Charles Howard died almost instantly and Eliza was rushed to the nearby London Hospital where immediate arrangements were made for a dying declaration to be taken from her. Alt went home but was taken to the London Hospital by his landlord. He refused to go inside and ended up at the busy German Hospital some distance away.

Abberline swiftly tracked him down, leaving one of his young detective constables, Henry Payne, to keep observation on the injured suspect until he was fit to be removed and charged. Not enough observation, apparently, as Alt managed to make another attempt on his own life, but again was saved. All to no purpose. For his part in what the newspapers referred to as 'The Tragedy in the East End', or 'The Whitechapel Murder', he was sentenced to death and, despite the jury's recommendation to mercy, the sentence was carried out. As the rope went around his neck Henry

Alt made his first utterance on the subject – beyond expressing sorrow for what he had done and a lack of recollection of the events. In a rush of recall, he exclaimed, 'This is all through that wicked and deceitful woman!'

'The drop fell and he appeared to die instantly,' reported one newspaper, and went on to satisfy the peculiar Victorian thirst for such morbid detail by pointing out that, 'the prisoner was only five-feet-four-inches high and he had a fall of eight feet six inches.'

The 'deceitful woman' (now, doubtless, only too aware of the murderous passions easily aroused in the unprepossessing when they feel cheated) had recovered enough to be wheeled into court to become the chief prosecution witness against the diminutive German baker who had robbed her of her second chance of happiness.

Obviously, the talents and application of the local inspectors varied. Ex-Chief Inspector Tom Divall, writing of the 1890s (in *Scoundrels and Scallywags*), said 'The Local Inspector was a big pot in his own way and never made an inquiry or affected an arrest; he would do nothing beyond supervising, reading and signing reports.' In contrast, Charles E. Leach, son of the local inspector at Kings Cross during the 1890s, paints a picture of a far more harassed individual whose workload forced him not only to neglect his son but to use his services to tail suspects.

> Those were sometimes hard days for me, for my father would often, through pressure of work, forget my needs in the commissariat and financial departments, and I would constantly be left to pace the streets of some such neighbourhood as Clerkenwell, from early morning until close on midnight, with neither food nor the wherewithal to purchase it.

Even when on an enquiry or an observation (he was twelve when he did his first) it seems his welfare was often forgotten. He makes no mention of a mother, so one presumes she was dead or had left. Once, with the son of another detective, he was watching a shop in Clerkenwell where one of the perpetrators of a silver ingot robbery was expected to visit:

> It was an extremely rough neighbourhood, and no detective could have remained there for five minutes without being discovered. Therefore we boys were put on the job. It was a bitterly cold day and we were put on watch in the morning and forgotten. No money

left to buy food, and to make matters worse, some local hooligans quarrelled with us, and we had a free fight on empty stomachs. You can imagine my relief, late that evening, to see my father and his men arrive on the scene and release us for a welcome meal.

On another occasion, these two young sons of detectives spent three weeks following the manager of a tea firm who was suspected of stealing from his company. They discovered that he was indeed taking tea and having it delivered to his wives and families (three wives and three families). 'It is interesting to record,' writes Leach (in *On Top of the Underworld*), 'that it was only after this man's arrest that the three wives learnt of each other's existence. Well, all this was good training, and I soon learnt discretion.'

This work doubtless helped his father to become a superintendent and, glancing at the son's career record, the father appears to have returned the compliment when Charles, too, joined the force, by having him seconded to the Convict Supervision Office, of which he was in charge, after serving only one year in uniform. The younger Leach, who had spent other moments of his formative years leafing through albums of wanted men, later became a successful local (or, by then, divisional) inspector.

Without doubt, Edmund John James Reid was a most colourful local inspector. The *Weekly Dispatch* went so far as to call him, 'one of the most remarkable men of the century'. While Reid appears to have been a successful enough detective, nailing criminals such as One Arm Steve – the king of the coiners, and the perpetrators of The Great Silk Robbery, his reputation for being 'one of the most versatile men of his generation' seems to have been gained largely from his social activities.

Before joining the force in 1872, at the age of twenty-six, this good-looking and genial man from Canterbury, had tried his hand at no less than seventeen jobs including pastry cook, and steward on a steamer plying the Thames to Margate and back. Obviously, he was a man who liked change, and it was the variety of detective work which finally took him in that direction. He got into the branch quickly, on P Division, which covered parts of south-east London and Kent, only two years after joining.

Off-duty, Reid was known as a daring balloonist who not only won medals for record height ascents at Crystal Palace (conveniently situated on P Division) but was claimed to have been the first to parachute from a balloon at a height of 1,000 feet. (Surprisingly, the first descent by parachute from a balloon took place as far back as 1797.) Reid was also an accomplished actor, a singer who had booking agents chasing after him, a conjurer of professional standard, and 'a Druid of distinction'. Many of the detectives were active Freemasons. There was no shyness about admitting it and the fact was usually mentioned in retirement and obituary profiles. Attendance at a meeting of the Domatic Lodge was even used as an alibi by Palmer at the Turf Fraud Trials. Fellow members were Williamson and Clarke.

Interest in detectives, real and fictional, was very keen at that time and Reid became one of the select band, along with Inspectors Field (fictionally, Inspector Bucket) and Whicher (likewise, Sergeant Cuff), to make the transition from one guise to the other. Although, in his case, it was no Charles Dickens or Wilkie Collins who used him as a model, but his friend, Charles Gibbon, one of the many Victorian writers whose detective works are unknown today. Gibbon's Detective Dier appeared in ten novels, being described in one of them thus:

> Meeting Sergeant Dier in the ordinary way, you would regard him as a successful commercial man. There was not the slightest flavour of Scotland Yard about him. The secret of his success lay partly in a natural gift for his business, his enthusiasm, and the good nature which underlay it all. He never allowed a scoundrel to escape, but he dealt very gently with any poor creature who might be betrayed into a first crime.

'The description is a true one', declared the *Weekly Dispatch* on Reid's retirement, in 1893, taking care to point out that Reid was no 'Sherlock Holmes' but a London detective whom everybody, including the criminals, admired. (The world's most famous fictional detective had only been on the scene since 'A Study in Scarlet' appeared in *Beeton's Christmas Annual* in 1887, but little notice had been taken of him until 'The Sign of the Four' appeared in the American, *Lippincott's Magazine*, in February, 1890. Fame followed rapidly – to what extent can be gauged by the fact that, by 1893, the *Weekly Dispatch* felt it unnecessary to elaborate further when they mentioned his name.)

As for Reid's career, by 1884 he had become a detective inspector, first at Scotland Yard, then as local inspector on the new J Division at Bethnal Green in East London. In 1887, he took over from Abberline on the notorious H – just as the shadow of Jack the Ripper fell over the division.

10 Sex

In England's proud capital city children were regularly raped, sodomized, whipped and tortured – sometimes in padded rooms so that their screams would not be heard outside – sometimes being permanently maimed or even dying from their injuries – and all for the sexual satisfaction of the British male. The series of articles on child prostitution in London, which appeared in the *Pall Mall Gazette* in 1885, made sobering reading. The final feature gave an account of the white slave traffic, by which means under-age English girls were sold into sexual slavery on the Continent, particularly in Belgium. The Metropolitan Police were not only in the pay of these people, was the accusation, but failed to save the children or offer any redress to those who managed to crawl back, maimed and bleeding, to their parents.

The child prostitution claims were true as far as London was concerned, Howard Vincent assured the investigation team which had come up with the story. They included the editor, W.T. Stead, members of the Salvation Army and Josephine Butler, whose work against the infamous Contagious Diseases Act 1866 (which allowed the intimate examination of women merely on the say so of a police officer that they were prostitutes) had resulted in its repeal in 1883.

The white slave traffic allegations were not new. Four years earlier, disturbed by the accusations of two reformers, Belgian lawyer Alexis Splinguard and English Quaker Alfred Dyer, the Belgians invited the British authorities to send an official representative to inspect their brothels. Detective Inspectors Greenham and Williams were charged with the duty and carried out a three-week tour which took in fourteen towns, cities and ports in Belgium, Holland and France. The detectives received most cordial assistance from all the police with whom they came in contact, Greenham was to report. M. Schroder, the Brussels

Commissaire de Moers, was particularly solicitous, not only rendering them every possible assistance but accompanying them to all the *maisons de tolerance* to enable them to inspect the women and interview the English girls.

Greenham did his job thoroughly, coming back with interview statements and curriculum vitae on each of the ten English girls he found in Brussels brothels and one or two more elsewhere. He reported back that the traffic was confined almost solely to women who were not under-age, were already prostitutes, knew what they were doing and were not virtual prisoners, as had been alleged, but were content with their new homes and wanted to stay. He admitted that he had discovered two English girls who had been victims of misrepresentation, but he had made arrangements for their return to England.

It so happened that M. Schroder, his chief M. Lenaers, and Lenaers' deputy, M. Lemoine not only turned a blind eye to the under-age traffic in English girls, but were deeply involved in their procuration and the running of the brothels. Naturally, before Greenham and Williams had crossed the Channel, they had cleared the houses of all young English girls – with the exception of one. She had been identified earlier by Splinguard and Dyer, whom she had begged to help her escape. There was no denying her presence but, the brothel-keeper had assured the morals police, she had been beaten sufficiently to induce her to change her story – or face the consequences. She did change her story, even accusing one of the two men who had tried to rescue her of kissing her, and the other of asking her to be his mistress – and both of them of attempting to induce her to leave the brothel against her will.

Ironically, the man who revealed the truth was one of the Belgian policemen who had escorted Greenham and Williams on their farcical tour. He had developed a conscience and told all he knew to Josephine Butler, who was in Paris at the time. Deputy Chief Lemoine actually owned two of the brothels, he revealed (when Dyer had tried to get Lemoine's help to free the English girl, he had been startled when Lemoine began acting as if he were a rival brothel-keeper, trying to steal his girls); Chief Lenaer's son was in a position, as superintendent-in-chief of immigration, to see that the importation of the girls went without a hitch, and Lenaers' family had a monopoly on the supplying of wine to the brothels. Further, the brothel-keepers had been instructed by police that on no account should they admit Dyer and Splinguard to their premises again and, if it became necessary, to kill them, to go ahead and do so as any subsequent investigations would be none too thorough.

Josephine contacted the home secretary who, this time, sent a barrister, T.W. Snagge, to Brussels. Her accusations and evidence were eventually aired in a leading Brussels newspaper and Lenaers had no choice but to sue for libel. This, as is so often the case, was his undoing. He broke down under Splinguard's ferocious cross-examination and the trio's dire deeds were uncovered.

T.W. Snagge's report revealed that the white slave traffic was a reality. The trade was systematic, the girls had often been tricked into going there, their treatment was cruel and they were detained under duress (sometimes never leaving the house again). Many were also under-age – copies of adults' birth certificates being easily obtainable from Somerset House. He gave his evidence to the 1882 House of Lords Select Committee on the 'Alleged Traffic in English Girls for Immoral Purposes in Foreign Towns', yet British consular officials, brought home to comment on the situation, pooh-poohed the whole idea of white slave traffic. The evidence of Howard Vincent and Superintendent Dunlop of C Division made a great impact, despite the fact that Vincent was obviously trying to protect his officers from too much criticism. He stressed that what the reformers should be paying *much more* attention to, was the child prostitution rife in London, and to a greater extent than in any other European capital. Dunlop backed him up, describing his own difficulties in attempting to bring prosecutions without adequate laws to support him. Even when he found old men in bed with 12- and 13-year-old girls (twelve was the age of consent) the difficulties in proving they had been violated against their will were enormous, particularly as it was frequently the parents who had sold them.

Most of the measures needed to make effective police action possible (where the spirit was willing, that is) were recommended by the Lords Committee and these formed the basis of the Criminal Law Amendment Bill which was introduced to Parliament – but, somehow, kept being shelved. The real resistance lay further up, with the brothel patrons from among the wealthy and powerful. Howard Vincent informed Stead that the very men who could not manage to find time to get the CLA Bill through, were in regular receipt of brochures describing the latest child attractions in the various houses of a Mrs Jeffries. Each of these brothels had their own specialities – such as the sodomizing of young children or flagellation. (One maid, in such an establishment, fled to Stead's organization after she saw the condition of a child beaten with a wire whip for the amusement of a wealthy man). Another brothel acted as a clearing house for girls about to be shipped to the continent.

In desperation at the stonewalling, Stead not only went into print with his series of articles in the *Pall Mall Gazette* in 1885 (which caused a sensation), but began hinting that if time were not found for the bill during the current session, he would start naming names among the high and mighty.

That did the trick. Miraculously, time was found, the bill passed and a clause was even inserted raising the age of consent to sixteen. It was, says Glen Petrie, author of *A Singular Iniquity: The Campaigns of Josephine Butler*, 'a notable victory'. The privileged could no longer assume that the children of the lower orders were freely available for their sexual enjoyment. The powerful extracted their revenge however. To show that it could be done, Stead had earlier purchased a young girl, Eliza Armstrong, and now his enemies found her previously absent father who laid information against Stead, Bramwell Booth (son of the founder of the Salvation Army) and reformed prostitute, Rebecca Jarrett. Bramwell Booth, who had been involved in the campaign, but not the specific offence, was acquitted, Stead went to prison for three months and Jarrett for two years. Stead was later to perish in the *Titanic* disaster. Eliza was returned to her alcoholic mother and brutal father. Justice had been done.

The year of the Queen's Golden Jubilee (1887) proved to be an unhappy one in general for the image of the Metropolitan Police. The summer saw the sensational 'Case of Miss Cass' in which an 'innocent young woman', arrested on a charge of soliciting in the West End, was vigorously defended by her female employer. This resulted in a publicity engendering tribunal and a charge of perjury against the PC in the case. On acquitting him, the judge had some tart words to say about the whole procedure – particularly the arraigning of someone before a dubious public tribunal before doing so in a court of law. Damage was done to the police, but the case was another small step forward for ordinary womankind who would from then on be handled a little more gingerly by them.

Later in the year, thousands of the unemployed and agitators camped out in Trafalgar Square for days on end. The Home Office shilly-shallying over what measures to use to regain control simply encouraged more public disorder, so that when, eventually, a notice banning any more meetings in the square was issued and enforced, The Battle of Trafalgar Square ensued. The police won, but only just, without the use of troops on standby.

To add to the Yard's worries, there were serious threats of renewed Fenian activity during the Jubilee celebrations. Belton Cobb tells the intriguing tale of police action in the face of just such a plot. A minor Irish-American leader (who had been in the pay of the British) wrote from Boulogne to say he had been sent across the Atlantic for the purpose of blowing up Westminster Abbey, during the Jubilee thanksgiving service. He offered to reveal details of the plot on receipt of a large sum of money. Assistant Commissioner Monro found such a payment unacceptable. Instead, the ever-game (now-retired) James J. Thomson took his wife to Boulogne for a holiday. They just happened to make the acquaintance of an Irish-American couple whom the Thomsons (with their knowledge of both the French language and the attractions of Boulogne) helped to enjoy themselves – while gradually revealing their sympathy with the Irish cause.

The gift of the gab is one of the greatest of Irish charms, but it was partly their love of good talk which had already caused their mainland campaign to be less successful than it might have been. Soon, the holiday chum was spilling to Thomson and he was certain this was their man. He sent for Williamson who informed the blackmailer that his information was not required and warned him of instant arrest should he attempt to enter Britain. Westminster Abbey remained bomb-free during the festivities. At least the police got that right.

Whilst 1887 had been bad for the Metropolitan Police, it was as nothing compared to the following year for the CID. In this, the tenth year since their founding, they were to come under intense fire – for 1888 was the year of Jack the Ripper. To consider it necessary to describe the Jack the Ripper murders in any detail would be to suppose that readers had been on another planet during the last twenty years. Suffice to say, that five prostitutes were murdered in less than three months, all within a short distance of each other in the Whitechapel and City area. Four of these murders were particularly gory. All five, and possibly more murders, were thought to have been committed by the same person.

Among those brought into the enquiry from the Yard was the now portly, softly-spoken, old Whitechapel hand, Inspector Abberline; the jovial and gentlemanly Inspector Walter Andrews who, as a sergeant had done much of the leg-work on the Bravo case; Chief Inspector Moore, who was as strong-minded as he was physically huge, and the capable Chief Inspector Donald Sutherland Swanson – who was in charge.

Playing minor roles were two young men who were later to make their mark in the branch: Police Constable Frederick Porter Wensley, Somerset born of yeoman stock, later to become a long-serving local inspector in Whitechapel and eventually to become head of the department, and Detective Constable Walter Dew, who was to gain fame in the Crippen case.

As one of the hundreds of extra constables drafted into the area, Wensley recalled nailing bits of rubber, 'usually old bicycle tyres', to the soles of his otherwise noisy boots to avoid giving the murderer too much warning of his approach. But, as the world knows, the murderer was never caught. Later, Wensley also made the pertinent remark that in those days there had been many uninvestigated deaths in the East End.

Like Inspector Reid, Walter Dew was new to Whitechapel CID, and though pleased to be there, was concerned about bringing his wife to live in such an area. By his own account, his chief attributes were his 'splendid memory' and his ability to gain the confidence of his superiors which resulted in his being entrusted with delicate enquiries usually assigned to men of higher rank. Dew saw the dreadfully mutilated body of one of the victims, Mary Ann Kelly, and unsurprisingly, it was a sight he later did not care to remember.

'There was one thing our critics overlooked,' he wrote in *I Caught Crippen*. 'This murder, as indeed were all the Ripper murders, was an added burden thrust upon a body of men already grievously overworked. Other crimes were being committed and other criminals had to be hunted. Life for the police officer in Whitechapel in those days was one long nightmare.' His only real criticism of police procedure was that he felt the way the press were held at arms length was a mistake.

The CID were not helped by the fact that their head, Assistant Commissioner Monro, after a period of quarrelling with the

Commissioner Sir Charles Warren, finally departed on the day
that the third body was discovered. Warren had refused to allow
him to appoint an old tea planter friend, as Assistant Chief
Constable. Monro was replaced by Sir Robert Anderson, who had
been the go-between for Fenian informer Le Caron and the British
authorities. The fourth body, that of Annie Chapman, was found
just after Anderson, for health reasons, had departed for two
months rest in Switzerland prior to taking up the post. Anderson
was recalled but it can't have helped matters to have had a new
man in charge at this crucial time and, indeed, one with no
experience of detection procedures but some rather fanciful ideas.
As he himself later admitted (as quoted by his son, A.P.
Moore-Anderson, in *The Life of Sir Robert Anderson*):

> When I took charge I was no novice in matters relating to criminals
> and crime. I was not a little surprised therefore to find occasion for
> suspecting that one of my principal subordinates was trying to
> impose on me as though I were an ignoramus. For when any
> important crime of a certain kind occurred, and I set myself to
> investigate it in Sherlock Holmes fashion, he used to listen to me in
> the way so many people listen to sermons in church; and when I was
> done he would stolidly announce that the crime was the work of A,
> B, C or D, naming one of his stock heroes. It was Old Carr, or
> Worth, or Sausage, or Shrimps, or Quiet Joe, or Red Bob, etc etc,
> one name or another being put forward according to the nature of
> the crime.
>   However, on putting the subordinates statements to the test, it
> appeared that he was generally right.

The person he is talking about may have been Williamson but,
more likely, 'Old Jack Shore' who was given to jotting down a list
of likely suspects as soon as an offence was reported.

With the failure of the massive Ripper operation much to the
fore, press attention was being strongly focused on the detective
department and there were accusations of their failing to acquire
the best brains for the job. Direct entry should be allowed. This
had long been a bone of contention with the uniform side who felt
there were already too many direct entry detectives. That was part
of the problem, these men lacked the essential background of
street experience. In November 1888, *The Times* published a
somewhat ambiguous statement by Warren, obviously intended to
clear up the matter but which appeared to be trying to keep both
the press and public happy without upsetting the ranks who had
shown some unrest earlier in the year.

He pointed out that there was no rule (and there never had been) that candidates had to serve two or three years as constables on divisions before appointment to the CID. They would consider a man who was shorter than the height usually required and even one not physically fit for normal police duties – though should he be removed from the CID he would be obliged to leave the force without compensation.

Having said all that, he concluded: 'As a general rule it has been ascertained by the Criminal Investigation Branch that the candidates who have applied to be appointed direct to detective duties have not possessed any special qualifications which would justify their being so appointed.'

In fact, as Williamson had informed the 1877 committee, there had been six direct entry detectives. One had been a French political refugee named Lavite who was useless to them after completing the task for which he was specifically appointed. Another was Saunders, who had been a businessman in Calais and spoke fluent French. He had become an alcoholic and finally committed suicide. Then there was Marchand, who had been dismissed for bad conduct, and Edwin Coathupe, a surgeon who took a fancy to detecting, joined the branch in the early 1860s, stayed for three years before going back to doctoring, and eventually became Chief Constable of Bristol City Police. Two direct entry officers were still serving and had given evidence to that same committee. These were the multilingual Lambert (the man who complained he wouldn't have joined had he known about the expenses) and Greenham. (There may have been more since 1877, though this seems unlikely as Williamson deemed the experiment a failure.)

In December 1888, four months after the resignation of Monro, Warren also resigned after getting into hot water with the Home Office for defending the police in print, without first submitting the article for approval. Monro was appointed commissioner in his place – and he brought his tea-planter friend with him as assistant chief constable CID. The following year the department suffered another body blow with the death of their beloved chief, Frederick Williamson.

On an autumn evening in 1891, outside a pub in the Waterloo Road, a 19-year-old girl collapsed in agony. A passing costermonger came to her rescue and took the trembling, shivering girl home. Such were her convulsions that, by the time a doctor arrived, several people were holding her down. She died on the way to St Thomas's Hospital later that night. The girl's name was Ellen Donworth and the post-mortem revealed the presence of strychnine in her stomach.

Before breathing her agonizing last, Ellen, who was a prostitute, described the man who had given her 'some white stuff' to drink from a bottle. He was tall, dark and 'cross-eyed'.

The division was L or Lambeth and the Local Inspector was George Harvey. Dorset-born Harvey was one of a new breed of post-Turf Fraud detectives inasmuch that not only was he hard-working, but also abstemious. Indeed he was most proud of the fact that he had never even tasted intoxicating drink of any description. Some of his predecessors, such as the convivial Inspector Field, might have regarded him with wonder. Despite having served for twenty-three years, Harvey had been an inspector for only the last two and a half. His numerous arrests of burglars, coiners, an abortionist, a child stealer and an attempted murderer indicated that he was one of the thief-taking variety of detectives whose sheer enthusiasm and doggedness, rather than flair or influence, got them promotion in the end. One criminal who had managed to slip through Harvey's fingers, albeit accidentally, was a forger who, in the desperate struggle to avoid arrest (penalties for the offence being severe) managed to shoot himself dead.

Inspector Harvey tried hard, but failed to trace either the cross-eyed man or the writer of some anonymous letters about the crime. One of these, signed 'O'Brien, detective' offered to find the murderer for a mere £300,000, while others accused Mr Frederick Smith, of the newsagent and bookseller family of that name, of the murder, but 'The South Lambeth Mystery' remained just that.

The death of another woman in the same area a week later failed to be connected with that of Donworth, despite the fact that the dying girl, Matilda Clover, had spoken of a man called 'Fred' giving her some pills. The reason for this was that her cause of death was registered as 'delirium tremors and syncope' by a doctor who had not seen her during her final brief illness nor inspected her body when she was dead.

The Yard received a letter, this time accusing a well-known physician of the 'murder' but, while attempting to trap the writer with an advertisement in a newspaper – with a view to punishing this blatant libel and possibly blackmail attempt – no one thought to check on how the girl had actually died, or to pass this information about the letter to the division concerned. The letter was filed under the Yard's equivalent of C for cranks and forgotten.

Six months later, at around 2 a.m. on a cold April night, a Constable Eversfield was called to a house in Stamford Street, once again, in the same dingy area south of the Thames. He found a young woman, Alice Marsh, lying face down in the passageway. She was obviously in agony, as was another girl, Emma Shrivell, in an upstairs bedroom. The PC gave them mustard and water emetics before he and a Constable Comley carried them into a cab and told the driver to make haste for St Thomas's Hospital. Alice Marsh died on the way but Emma Shrivell remained coherent and, between her dreadful convulsions, managed to describe the 'gentleman' with whom they had spent the evening – and who, by a ruse, had given them three pills each to swallow. He was tall, wore a silk hat, and was bald. 'Was that the gentleman you let out at a quarter to two, with glasses on?' asked PC Comley. 'Yes,' Emma replied, 'we called him Fred.'

After a night of dreadful suffering, Emma also died. At first, it was supposed that 'fish poisoning' from their supper had killed the women, but later analysis of their stomach contents revealed the presence of strychnine.

During the murder investigation which followed, someone thought to mention the death of Matilda Clover. Inspector Harvey obtained an order to have her body exhumed. Shortly afterwards, a Detective Sergeant McIntyre, of the Special Irish Branch, became acquainted with a political informant by the name of Haynes. Haynes lodged with a photographer and the photographer had a regular customer – Doctor Neill, a man who seemed to love having his picture taken, despite a prominent cast in his eye. Sergeant McIntyre was introduced to this friendly medical man, who said he acted as an agent for a US drug company, and who soon began complaining to McIntyre that he was being followed by the police. Indeed he was.

Harvey's assistant, Detective Sergeant Alfred Ward, and PC Comley, had spotted the doctor in the street and it had struck them that he resembled the description of 'Fred'. Since the sighting, he had been tailed intermittently. Sergeant McIntyre asked the doctor why anyone should want to follow him, and Neill confided that it was obvious he was being mistaken for a fellow lodger, a medical student named Harper, who had been blackmailed by Emma Shrivell and Alice Marsh and who had asked his advice about the purchase of strychnine. Dr Neill now had the detective sergeant's full attention, particularly when he began to include Matilda Clover in his murmurings.

Neill was assured that the police interest had merely been focused on him because he was a stranger in the area – if he could just prove his identity and state his business everything would be all right. The doctor was eager to comply, saying he would produce his medicine case to prove he was a bona fide commercial traveller. McIntyre took along Inspector Harvey and Chief Inspector Mulvaney and they all retired to a pub where they inspected the case and some unopened mail addressed to 'Dr Neill', who opened one of the letters to show that it contained details of medicine prices.

The detectives were convinced that this was their man, but were in a cleft stick. Such cases were notoriously difficult to prove, as events of the previous decade had demonstrated. Poisoning was a popular murder method at the time, for two reasons. Several lethal drugs were not yet controlled so were easily available. Some, such as arsenic, were even in common domestic use for, for instance, killing rats. Consequently, possession of them could be justified. In addition, toxicology was still in its infancy. Potential murderers, therefore, might reasonably suppose that, despite suspicious circumstances, the chances of a conviction could be slim – and they were right. It was true that Dr Lamson, who poisoned his nephew in 1881, was convicted despite the use of a rare drug, aconitine, but he had administered it in a manner bound to give rise to suspicion. When he went to visit the boy, he had taken some ready-cut Dundee cake with him – and the boy just happened to collapse and die after eating it. He was arrested, convicted and hanged.

Two similar cases in the mid and late 1880s had differing outcomes. Adelaide Bartlett and Florence Maybrick were each accused of murdering their husbands, in 1886 and 1889 respectively. Both women were of foreign stock and both were married to older men whom they were cuckolding. Bartlett was acquitted largely because there was no way of telling how a substantial quantity of chloroform had got into her husband's stomach without corroding his lips and gullet. Maybrick was convicted – on fairly flimsy evidence and despite the fact that her husband was known to take arsenic as an aphrodisiac.

The difference between Doctor Neill and these other suspected poisoners was that with the latter the victims were relatives, not strangers, and the suspects had a discernible motive. Neill had not even witnessed the dying of these girls so even a virulent sadism was difficult to prove, as might have been possible had he been with any of them immediately before their deaths. Added to which, detectives were often accused of making arrests too early, and there was some justification for this complaint. Harvey did not want to move until satisfied that he had sufficient proof to sustain the charge – yet, on the other hand, this man was dangerous.

Inspector Tunbridge of the Yard was called in to take charge of the investigation and Detective Sergeant McIntyre was seconded to the full-time cultivation of his friendship with the doctor. He asked Neill to provide him with a sample of his handwriting and a note of his movements and his complaints about the unwanted police attention. His writing proved to be similar to that in some of the anonymous letters, but not all. The ploy bore fruit, nonetheless. When the writing-paper was held up to the light, a watermark was revealed – the same watermark as that on the paper used for a particularly damning anonymous letter. That paper was available only in the US.

Suddenly, Detective Sergeant McIntyre reported that the doctor was becoming restless and looked liable to move at any time. There was no choice but to go in. Tunbridge arrested him – for attempted extortion by way of the letters. 'Fire away,' said the unruffled Neill, 'you have got the wrong man.'

In his room detectives discovered strychnine (but then, he sold drugs) and notes about the murdered girls. Police were still doubtful that they would be able to prove their case and requested the first of what was to be a series of remands at Bow Street. This first was granted, pending the result of the inquest on Matilda Clover who, at last, was getting the attention that her doctor (paid for by club subscription) had denied her. 'It was a case of murder made easy,' commented prosecuting counsel Mr C.F. Gill, after it had been pointed out to Matilda's doctor that he had signed a death certificate which stated that he had tended her in her last illness when, in fact, he had failed to attend on both occasions when he was called as she lay dying. Initially, he had sent his unqualified assistant and, on the second occasion, he had sent medicine. He had signed the death certificate without thinking, he claimed.

The inquest jury brought in a verdict of murder by Dr Neill and the coroner agreed with that. The poor local inspector must have felt somewhat slighted when the coroner added that, although the greatest credit was due to Inspector Harvey and Sergeant McIntyre, Inspector Tunbridge had aided him materially by presenting his evidence in such a clear way. Harvey already felt aggrieved that the first he had heard about the letter, which claimed Matilda's death was 'murder', was when Neill was taken before the Bow Street magistrates. At that time, too, he was first let into the results of the examination of Matilda's body – that strychnine was present. It seems that the lack of co-operation, complained about when the old guard were at the Yard, was still a problem.

The charge against Neill now became one of murder but Tunbridge was obliged to ask for further remands, while awaiting a witness from America (where Inspector Jarvis had gone in the course of further enquiries). Among the witnesses Tunbridge called, while they were waiting, was a woman who had been given pills by Neill for some spots, but had only pretended to take them and had thus survived. By the time the waiting had stretched to nearly three months, defence counsel were, not surprisingly, complaining bitterly. When a witness finally arrived, he turned out to be a fellow commercial traveller to whom Neill had shown the poisons he claimed to give to women – usually to induce abortion.

The other findings of Inspector Jarvis (a man of the world as familiar with New York as with London) proved startling. Neill's real name was Thomas Neill Cream and he had been born in Glasgow in 1850 or thereabouts, but had emigrated to Canada with his parents a few years later. Surprisingly enough, his medical credentials appeared to be genuine (indeed, he had studied for a while at the hospital he was later to keep busy with the care of dying girls – St Thomas's), but he had fled to Ontario after being implicated in the suspicious death of a girl (by the administration of chloroform). He settled in Chicago where, in 1880, he was charged with causing the death of a young woman during an abortion but had been discharged due to lack of evidence. Soon after that he was arrested for the murder of Daniel Storr, the husband of his mistress and, this time, was convicted and sentenced to life imprisonment. The method had been strychnine poisoning and he had been apprehended as a result of his drawing attention to the case by writing anonymous letters accusing others of the crime.

Under the sentencing system, he had not been obliged to complete his life term – merely serving ten years before being released in July 1891. Shortly afterwards he was in London, during which time he killed Ellen Donworth and Matilda Clover, before returning to Canada. He was soon back again – to kill again.

During the trial, the tensions between the Yard men and the Divisional CID resurfaced but suggestions of jealousy between the two were denied. The jury took only twelve minutes to find Doctor Neill Cream guilty of wilful murder and, this time, action was taken to ensure that no other young girls would die terrible deaths at his hands. He is reputed to have had one last attempt to cause mayhem. As he was hanged, it is said that he exclaimed, 'I am Jack the R ... '

The degree of acrimony that obviously existed between divisional and Yard detectives cannot have been helped by the fact that, while many of the former were still grubbing away in comparatively primitive conditions, the latter were moving to quarters in the splendid New Scotland Yard which overlooked the Thames, was adjacent to the Houses of Parliament, and had, if you please, been originally designed as an opera house.

Day-to-day working in the 'dingy collection of mean buildings' spread around Great Scotland Yard had become nigh impossible. *The Times*, describing the 'hopeless confusion' which reigned there, told of books piled on staircases, making them almost impassable, and piles of clothing, saddles, horse-furniture and blankets heaped up in little garrets.

Thirty years earlier, when the splendid, new Victoria Embankment began sweeping away grubby old alleys and wharves from Chelsea Bridge to Blackfriars, one site, near Westminster Bridge, had been left empty of buildings. Being partly reclaimed land, it remained waterlogged and, as such, was considered unfit for development. But such a prime site could not remain neglected for long and, in 1875, an ambitious scheme had been launched to build a huge, grand opera house. But so much money was spent in sinking the necessarily deep foundations that there was insufficient remaining to put a roof on the building. There were rumours that it might be converted into a hotel, but Commissioner Henderson saw it as an answer to the Yard's chronic, overcrowding problems. The site was purchased, the partly constructed opera house demolished to its foundations, and New Scotland Yard was erected to a design by Norman Shaw. This turreted, Victorian Gothic fantasy was certainly unique and was destined to represent Scotland Yard around the world. As Douglas Browne wrote in his splendid book, *The Rise of Scotland Yard*, one particularly useful feature retained was a tunnel 'designed to bring opera addicts direct to the auditorium from the platform of Westminster Bridge Station. By this means, in time of emergency, 2,000 policemen could be fetched by rail from all over London and concentrated unseen at the nerve centre of operations'.

The incoming occupants fought over all the available space in the new building – the CID, alone, wanted forty rooms – and so, by the time the grand edifice was completed, it was already too small. New Scotland Yard received a mixed reception from the press, though many thought it splendid. Moving-in took place during November and December 1890, before drying out was complete. Soon, there were complaints about damp, so more fires had to be sanctioned by the receiver. Shortly afterwards, a twin building was erected alongside and joined to the original by means of an enclosed bridge. Later, further space was taken in offices on the other side of the first building. The whole was as complex as a rabbit warren – as I know to my cost, having become quite lost in the middle of the night in its echoing corridors, when, in the 1950s, I was sent to consult records of missing girls.

11 The Naughty Nineties?

It was a shepherd who found the body at dawn as he was moving his flock across Wormwood Scrubs, within sight of London's most up-to-date prison. The common was the haunt of roughs, a number of whom slept there during the summer. On that June night in 1893, however, it had rained for several hours so the shepherd was surprised when he came upon a 'respectably dressed' woman lying on her back in a hollow. He would have been content to give her a wide berth had his dog not insisted on going up to the woman and sniffing her face – which drew his attention to its awful condition. The whole of the left side was heavy with congealed blood and, on touching one of her clenched fists he found it icy cold. She was dead.

The shepherd hurried to fetch Constable Parrish from his prison perimeter patrol duty. He, in turn, sent for Notting Dale's Inspector Gilham and the divisional surgeon. They found the woman's injuries to be terrible. On her forehead were two large wounds with another under her chin – all of which showed fractures of the bone, and her right eye was 'completely smashed'. On the ground beside her lay an umbrella and a purse, but the latter contained nothing to identify the victim. The surgeon estimated her age to be thirty, and guessed that she had met her death about five or six hours earlier – certainly she must have been there since before midnight as the grass beneath her body was dry.

The local detective inspector, Daniel Morgan, had been in the department since before the Turf Fraud Trial and, indeed, had been called to give evidence in favour of Nathaniel Druscovich – but only to say that his behaviour towards his turf fraud captives had been perfectly proper and not at all suspicious during the journey back from Rotterdam with them in his custody. Morgan had survived the subsequently imposed probation period and went on to become Local Inspector of X Division, in West London.

Now, after twenty-nine years' service, he was nearing retirement age.

He began the Wormwood Scrubs investigation with no clue as to either the identity of the victim or the assailant – never a good start. The first priority was to name his corpse so, to this end, he supplied the press with a detailed description before attempting to find any witnesses to the crime itself.

The night-duty perimeter patrol policemen claimed to have seen or heard nothing at all unusual during that night. This surprised PC Parrish and when, at 7 a.m. the next day, he took over from one of them, PC George Cook, he remarked, 'You left a pretty fine job behind you yesterday morning'. The tall and powerfully built Cooke agreed. Yes, he had heard it had been a nasty job. Why, persisted Parrish, (who obviously resented the stressful time he had suffered since being called to the body) had neither of them seen the body from the corner of the prison wall? – it was light enough these mornings. Here, Cooke disagreed – no-one would have noticed it unless it had been pointed out, he insisted – there were sheep feeding in that area. Of course, it is not unknown for policemen to studiously avoid noticing something which may bring upon them a great deal of hard work, particularly when they are tired or approaching the end of their shift.

That afternoon, 27-year-old PC Cooke was roused from his bed for an interview with Detective Inspector Morgan. The constable, whose manner some found rather reserved, had been attached to Notting Dale Police Station for only a few weeks and it was common knowledge that he had come there under a bit of a cloud. There was no way it could be kept secret when the results of his transgression had been blazoned, as was the custom, in the regularly issued *Police Orders*. Cooke had been serving at Bow Street when he was suspended from duty, and his later reinstatement had been accompanied by a very strict caution and a transfer to X division. Police Orders had not revealed any details of his offence but rumour had it that a woman was involved. So far, it had been a happy move for him. While at Bow Street he had lived in the spartan section house above the station whereas on X, he had found pleasant lodgings with a fellow-officer, PC Robinson and his wife. They had introduced him to a charming girl, a ladies' maid, to whom he had quickly become engaged. The wedding was to take place in October, three months hence.

Detective Inspector Morgan told PC Cooke that the body had

now been identified – by Mrs Robinson – as a woman named Maude, who had come to the house, looking for Cooke, on the evening before her body was found. Several policemen also recognized her as the woman who had been asking for Cooke at the police station and on the beat. Who was this woman, Morgan asked?

Cooke admitted that he had known her for about two-and-a-half years, having first encountered her in the Strand, 'where I knew her as an unfortunate woman'. He had last seen her, he claimed, on the previous Saturday evening (it was now Thursday) and had received a letter from her on Tuesday, to say she would come to Wormwood Scrubs station that evening and wanting to know what time he would meet her. 'But I did not see her that night,' he insisted. No, he didn't have the letter, he had burned it.

Cooke was not to know but was soon to find out that that very afternoon Mr Grimshaw, the prison chemist, who lived in a cottage on the common, had come to the police station. He reported that at 10.45 p.m. on the night in question, he had seen a PC talking to a young woman on the path just outside his home. He remembered clearly because he was obliged to brush past them to get in and, while doing so, had wished the constable goodnight. The greeting had been returned in calm and respectful tones. Later, he had overheard an altercation between the couple.

'You were the only constable on duty there,' Morgan pointed out.

'I neither saw nor spoke to any woman all night,' Cooke replied firmly.

But there was more. Detective Inspector Morgan produced a whistle and truncheon, saying, 'You were seen to bury these in the back garden early yesterday morning.' Cooke could only follow the golden rule – agree with unassailable evidence but put a different, innocent, interpretation on it. He admitted that he had buried a whistle and truncheon, explaining that he had been worried that the station inspector would be coming to visit his lodgings. (Policemen's residences were inspected for suitability by a senior officer even in my day – the 1950s – but Cooke may have been referring to a possible search with regard to the murder.) He admitted that, this particular truncheon and whistle were surplus to issue (a useful thing to have as insurance against loss, but possession of them would not be approved). He had bought them, he explained (not stolen them) about three years earlier – for sixpence, from a constable on A division.

Morgan was still not finished. He pointed out to Cooke that his trousers appeared to be bloodstained. The cool constable could not account for that but suggested that the stains might have got there on Monday, when he had injured his thumb while cutting tobacco.

Mr Grimshaw identified the body as that of the woman he had seen with the constable, but was unable to recognize PC Cooke. There was nothing surprising in that. For some odd reason, members of the public rarely remember the face of a policeman they have seen previously in another setting and wearing a helmet. Nonetheless, at 6 p.m. on Thursday, 8 June 1893, PC George Samuel Cooke was charged with the murder of Maude Smith/Merton/Cooke, a charge he vigorously denied. Predictably, the case caused a sensation. The public were quite accustomed to seeing policemen as murder victims – not suspects. Cooke, however, did not deny it for long.

The following day, after his appearance at West London Magistrates Court, he murmured to the uniformed Inspector Hatcher who was looking after him, 'I suppose it is no use trying to get out of it.' The unhappy inspector replied that he did not know, whereupon Cooke remarked, 'You have not got the right tool it was done with.' (It is curious that some murderers give the impression that they are confessing merely to put the investigating team right on some niggling point. James Greenacre, who murdered Hannah Brown in 1837, couldn't wait to tell the police they were wrong about the order in which he had distributed her dismembered remains about the capital.) In this instance, Cooke wanted it known that he had killed Maude with his regular issue truncheon – *not* the one they had dug up from the garden.

It transpired that the well set-up young PC had once cohabited with prostitute Maude Merton but had wanted to finish the affair. She did not, and had gone to Bow Street Police Station to complain that he ill-treated her – though there was other evidence to suggest that he had been kind and generous to her. Consequently, he had been suspended and transferred to X division – so as to put an end to the matter. He was a good officer, a senior policeman assured the trial jury.

Maude was not to be so easily fobbed off and had pursued him to X division. That night, she had refused to leave him alone and threatened (so he claimed) to make more trouble for him – ruining his career and his marriage plans. Eventually, in a rage, he struck out at her with his truncheon. She had fallen down, but once he had started he couldn't stop and he struck her two or three more times, before keeping his foot on her neck for five minutes. When his colleague joined him later, he claimed, 'we were jolly all night afterwards'. He had gone from saying nothing to saying far too much. He concluded this suicidal confession by admitting, 'I have been much happier since she has been dead than I was before. She was always annoying me and I was in misery.'

It is hardly surprising that the judge (known as Hanging Hawkins), who had given a vitriolic summing up, would have no truck with the jury's recommendation to mercy on the grounds of provocation, but sentenced PC Cooke to death. Cooke's fiancée, possibly egged on by the press, tried desperately to save him, appealing to MPs, the new Duchess of York, the commission (for permission to launch a Metropolitan Police petition such as the City Police had agreed to) and even Queen Victoria – contrasting her own despair with the happiness of the sovereign's newly wedded son (The Duke of York). All to no avail. On Tuesday, 25 July 1893, exactly seven weeks after that wet night when Maude Merton had come looking for her lost love, PC George Cooke was hanged. Justice was swift in those days.

Shortly after PC Cooke was hanged there were two important developments concerning the British Police. The first was the launching of *Police Review and Parade Gossip*, and the second, the inauguration of scientific identification procedures.

The primary aims of the new magazine were to support, educate and give voice to police officers while providing a means of communication between them – thereby raising their status and professionalism. This applied as much to the ordinary man on the beat as to the chiefs but, probably to prevent consternation among the latter, they insisted that they would always encourage respect for superior authority and the maintenance of good discipline. All of which made the magazine more likely to be of influence when it later chastised policemen for not taking full advantage of what they termed 'the revolutionary change' in police methods of identification. Instead, it claimed, policemen were clinging to 'old, cumbrous, time-wasting and uncertain methods, greatly to the advantage of the astute criminal who has reason to conceal his identity'.

Identification was, and probably always will be, the greatest of detection problems. Identification not only of suspects and bodies of victims but, in those days, of those caught in the act and charged. Before the days of fingerprinting there was no sure way to check that those charged were who they claimed to be, so habitual criminals invariably gave false names to prevent a bad, past record coming to light. This was particularly the case with habitual offenders who might be eligible for the swingeing preventive detention sentences. Up to 1893, the British police had relied on personal visual identification and, to this end, the viewing of prisoners in custody was a regular part of a detective's duties – and a hugely time-wasting one.

The French police were well ahead in this respect. In 1882, the Parisian Police had begun experimenting with the new identification system developed by Alphonse Bertillon. This involved the taking of the prisoner's physical measurements – the length of the head (back to front), feet, hands, fingers, height (standing and sitting) and arm-span. Scars, other marks and eye and hair colouring were also noted. The premise being that no two persons would have the identical assortment of physical characteristics. The details taken were then classified 'by a process of continual sub-division'. Bertillonage or The Anthropometric System was deemed a success after its first trial when it had proved the means of correctly identifying twenty-seven prisoners in just over twelve months.

By 1893, it had become obvious that not only was Britain lagging behind in identification methodology but as the population of London continued its relentless expansion the Metropolitan Police desperately needed something better than the existing system. Visual identification was all very well but, as Littlechild pointed out, 'people often bear an astonishing resemblance to each other, and this similarity has sometimes been sorely perplexing and misleading to the detective'. As well as quoting his own experiences on the subject, he claims that the Yard once arrested the wrong twin, who subsequently brought an action for false imprisonment, and goes on to tell the tale of a wooden-legged man 'who was, one might think, easily to be identified'. When arrested, he protested his innocence saying, 'Yes, I know you want a wooden-legged man; but you see I've lost my *right* leg, and the man you want has lost his *left*. He lives next door to me ...'

Of course, he may have been pulling our legs.

With the identification problem, as with so many others, the thing to do seemed to be to raise a committee to discuss the matter, although on this occasion it was the British Association for the Advancement of Science which prodded the Home Office into action. The committee considered both the anthropometric system and the possibility of utilizing 'finger marks'.

The idea of identification by finger marks (i.e. thumbprints in lieu of signature) is thought to have been in existence since ancient times when used by the Chinese and other Asians in lieu of a signature but, typically, when the expansion of this use began to be considered seriously, the idea took root in several different places: Germany, in 1823, when a Professor Purkenje read a thesis on the subject; Bengal, in 1858, where English civil servant, William Herschel, developed a fingerprint system to (as Cherrill put it) 'frighten the natives' who impersonated one another to collect their pension or allowance; and in New Mexico, in 1882, by the leader of a geological survey to register local workers. A great leap forward occurred in Britain when Francis Galton using some of Herschel's data, demonstrated that the fingerprint was individual to a person and that the patterns persisted throughout life, and in 1892, he published a fingerprint classification study. The Argentinian police began experimenting with a fingerprint system based on his work, and they are credited with the first conviction obtained on the basis of the new science – a woman who murdered her own children because her new lover did not like them – but the bloody fingerprint she left at the scene subsequently identified her and led to her confession. (Though the belief is widely held that identification by finger marks has been in existence since ancient times, Fred Cherrill – who spent most of his service in the Yard's Fingerprint Bureau and became its head – disputes the theory, saying that in his own thirty years of research he has found no evidence whatsoever to support such a contention. *Cherrill of the Yard.*)

It soon became clear that the fingerprint was the practically foolproof method of identification. Not only that, the means of taking them – rolling each finger in printer's ink and transferring the image on to white card – was a simple matter requiring the minimum of time, equipment, expense and training (and this simple procedure has never been changed). Where the difficulty arose, was in the classification. The sorting of prints so as to be able to extract the vital information required was a monumental task which seemed to make fingerprinting impractical as an everyday aid. Galton had formulated a selection process which he demonstrated to the committee (of Home Office personnel, Melville Macnaghten, now chief constable of the CID, and Major Arthur Griffiths, Inspector of Prisons) using a collection of 2,500 sets. Although impressed by his expertise, they foresaw great difficulties when it came to its use by lesser-skilled men sorting through even larger numbers.

Two other matters concerned the committee: the likelihood of criminals attempting to destroy or alter their fingerprints, and the possibility of them becoming obscured by manual labour. The first concern was disposed of when it was shown that attempts to destroy or alter fingerprints tended to make them more identifiable rather than less. As to the second, the *Police Review* reported:

> ... the habitual criminal is of all persons the least likely to engage in hard manual labour unless it is forced upon him in the shape of oakum-picking, while the committee found from the examination of the fingerprints of 100 prisoners at Pentonville, variously engaged as oakum-pickers, stokers, bakers, or tailors, that though the lines might be slightly thickened, there was no difficulty in obtaining a perfectly clear print – 'the only exceptions,' they [the committee] say, with perhaps unconscious humour, 'being a prisoner who had lost a hand, and another who had lost one of his fingers.'

The Home Office plumped for a trial period of a modified Bertillon system (they added face-breadth or bizygomatic measurement) backed up by final identification by fingerprinting. How this was meant to work was, for example, in the case of two men having very similar measurements, the fingerprint could then be used to differentiate between the two.

There were the usual doubts about the wisdom of adopting these unpleasant foreign habits. A letter to *The Times* from 'Observer', for instance, pointed out that not only might some offenders find all this measuring an indignity but, if they consequently resisted, proper accuracy could only be achieved by the use of some kind of muscular restraint by the warders or police. 'That may answer very well on the Continent, where everyone submits patiently to the inevitable, but it would not do in England, and I trust the recommendations of the Committee – opposed as they are to the sentiments and principles of Englishmen – will not meet with the approval of the Secretary of

State.' He did approve, however, and in July 1894 an Anthropometric Office was attached to the Home Office Registry of Habitual Criminals. The system even went so far as to employ the metric measuring system which had been deemed not only easier to use but less liable to error. Inevitably, the title of the department was shortened to 'The Metric Office'.

One of the biggest headaches for the CID in the late 1890s was Queen Victoria's Diamond Jubilee which brought not only a glittering array of the rich, the royal and the fashionable to London, but also 'the aristocracy of the criminal world' to prey upon them. Con men were everywhere and one of the detectives put on their trail was Charles Arrow, who had gained his investigative spurs in the West rather than the East End of London. Arrow was from a middle-class background, had left school at nineteen, and greatly disappointed his parents (who had a civil service career planned for him) by enrolling in the Metropolitan Police. He had, he explained, gained a taste for the man-hunt when helping to capture a thief stealing from his school.

The young Arrow's first beat was in Westminster, parts of which were very rough, and, unlike some detectives who can't wait to tell you how quickly they got out of uniform, he obviously had some very fond memories of those first three years. He admits in *Rogues and Others* that his enthusiasm was somewhat dampened by guarding government offices from Fenian bombs on wet and freezing winter nights. But he tells endearing tales of heating his coffee tin on the top of a street gas lamp and being caught by his inspector when accepting some hot elderberry wine from a lady of quality on Christmas night. She, on seeing his horror at such discovery, similarly plied the inspector on his next patrol. He also waxes lyrical about the four jolly days a year spent living and working at Ascot during race week – the camaraderie, the fresh air, bird song at dawn over the race track, the noisy throng and the glitter of diamonds at a nearby house party.

He claimed he was given a start in his career as a detective by a woman to whom he had shown some sympathy, who told him where to find some coiners. While pleased to get into the CID he missed the greater *esprit de corps* he had found in the uniform branch, and said so. Another woman he credited with assisting him with his enquiries on one occasion was his wife. He had arrested a man who, he thought, was involved in the theft of some of Nelson's relics from Greenwich Hospital, but had found nothing in the suspects baggage but some old clothes and a concertina. 'Did you look *inside* the concertina?' asked the clever Mrs Arrow. Opening up that convivial instrument, he found the famous Admiral's watch and seal. (In a *Police Review* profile on him in 1907 her role was not mentioned, the find being put down to the particular astuteness of Arrow – but he put this right in his book.)

Arrow believed that for an enthusiastic detective there could be no rank more enviable than that of local inspector and so was delighted when he achieved that status on C Division which covered the West End. Among the con men he netted during the celebrations of Victoria's sixty glorious years in 1897, were an 'American Colonel', an 'Austrian Count' and a 'German Baron'. They ended up making, 'a much longer stay in this country than they intended – as the guests of the nation'. Working among the well-to-do, it was inevitable that diamond robberies and the like were more to the fore than coining and cargo-stealing, and that he would come in contact with the crime of blackmail more often than his East End colleagues. Indeed, Arrow became something of an expert on the subject. Many of the cases concerned threats of revelations of homosexuality but, while claiming to speak plainly about the crime, Arrow assumes, or merely pretends to assume, that all of the allegations so made were false.

> Any gentleman strolling home at night or in the early morning from his club or from some function or even from the House, is looked upon as a possible victim and may be followed by the youth under the observation of his accomplices. The youth will ask the gentleman for a light, or beg from him – anything to get into conversation; and, if he can gain sympathy by a tale of woe sufficiently to induce the gentleman to ask him into his house or chambers, for food or other assistance, this is a consummation devoutly to be wished, and the rest is easy, especially if the youth manages, as he often does, to steal some article from the gentleman's rooms as a proof of his having been in them.

What followed, of course, was an accusation of 'something unnatural' having taken place. The problem was, inevitably, to get the blackmailed to come forward. That homosexuals should be placed in a position of such vulnerability was unpleasant to say the least, but coming in the wake of the Cleveland Street scandal and the trials of Oscar Wilde, to pretend that none of the upper class

The multilingual James Jacob Thomson who was typical of the more educated second generation of detectives. He rose to the rank of superintendent

Detective Inspector Charles E. Leach who formed a squad to combat the many con men who flooded into London after the Great War

Florence Bravo

Superintendent Walter Hambrook, first chief of the Flying Squad

Superintendent Hambrook in earlier days wearing Beefeater fancy dress ready for duty at Chelsea Arts Ball

Chief Inspector Charles Arrow as a young uniformed PC in the early 1880s. Later he became one of the first members of the Murder Squad

Conference at the siege of Sidney Street: far left is Inspector Wensley, second from right ex-tea planter, Assistant Commissioner CID, Sir Melville Macnaghten

The first vehicles used by the Flying Squad were Crossley tenders. Attaching radio aerials as shown allowed the first mobile communication but earned the van the nickname of The Bedstead and made it easily recognizable

males were so indulging seems – well, perverse.

Edward Drew was a West End detective with a career similar to that of Arrow. He served for twelve years in Vine Street CID, went on to do a stint at the Yard, then returned to the diamond belt as a local inspector. An elegant and handsome man but also 'a great adept in the art of personal disguise' he was always given the job of looking after any valuable presents *en route* to the King at Sandringham and was entrusted with the care of the massive Cullinan diamond when it was sent to Amsterdam to be cut. He solved several famous jewel robbery cases recovering some fabulous sparklers in the process so it is not surprising that when he married a solicitor's widow in 1904 his wedding presents 'included gifts from the nobility'. By the time Drew retired, in 1908 on, according to the *Police Review*, 'the largest pension it was possible for him to get', he had become senior detective chief inspector at Scotland Yard.

A policeman of quite a different stamp had said a sad goodbye to Scotland Yard in 1896. Superintendent John Shore, the last of the second generation of Yard detectives, was, wrote Macnaghten in *Days of My Years*, 'a fine old policeman of a type now obsolete'. His reports were laboured, and his spelling indifferent, 'but his knowledge of the thieving fraternity was unrivalled, and he possessed a very remarkable memory for their names and faces ... his physical strength was enormous, and he could eject a welsher in each hand from any ring on any racecourse over which the Metropolitan Police had control. Rough as his methods were, the criminal classes trusted and respected him, and few officers before or after his time could get more 'information received' out of them'.

Shore had, claimed Macnaghten, few other interests outside his work and when asked by an old colleague how he liked being free from the trammels of office he snapped, 'I never had no trammels, and I don't know that I rightly understand what the word means!'

Within two years 'Old Jack Shore' had died from diabetes. His long and faithful service (37 years 111 days) doubtless attributed to his death at the early age of fifty-eight, commented the new police champion, *Police Review and Parade Gossip*. They made it clear that they felt this devotion had not received its just reward: '... it was generally anticipated that upon the death of Mr Williamson, Mr Shore would be appointed chief constable. (The rank attained by Williamson – district superintendents were now termed chief constables). But red-tape and favouritism blocked the way to his further advancement, and after an interval the Home Office foisted one of its own Prisons' Commission staff, an inexperienced gentleman to boot, over the head of the old Detective'.

12 Escort Duty

Despite having so many responsibilities in London, Scotland Yard detectives continued to make frequent routine journeys, escorting wanted men to France and Germany as well as the occasional long distance sorties. The shorter journeys were certainly no sinecure. For example, when taking a prisoner to France, they would pick him up from the House of Detention in Clerkenwell at about 7.45 a.m., take him to Dover by the morning mail train, then cross the Channel to Calais, arriving around midday. The officer, Moser reports, was then compelled to return immediately and to catch the first available train back from Dover to London, 'thus making it an extremely hard day's work'. For the round trip to Hamburg with prisoners for Germany or Austria, seven days were allowed, 'giving the officer only one day for rest'. No allowances were made for rough weather which could make the journey much longer – Greenham recalled one gale-ridden occasion when it took an extra sixteen hours.

Despite these trials and tribulations, escort duty might still appear to have been a privileged travel opportunity – the only element of duty being to keep an eye on your companion. But, as I know from personal experience, constant vigilance over a long period in an insecure environment can be very wearing. Not only does the officer have to stay alert for any opportunist escape attempts but he has also to watch out for sudden suicide bids. Moser describes a French youth who firstly attempted suicide before capture; secondly, in his cell at Bow Street; and finally on the train while *en route* for Dover – when he tried to choke himself by stuffing a whole hard-boiled egg in his mouth. That it was an egg given him, in kindness by Moser, doubtless choked him as well.

Constant surveillance (even in the lavatory) is also wearing for the prisoner. Fraudster, Jabez Balfour, who was escorted from

Argentina by Detective Inspector Frank Froest, said the officer was a kindly enough man, but obsessed with the idea that his prisoner was bent on committing suicide. According to Balfour, Froest could not drive from his mind the possibility that he might arrive in England minus his prisoner. Given the trouble the inspector had gone to in getting his man (as will be described) it is hardly surprising he should feel like this, particularly as he would be only too aware of some of the harrowing ordeals experienced by colleagues while on escort duty.

Greenham referred to an escort incident as one of the most disagreeable experiences in his life. On a journey from Jersey to Southampton shorter than that made by Froest and Balfour – one of the two prisoners in his charge was found to have hanged himself. Ironically, it was due to Greenham's own keenness and exertions that he had ended up with two prisoners rather than just the one. Of the two warrants he had brought with him – the first, for 'an old man, a Belgian professor, on trumpery charges of fraud' – he had executed with ease. As for the second, the Jersey police had assured him that they had looked long and hard for the man (a Frenchman, wanted in France on charges of arson, robbery and attempted murder) but that he was nowhere to be found. Greenham tracked him down nonetheless (he says) and then he borrowed a Jersey policeman to help him keep an eye on both prisoners on the journey to the mainland.

But the Jerseyman proved to be a bad sailor and as the weather was rough, he asked to stay on deck. The elderly, Belgian professor had a severe cold and wanted to go below to the warm saloon. Greenham solved the problem by putting the French prisoner in a deck cabin, stripped, so he thought – 'of all articles with which he might injure himself' – the man was known to be suicidal. The seasick Jersey policeman was left nearby, to keep an eye on the Frenchman but, when Greenham came up from the saloon to see whether the prisoner wanted anything to eat he discovered that the man had managed to hang himself from a hat peg on the wall. The frantic inspector tried to revive him, 'by working his arms up and down', but a doctor on board told him he was wasting his time. The spinal cord had been snapped.

Greenham also relates how Inspector Von Tornow had a similar experience with a prisoner bound for Hamburg, but, subsequently, contrived to hoodwink the Germans into accepting the man's dead body. By Greenham's account, Von Tornow was an extremely well-educated man who had a rare degree of courage, daring and resourcefulness (though his courage appears to have deserted him when the Turf Fraud Scandal loomed, and he fled back to Germany).

His resourcefulness surfaced, however, when his prisoner, a fraudulent bankrupt, jumped overboard just after leaving British waters. The man did not drown but died of the shock of hitting the cold water – a common occurrence. Since they were still only just outside British waters the Captain offered to turn back, knowing that the Germans would not allow him to land a dead body. But Von Tornow insisted they continue, claiming that the warrant requested delivery – dead or alive. On arrival in Hamburg, Von Tornow informed the German police officer who met him that his prisoner was safely locked in a cabin and requesting his assistance in carrying his considerable luggage onto the dockside. Among the luggage was a large and heavy wicker basket which, of course, contained the body. Once safely on German soil, Von Tornow opened the basket to reveal the corpse to the angry but impotent Germans.

One way the detectives could ensure that their prisoner was always with them was by the use of handcuffs, but some found that these could be more of a nuisance than they were worth, particularly on long journeys. Moser was to write (and illustrate) an article on the subject of handcuffs for the *Strand Magazine* in 1894. It was apparent that he didn't care much for their use in general and he was particularly derisory about the British design, 'The Flexible'. They were, he declared, heavy, unwieldy, awkward and – even under the best of circumstances – extremely difficult to apply. 'They weigh over a pound, and have to be unlocked with a key in a manner not greatly differing from the operation of the winding up of the average eight-day clock.'

Furthermore, not only did the prisoner have to be overpowered or voluntarily submit to their application, but he could then use them as weapons against his captor. When going to arrest one of the Russian rouble forgers, he had taken along several different sizes of 'flexibles'. But not until he received assistance was he able to find the suitable 'darbies'. Then, having put them on, and forced his prisoner into a four-wheeler to take him to the police station, he was savagely attacked. The forger lifted his manacled wrists and brought them down heavily on the inspector's head, 'completely crushing my bowler hat'. Well, you can't get more dastardly than that.

French and Belgian handcuffs (long, nobbly chains of steel piano wire or whipcord bound together) were much better, Moser found, because you could simply twist 'La Ligotte' around the wrist and the slightest struggle could be met 'with the infliction of torture'. The South American 'Twister', once used in the UK but banned by then, could be even more painfully applied – a thick metal chain with a flat metal handle at one end. 'Its simplicity and its efficacy, together with the cruelty, have recommended it for use in those wild parts of South America where the upholder of the law literally travels with his life in his hands.' The extraordinarily clumsy and awkward Mexican handcuff was *not* approved of, being dismissed as 'quite worthy of the retrograde country of its origin'.

The Americans, however, had 'perfected the article'. In fact, they used a type similar to the British (two solid metal snap bracelets joined by a short chain) but their version was lighter, less clumsy, and easier to apply and conceal. As such, they found general favour with Scotland Yard officers. Better still, Moser felt, would be some device which gripped the prisoner tightly across the back 'imprisoning his arms above the elbow joints'. Such an instrument would cause no unnecessary pain, 'while relieving the officers from that part of their duty which is particularly obnoxious to them, viz, having a prolonged struggle with low and savage ruffians'.

Inspector Lansdowne was not in favour of handcuffs either and claimed never to have used them. 'I took a man from London to Ceylon. We occupied the same cabin, as first class passengers, and he was never handcuffed. Handcuffs and leg irons are only needed for very desperate men.'

(The handcuff problem is still with us. A recent 'solution' featured in the *Police Review* is the US designed 'Quick-Kuf' – a rigid handle which can be fitted over existing models. Apparently, because it does away with the play of a connecting-chain, it allows more control. The adapted handcuffs can be easily clipped on by a lone officer, instead of up to three when a prisoner is struggling, and I was amused to learn, the officer can make his captor more compliant by exerting pressure on the radial and ulnar nerves 'causing temporary but intense pain' – with no after effects. La Ligotte reborn?)

Tedious though they were in many respects, one of these

extradition journeys was to bring fame and promotion to one detective inspector, Frank Castle Froest. Froest, who hailed from Bristol, was a short man in an era when even the detectives were becoming taller – only five foot seven and a quarter inches – but sturdy and tough, and good at instant decisions. Moreover, he had charm, good dress sense and grooming, delicate hands, and a twinkle in his eye. He joined the Metropolitan Police in 1879, just after the Turf Fraud Trials, but had not gained entrance to the CID until eight years later, and then it seemed to be due (judging by the stream of commendations and rewards recorded in *Police Orders*) as much to his keenness at thief-catching as to his knowledge of languages. Whilst still in the uniform branch he had been sent to Paris with Moser, as one of the men drafted into plain clothes to watch for Fenians at the height of their activities in 1884.

Once in the CID at Scotland Yard, Froest was again teamed up with Moser, for a seemingly impossible task handed to them by Superintendent John Shore, who had replaced Williamson as operational head of branch. They were asked to find a man who had murdered a gamekeeper in a Westphalian forest before (the German police believed) fleeing to England via Hamburg. The only thing known about him was that he had probably taken the gamekeeper's silver watch, which had a dachshund's head engraved on its case.

At the time, there was a constant traffic of Germans going back and forth between their home country and Britain. Many were looking for work or escaping justice and they entered the country through a number of busy ports. This made the detectives task that much more difficult but a fact which Moser greeted with his usual cheery optimism. He ranted and raved for a while, as was his custom, but both he and Froest were hard workers and, eventually, they found the gamekeeper's watch in a pawn shop in Hull – an entry port for ships from Hamburg. There was no sign of the man who had pawned it, but local information suggested he may have gone on to Newcastle. The detectives followed this lead, combing the docks, lodging houses, coal pits and, lastly, the railway workings – where they found him. They even got him to confess and were able to strengthen the evidence by identifying him from an old photograph (in the Convict Supervision Office) as a fraudster. (Apparently, the poor gamekeeper had been on the point of realizing he was being duped – and needed to be silenced.)

Froest began to be employed regularly for extradition work and (at least, according to his own account in 'Bringing Famous Criminals from Abroad', an interview reprinted in *Police Review*, 17 May 1895) had some very tricky and dangerous moments in the process. Such as the time he persuaded a daring bank thief to come out of 'a low saloon down the Bowery' in New York so as to be able to effect an arrest. On another occasion, he cajoled a channel-steamer captain into turning back to Folkestone when he realized his quarry, a forger, was on board; not to mention his single-handed retrieval of an Italian murderer (who had knifed two men in Saffron Hill) from a village in the south of France.

But his most extraordinary exploit, worthy of today's Mossad, and the one which was to bring him instant fame, took place in 1895. Sir Robert Anderson, Assistant Commissioner CID, instructed Froest to go to Argentina and arrest the super embezzler, Jabez Spencer Balfour, adding, 'Don't come back without him.' Anderson knew full well the task he was setting the detective inspector.

During the late nineteenth century, lax company law and an expanding middle class prepared to speculate, led to a spate of large-scale financial frauds. One of the most ambitious of these concerned the Liberator Permanent Benefit Building Society run by the pious teetotaller and MP for Burnley, Jabez Balfour. While advocating good works, Balfour was busily lining his pockets by cooking the books. When, in 1892, the bubble finally burst, he fled to Argentina, leaving his investors short of about 6 million – a colossal sum at the time.

Despite the fact that Britain's extradition treaty with Argentina had yet to be ratified Inspector Tunbridge and Sergeant Craggs were sent out with a warrant for Balfour, but the speculator's ample funds had enabled him to buy off officials and hire a bevy of protectors. While negotiations were in progress, Balfour disappeared, only to be located again, in January 1895 – a thousand miles up country at Salta, in the foothills of the Andes. He must have felt very secure there, deep inland, with the towering mountain chain behind him, and the Chilean and Bolivian borders nearby. The following month, Froest was sent out to relieve Tunbridge, and intense diplomatic activity resulted in a promise that the fugitive would, at last, be handed over by officials at Salta. But such promises had been given before, only to be blocked at the last moment with a variety of spurious law suits issued by Balfour's cronies and technical objections by his counsel.

There were more stalling tactics until, finally, a federal judge ordered the Salta authorities to hand over the prisoner to the British.

Froest and the British Consul were in Salta to receive him but discovered that the handover had been arranged to take place twenty-four hours before the next train was due to leave for Buenos Aires – thus allowing plenty of time for more obstructive tactics, or even an actual attempt to spring Balfour. The ever-resourceful Froest promptly hired a train and had it waiting, with steam-up, ready to leave immediately. When it did so – with the armed British Consul guarding Balfour in a carriage, while Froest rode on the engine footplate with his revolver at the ready – officials were taken completely by surprise. Further down the track, a sheriff's officer rode out to intercept them, waving a writ and shouting for the train to stop as he galloped alongside. Froest and his revolver persuaded the train driver to keep going as they still had a thousand miles of wild country to cross but, unfortunately, the sheriff's officer was killed when he fell from his horse while attempting to board.

Eight hundred miles further on, the train broke down at a station, and a party of local police soon arrived to detain them. By then, Froest had already ordered another train and he continued to argue with the officials until he received a signal that Balfour was aboard and steam was up. He excused himself to go to the toilet, eluded his would-be captors, and boarded the train. It steamed away followed by agitated shouts and shots. Assistant Commissioner CID, Sir Robert Anderson, who gleefully related this tale in his *The Lighter Side of My Official Life* assured readers that, 'the relatives of the unfortunate sheriff's officer received compensation for his death'.

At Buenos Aires, the party headed for the steamship *Tartar Prince* which was supposed to be about to leave for Southampton, but her departure had been delayed by unusually low tides. An Argentinian cutter came alongside, carrying two agents of the Salta judge with an order demanding the release of their prisoner. The captain insisted he had no choice but to obey the laws of his own country and was backed up by his crew and some British cattlemen. Eventually, a detachment of Argentinian soldiers was sent to ensure their safe departure.

Almost daily reports in the press had charted Balfour's progress back to retribution. On his arrival at Buenos Aires, *The Times* reported that Balfour seemed to be 'very low spirited', and the captain was later to confess to a reporter that they had been very anxious as he was supposed to have sworn never to be taken back to England alive. But after a few days on board, 'he seemed reconciled to his position' and the restrictions imposed on him were relaxed somewhat. His food remained diced, however, so that he needed only a spoon to eat it, knives and forks were strictly taboo. He was in a cabin amidships, next to that of Froest, *The Times* reporter later gleaned, with spy-holes cut in the bulkheads between, a guard outside and an iron bar and padlock on the door. But he was permitted an accompanied walk up to the bridge in the morning, strolls round the deck at night, and to welcome visitors to his cabin for conversation and games of chess. Other passengers asked that he be allowed to participate in the social life, but Froest refused to allow it unless he was handcuffed, so it 'came to nothing'. Froest had come too far to jeopardize the final outcome.

Another ambush was planned for the climax of this penultimate part of the journey but, this time, it was the press lying in wait. News had been flashed ahead that the *Tartar Prince* had arrived at Las Palmas and later that she had passed the semaphore at Cape Ushant as she came into the mouth of the English Channel. If the authorities knew what time she was due to be at Southampton, they were not saying, but there was no hiding the two Scotland Yard officials and a large force of detectives and police on the dockside on 5 May. It was understood that a special train was standing by for the journey to London. This, however, might merely be a ruse, *The Times* reported, as there were various rumours afloat that Balfour would be landed before the *Tartar Prince* reached the Solent. The docks were rigorously closed to the public, while the press was finding it difficult to charter a special tug to take out to the arriving ship. What police feared was a large and violent demonstration of robbed investors (thousands of poor people had also suffered through the crash).

Some of the press did manage to get aboard the tender *Albert Edward* and, on the afternoon of 6 May, they suddenly realized that the waiting detectives had disappeared. The *Tartar Prince* was sighted off Calcott Castle, at the entrance to Southampton Water, and the *Albert Edward* sped out to greet her. As they did so, a small launch, *The Solent*, left the steamship and dashed towards Southampton harbour. The *Albert Edward* gave chase but *The Solent* slowed suddenly which made the tender pass and, by the time they had turned around they had lost sight of their quarry. '*The Solent*,' reported *The Times* without rancour, 'having outwitted her pursuers, was thus left free to land the prisoner at the eastern extremity of the dock.'

The last leg of this marathon journey was completed, not by special train, but in a first class compartment of the regular 7.45 p.m. London-bound express and, although a number of passengers crowded around the carriage when they arrived at Vauxhall Station, there was no demonstration as they left for Bow Street Magistrates Court, 'followed by quite a procession of hansom cabs'.

Balfour was found guilty of numerous frauds and sentenced to fourteen years imprisonment, but was released in 1906 for good behaviour and he later wrote a book about his prison experiences. His exploits led to reform of the laws governing building societies, and the chase made Froest famous.

The following year Froest was off again, this time to South Africa, to bring back Dr Jameson, whose raid on the Transvaal, in an attempt to overthrow the Afrikaaner Government, resulted in a worsening of Anglo-Boer relations and, eventually, led to the second Boer war.

But no career is without its setbacks and errors of judgement (despite what some writers of police autobiographies would have you believe), and there is an unwritten rule which says that the harder you work the more liable you are to make some mistakes. The year after his great Argentinian adventure, Froest was a leading player in the Yard's involvement in one of the most serious miscarriages of justice (among those which have come to light that is) as the result of that continuously thorny problem – identification.

13   The Magic Mark

In 1895, Froest was dealing with a case in which a con man, Adolph Beck, was accused of fraudulently relieving a Frenchwoman, Ottilie Meissonier, of her jewellery. It occurred to him that the crime bore a distinct similarity to those of one John Smith who, shortly before, had been released from prison on licence. Froest began to suspect that Smith and Beck might be the same man. Several of Smith's victims identified Beck as the man who had duped them. The PC who had arrested John Smith also thought Beck was Smith. At Beck's trial, the judge, under the impression that Beck was a man with a bad record, sentenced him to seven years penal servitude – ignoring Beck's insistence that he had been in Peru when Smith's offences had been committed. In fact, had they known it, there was a simple way of differentiating between the two: 'John Smith' was a Jew, while Adolph Beck was an uncircumcized gentile. This case is habitually (and rightly) cited by writers as demonstrating the desperate need for an efficient identification system (although the impression is sometimes given that Beck was a complete innocent, which is not the case).

Another earlier identification saga was the strangely convoluted case of the Edlingham Burglary. Edlingham is a hamlet in a fold of the Northumberland Moors between Alnwick and Rothbury. One February morning in 1879, at about 1 a.m., the 77-year-old Reverend Buckle, vicar of Edlingham, and his 30-year-old daughter, were awakened by the sound of intruders. Grabbing a candle to light their way and a sword with which to protect themselves, they rushed downstairs where they found two burglars ransacking the drawing-room. The Reverend Buckle thrust his sword at one of the men who retaliated by firing a shotgun – wounding both the old man and his daughter. The intruders fled – leaving behind them the chisel which had helped them gain entry, and footprints on the soft soil of a garden bed under the window, and on the pathway outside.

Alnwick Police, led by Superintendent Harkes, established that two local poachers, Michael Brannagan and Peter Murphy, had been out that night, but neither Mr Buckle nor his daughter could identify the men (although, later, the vicar was to change his mind). No matter, their boots and clogs fitted the footmarks and Murphy's brother-in-law identified the chisel as his property. To clinch the matter, a scrap of newspaper was found in Murphy's pocket which matched a torn newspaper from the vicarage. The pair were charged with burglary and attempted murder. Although the case against them was relatively flimsy, the judge summed up strongly against them, and they were duly convicted and sentenced to life – which then amounted to about twenty years.

Seven years on, a local solicitor and the Reverend Muschamp Perry, vicar of St Paul's, Alnwick, learned that two other men, George Edgell and Charles Richardson, had been out poaching that night. Richardson was described as, 'a quarrelsome desperado of great stature', who had once been charged with the murder of a policeman but had been acquitted for want of sufficient evidence. George Edgell was questioned by the vicar and the solicitor about his movements on the fateful night and, while giving nothing away, 'seemed greatly agitated and upset'. Furthermore, rumour had it that Superintendent Harkes, who had since died, had admitted that he realized that he had arrested the wrong men, but it was too late to do anything about it.

George Edgell was prevailed upon to confess to the Edlingham Burglary. An enquiry was ordered. The conviction of Murphy and Branagan was quashed, and Inspector Butcher of Scotland Yard, sent up to investigate police behaviour in the case. James Butcher had an analytical mind and submitted the most convincing of reports but, according to his later chief Melville Macnaghten, he was a man of quick judgment and hasty temper who tended to nurse grievances. His colleagues thought he was never happy unless he was miserable.

Evidently, he unearthed sufficient evidence of wrongdoing and filed a convincing report on the Edlingham Burglary, because the four constables concerned were prosecuted for 'procuring, making and giving false evidence'. The defence, which employed Detective Brett of the City of London Police, claimed that the Edgell confession was a sham. Edgell gave evidence that he had been informed he could not be prosecuted – so was obviously horrified when he and Richardson were charged, convicted, and sentenced to five years imprisonment. As for the constables, telling in their favour was the fact that the man who had been in charge of the enquiry was now dead – and the machinations of the enquiring vicar were beginning to appear dubious. They were found not guilty.

Conclusions drawn about the Edlingham Burglary by contemporary writers are at odds. In his *Mysteries of Police and Crime*, Major Arthur Griffiths makes it clear that he believed Edgell and that the policemen were culpable. He describes winningly how, after Branagan and Murphy were released from their 'durance vile', they were given £800 each in recompense and this was duly invested for them. 'Branagan,' he goes on, 'at once obtained employment as a wheelwright, the handicraft he had acquired in prison, and Murphy, who was a prison-taught baker, adopted that trade, and married the girl, Agnes Simm, who had befriended him in regard to the coat on the morning after the burglary.' (She was supposed to have given police someone else's jacket instead of Murphy's.)

A less rose-tinted view was offered by Lt. Col. Smith, the retired commissioner of the City of London Police, in his book, *From Constable to Commissioner*. At the time of the burglary, Colonel Smith was a gentleman of leisure living in nearby Alnmouth and was acquainted with the suspects, the area, the vicarage, and the vicar of Edlingham. He was, he revealed, asked by the county magistrates to find a good counsel for the policemen – whom they believed to be innocent. This counsel, Mr E.E.T. Besley, told him that there was not enough evidence against the policemen to hang a dog but, on the other hand, the additional evidence now brought forward against the *original accused* was, 'ten thousand times stronger'. 'Besley was certain – as I always was, and am to this day – that the original men were the guilty men, and that the police, whose animus, looking to the murder of PC Gray, must have been far stronger against Edgell and Richardson, than against them, made no mistake from start to finish.'

(The Reverend Muschamp wrote a book: *The Edlingham Burglary or Circumstantial Evidence*, while *The Massingham Affair* (Chatto & Windus) 1962, by Edward Grierson, is a novel based upon the case.)

Whatever the truth of the matter, it was clear that further aids to identification were sorely needed and, by the late 1890s, it was also becoming obvious that anthropometrics were not living up to expectations. There were several reasons for this: procedural difficulties and misunderstandings, variations in the skill and patience of the police and prison officers who were taking the measurements – and a certain lack of appreciation on their part for these new-fangled, foreign notions. The science may have become bracketed in their minds with the newly popular criminology, some areas of which also involved the taking of measurements and which threw up some rather risible propositions.

While searching for evidence to uphold the perfectly legitimate notion that criminals might be born and not made, devotees had homed in on physical factors which might help pinpoint these unfortunates. They had 'discovered' that 44% of habitual criminals possessed noses which deviated to one side, and 57% of recidivists had projecting ears. After execution, the brains of killers were weighed and found wanting, while even hair growth, or lack of it, was found to be significant. Baldness in criminals was rare (two per cent in thieves, thirteen per cent in swindlers) and their eyebrows tended to be thick. Beards, however, were scanty 'with a tendency to the contrary in females'. (*The Criminal*, by August Drahms).

The Home Office Belper Committee, formed to enquire on the progress of the identification procedures, reported in December 1900. Fortunately, they had been able to call for evidence from Edward Henry, Inspector General of Police for the Lower Provinces in Bengal. Inspired by the work of Frances Galton, he had been enthusiastically refining a workable fingerprint classification system which had not been adopted by the Indian government. He demonstrated his retrieval facility from a collection of about seven thousand prints. The committee were impressed and, when reporting, recommended the gradual introduction of his fingerprint-only system.

The following year, Dr Robert Anderson retired from his post as head of CID, and the job went to Edward Henry. Commenting on the fact that doubts were expressed as to his suitability for the role, an ex-fingerprint branch commander (Gerald Lambourne) writes: 'The dissenters obviously did not appreciate that Henry was able to place in their hands one of the most efficient detection systems of all time – fingerprints.'

Indeed, it was not only revolutionary in its effect but it also did wonders for the reputation of Scotland Yard worldwide.

On the first of July, 1901, three men from the Anthropometric Office were selected to form the new Fingerprint Branch. They were Detective Inspector Charles H. Stedman, Detective Sergeant Charles Stockley Collins and Detective Constable Frederick Hunt. This identification system, far simpler to operate, took off as Anthropometrics had never done, and soon, the range of persons fingerprinted was extended to include all persons convicted at Assizes or Sessions who had received a term of imprisonment of a month or more. Previously, only habitual criminals had been measured and fingerprinted. During the first six months, ninety-three identifications were achieved by fingerprints, and before the end of 1902, the number had well exceeded that made throughout the six years of the previous system. By then, another five officers had been drafted in to assist. The identification revolution had begun.

One man in the new department stood out from the rest – a 36-year-old, ex-greengrocer's assistant from Surbiton, Detective Sergeant Charles Stockley Collins who, like Edward Henry (who had already run a test case in India), was keen to link fingerprints at the scene of crime with known criminals – not just use them to identify persons already in custody. To this end, he studied photography so that he might record prints at the scene if necessary. His big chance came in June 1902, after a burglary at a house in Denmark Hill. Dirty fingermarks were found on a window sill, Collins photographed the one he judged to be the most clear – made by a left thumb – then, with his colleagues, set about the task of matching it with a set in the files.

Once they had identified and captured their man, a previous offender named Harry Jackson, their next hurdle was getting the print accepted by the court as primary evidence. Nowadays, we accept, the perhaps remarkable fact that fingerprints are absolutely individual – thus making the system, properly operated, almost infallible. But at the outset, that idea was a large pill to swallow, and the public and judiciary were, understandably, not totally persuaded. Consequently, Henry, his detectives Stedman and Collins, and Treasury Counsel, Mr Richard Muir, prepared well for this début. In the event, they virtually treated the jury to a crash course in the science of fingerprinting – enlarged photographs and all. 'Surprisingly,' writes Gerald Lambourne, 'there was no strong attack on the fingerprint evidence by the defence. Jackson was found guilty of all charges by the jury, and thereby set a profound precedent.'

The next big success for the fingerprint department occurred after its officers went to Epsom on Derby Day to fingerprint sixty men in custody, many of them petty criminals who regularly plagued the racecourses. Usually, there was insufficient time to identify them before they appeared before magistrates the next morning. They were well aware of this and frequently gave false names to escape the fate their known records might visit upon them. On this occasion, the sixty sets of fingerprints were rushed back to the Yard and, in court on the following morning, no less than twenty-seven offenders were identified as old hands.

News of this wonderful new system was spread abroad when Detective Constable John Ferrier gave a demonstration at the International Police Exhibition and the World Fair, held in St Louis, Missouri, in 1904. He was overwhelmed with enquiries, and there is little doubt that the exercise sounded the death knell for anthropometrics and heralded the worldwide swing to the Henry fingerprinting system. (It may be some consolation to the French that the first automatic fingerprint system in Britain, adopted by the Scottish Criminal Records Office, in 1991, was made in France.)

The first English murder in which fingerprinting evidence played a vital role was of a familiar type – the battering to death in South London, of an elderly shopkeeper couple for their takings. Even the discovery of the crime, at Chapman's Oil Shop in Deptford, followed the classic pattern – a shop assistant unable to gain entry, going to get help, an entrance effected through the back – and bloodied bodies found. (In fact, the wife, Ann Farrow, was still alive but died four days later.) It was later ascertained that her husband, Thomas, had not died at the time of the attack. A witness came forward to say that, at 7.30 a.m. that morning, he had seen a bloodied old man come to the open door of the shop and stand looking around dazedly for a moment, before closing it. This witness had been unable to find a policeman so had continued his journey to London by train. Found inside the premises were crude masks made from the tops of black stockings – the search was on for 'The Masked Murderers of Deptford'.

Witnesses were found who claimed that they had seen two men leaving the shop at around 7.15 a.m. The pair had slammed the door behind them but it had swung open again. Another witness had seen the brothers, Albert and Alfred Stratton, around at that time and the description of the clothes they were wearing tallied with those of the men seen leaving the shop. Albert Stratton's landlady revealed that he had asked her if she had any old stockings she didn't want – and later she had seen the rudimentary masks tucked between his mattresses. The most crucial find was a thumbprint on the inner tray of an empty cash box. It proved to be that of Alfred Stratton.

The brothers were arrested and charged. At the Old Bailey, Detective Sergeant Collins gave another of his crash courses in fingerprinting, even taking the fingerprints of one of the jury just to demonstrate how the variations called into question by defence counsel, were caused merely by differences in pressure exerted when the impression was made. This time, the fingerprint evidence *was* strongly attacked. The defence called Doctor Garson, formerly of the Anthropometric Office, who claimed that the two impressions had not been made by the same digit. Unfortunately for the Stratton brothers, Garson made a poor showing under cross-examination by counsel, Richard Muir.

In addition, it was revealed that Garson (said to have been removed from the Anthropometric Office because he resisted the move to a fingerprint-only system) had initially written to the public prosecutor to ask whether he was going to call him as an expert, and warning that, should he not, he would probably give evidence for the defence. On the same day, without seeing copies of the prints in question, he also wrote to the defence solicitor, offering his services if the prosecution did not require him, adding, 'It (the fingerprint system) is a splendid means of identification when properly used, but I have no hesitation in saying that the way it is being used by the police is that which will bring it into disrepute.' Under cross examination, he admitted to Richard Muir that, although he had often given expert opinion on anthropometric measurements and fingerprints from 1895–1901, he had not given any since that time – but he did know that Inspector Collins had spoken a great deal of nonsense about them in the police court.

The judge, Mr Justice Channell, was not impressed by Garson who had seemed to be acting out of pique. He thought the doctor's evidence had harmed the accused. However, he warned the jury that, although the print might be regarded as corroborative to a certain extent he did not think they should act on it alone. 'The fingerprint system is used for the purpose of identifying a criminal who has been convicted once, and has been convicted again, in each of which cases a proper impression has been taken for the purpose; but it is a different thing to apply it to a casual mark made through the perspiration of a thumb.'

The jury deliberated for two hours before finding the brothers guilty, and both were hanged just over two weeks later.

The *Daily Express* took advantage of the enormous public interest in the new science by running a £100 prize serial detective story in which the clue was a fingerprint which had been left on a tumbler. Oddly, the fingerprint crash course *they* offered to their readers the day before the competition, came from the pen of the discredited Doctor Garson. It is possible they had heeded the cries from the *Lancet* and some other sources, who deplored the fact that fingerprinting should be left in the hands of clodhopping policemen, rather than medical men whose evidence would not only be accurate but above suspicion. This claim was countered in a letter to the *Daily Express* from the Chief Constable of Staffordshire, who said this was all very well but, 'nine doctors out of ten make the worst witnesses in the world'.

The *Daily Express* did try to have it both ways by announcing that, 'In the competition for the hundred pounds, Police Officers stand a splendid chance. Their experience in dealing with crime must materially assist them in solving the mystery. The story and problem form a practical lesson in a branch of detective work that is coming more and more into prominence.'

Obviously, it was not their experience with fingerprinting which was going to help them.

Although fingerprinting was the greatest identification aid ever devised, strides were also being made in other fields which would help police with their enquiries. These were not always given the welcome they deserved.

Improvements in the public transport systems and the widening of the railway network had gradually made extended enquiries easier for the detectives, who had no allocated transport. Development of the electric telegraph had eased the problems of communication but, nonetheless, instant, two-way communication, such as was offered by the telephone, would have made all the difference to the progress of enquiries in which the situation could change from minute to minute. In *At Scotland Yard* ex-Detective Inspector Sweeney gives an example of the inconvenience when he describes how, when tailing a suspect, he might well land up at a considerable distance from his starting point in, say, the Euston Road. He would then telegraph the Yard for his relief officer to meet him there. Meanwhile, the suspect might be on the move again soon after to, say, Finsbury, and the detective would have to send another telegraph. 'I have known three such telegraphs sent in succession, and all to no purpose.'

The Metropolitan Police were particularly slow to take advantage of this marvellous new invention. Walter Hambrook, an ex-footman from Kent, describes his reactions when he was posted to Paddington Green Police Station, just after joining in 1898. 'To my amazement, I found that, although at that time there was not a single provincial force of any importance that was not on the public telephone, neither Scotland Yard nor any of the two-hundred police-stations in the Metropolis possessed such a thing.' He was all the more astonished because, in his little home hamlet of Betteshanger which lay between Deal and Ramsgate in Kent, 'I had frequently had occasion to use the telephone, and knew how indispensable it was in all matters of urgency, and how simple it was to operate and to talk to people miles away at the other end'. What was even more surprising to him was the slow and primitive telegraph system which took him some considerable time to master.

The Yard did have *some* direct external telephone lines – to the Home Office, Wellington Barracks, the Fire Brigade and the like – but it was the public and inter-station connection which had been resisted for so long. Oddly, some home counties police stations were linked to their nearest Metropolitan counterparts, usually at their own instigation and, often, their own expense.

The *Daily Mail* launched a campaign to persuade the Metropolitan Police to change their attitude. This stimulated comment from the chief constable of Reigate who pointed out that his force had been on the telephone for sixteen years. He went on to describe one unusual use which was scarcely calculated to win the Yard round. A lady, who had reported the loss of her pet dog, was asked to speak over the phone to an animal of similar description which had just been brought in. 'The effect was electrical and amusing,' said the chief constable, 'for there was a mutual recognition of voices.'

The *Daily Mail* campaign failed, probably because the idea of the public actually being able to make a nuisance of themselves by ringing the police direct, was still quite horrifying to some senior officers. But, in 1903, the forward-looking Edward Henry became commissioner, and shortly afterwards, installation began. But it was to be 1906 before a significant number of police stations were linked. Even as late as 1917, two minor police stations remained unconnected to public telephone exchanges.

Another area in which improvements were long overdue was in initial training. In effect it was minimal – only three weeks drill, interspersed with five lectures on 'ambulance work' and an hour a week instruction on police duties. When the constable was posted to division, he attended police courts for a fortnight to see how to give evidence. In addition, recruits were given an instruction book which they were expected to study in their spare time.

Even this meagre attempt at training was casually organized by a chief inspector who was out of touch with the current street scene. In 1904, a board of superintendents was drawn up to look into the matter. One of the witnesses was Howard Vincent, who reiterated his belief in the urgent need for better training and declared that, in his experience, 'The best recruits come from the farms and the worst from domestic service.'

The committee recommended that there should be less drill and more police duty instruction – which should be given by younger, keener, and more up-to-date men. But Edward Henry saw that a proper training school was needed and, in due course, a suitable site was found in Regency Street, off the Vauxhall Bridge Road in Victoria. Peel House Training School was opened in 1907.

Despite the committee's recommendation, a considerable amount of drill remained on the curriculum. This was justified by the officer in charge, Chief Inspector Albert Gooding, as being essential to pull together such a mix of men. The recruits were, he declared, in a great many instances, fresh from the country and therefore 'awkward in gait, manner and general bearing' (as quoted in the *Metropolitan Police Training School Magazine*, 1963).

In addition to police duties, recruits were now to receive educational instruction (writing, spelling, composition, dictation, grammar, use of maps and plans etc.), self-defence training (eight simple holds) – and revolver practice. This last was no longer on the syllabus when I went there, forty-seven years later, but, at that time, the need was urgent.

14   Getting Booked

Many of the capital's more sensational cases continued to involve the immigrant population. Their crimes were a mix of the politically motivated, the straightforwardly criminal, and, sometimes, an amalgam of the two. Even now, it can be difficult to sort out which was which.

There is certainly no doubt about the motives of, 'The Walsall Anarchists', a group of British and Italian revolutionaries, arrested by the Staffordshire Police and the Special Branch in 1892. They had been planning the production of 'pear-shaped bombs with nipples' – the idea being that when thrown, the nipples would stick into the person or object. Police learned that there were probably other locations where bomb factories were in production and that plans were afoot to blow up the Stock Exchange. Bombings and assassinations in several other European countries convinced the Yard that, despite their ridiculously high profile in this country, anarchists (an all-embracing term) meant business. They were further alerted when, in 1894, a French anarchist blew himself up in Greenwich Park – apparently while *en route* to the unlikely target of the Observatory and the Meridian.

Special Branch officers began tailing two particular Italian anarchist suspects: 17-year-old Francesco Polti and 44-year-old Giuseppe Farnara. One day two detectives (Sweeney and Maguire) followed Polti on to a bus where they sat down beside and behind him while he unwrapped a brown paper parcel he had just collected from an iron foundry. It contained a bomb case which, when arrested, Polti claimed was a present for his brother in Italy.

The politically motivated crimes were not always committed by the refugees and revolutionaries. Take the kidnap, in 1896, of Doctor Sun Yat Sen, and his subsequent incarceration in the Chinese legation. The doctor, later to be acknowledged as the

174

father of the Chinese Republic, had been organizing and canvassing support for Chinese uprisings. A smuggled-out letter and diplomatic pressure secured his release. But the still radical, *Reynolds Newspaper* (an earlier commentator thought it might be a good family newspaper if it wasn't for its violent politics) claimed that such political kidnaps were commonplace in London – with the connivance of the police – and that most did not end so happily. The victims were usually spirited aboard vessels lying on the Thames and then away to who knows where, and what terrible fate. The Russian revolutionary, Sergius Stepniak (thought to be the assassin of the head of the St Petersburg Police), had lived with the dread of this happening to him. In the event, he had been killed by a train in a London suburb. (According to eye witnesses, he had been so busy reading that he had not heard the train coming and had suddenly rushed across the track at the last moment only to be struck by a buffer.)

Meanwhile, the East End was in the grip of a number of violent foreign gangs. Two of the principal ones were largely Russian in origin, with Kray-like protection tendencies and exotic-sounding names at odds with their activities. But the Bessarabians and the Odessians were only the tip of the iceberg.

Young Constable Wensley who was patrolling Whitechapel at that time, noticed that, as well as many genuine, hard-working (dreadfully sweated, in fact) immigrants in the area, there were also, 'the off-scourings of the criminal population of Europe – Russians, Poles, Germans, Austrians and Frenchmen'. Not only were these (together with the poorer English people) crammed together in the crowded slums, but vast numbers of single men (Wensley reckoned 30,000 to 40,000) lived in lodging houses. This encouraged the formation of gangs (often armed) which infested the streets and 'levied blackmail on timorous shopkeepers'. Some gang members were genuine revolutionaries who regarded theft as merely the expropriation of wealth in a good cause and, in any case, it was better than working in a sweatshop. But their activities didn't make the lives of fellow refugees any easier. As Wensley recalled in *Detective Days*: 'There was an enormous amount of personal robbery with violence. The maze of narrow, ill-lit alleys offered easy ways of escape after a man had been knocked down and his watch and money stolen.' He claimed that murder was probably far more common in those days than official statistics ever revealed. Bodies were frequently found near disreputable houses and many of these victims had obviously been knocked on the head but, unless there was any other obvious evidence of foul play, the inquest verdicts were usually left open.

One of the reasons for this state of affairs was the complete lack of control on alien entry. A bill to rectify this had been introduced into Parliament, following the anarchist antics in the early 1890s, but it was dropped after the second reading. The refugees kept coming in ever-increasing numbers, particularly (following the pogroms) the Poles, Russians and Rumanians. This influx proved not only disturbing socially but had a disastrous effect on certain sections of the labour market, lowering the wages in some instances to starvation level for alien and Englishman alike. The fact that almost all the aliens settled in the same areas; the East End of London, Clerkenwell, and, increasingly, in Soho, led to horrendous overcrowding. Landlords squeezed enormous numbers into each house, raised rents and extracted key money – exacerbating the situation further.

But it's an ill wind … Wensley found, as others such as Abberline had before him, that Whitechapel was a marvellous training ground for the detective, due to the amount and variety of crime. PC Wensley was highly intelligent, hard-working and a very determined young constable with a great many rewards and commendations to his credit but, nonetheless, it took him seven years to get into 'the department'. The reason, he claimed, was that his face did not fit as far as the local inspector was concerned. Such was Wensley's determination to join the CID that when he wasn't engaged in unpaid, off-duty, plain-clothes suspect-shadowing, he was 'getting up the subjects in which a candidate for the CID had to pass'.

The educational exams for entry into the department were something of a bone of contention, some senior CID officers complaining that the standards required deprived them of the services of some of the best thief-takers. Tom Divall, by then a detective sergeant at Hackney, was one of those who, with a great deal of effort, managed to jump this hurdle. Tom had never even been to school, having worked on a farm from the age of eight, (although he must have had some writing ability as this was a condition of service). He later recalled attending Board School:

> … and every possible place where I could learn something to my advantage. Sometimes I did not get to bed until 3 a.m., and at others I would be up at 5 a.m. practising writing, spelling etc.,

whilst my wife and kids were asleep and snoring, I found these early hours the best for study for my brain was clear and my mind free and calm.

But Divall's local inspector wanted him aboard and managed to get him into plain clothes 'as a supernumerary' while he continued swotting to gain proper entry.

Wensley's chance came, while trudging his beat one day in 1895, when he bumped into Divisional Superintendent Dodd, 'a queer old bird but mightily efficient in his work,' who asked him why he hadn't joined the CID yet?

'I don't think I'm wanted, Sir,' Wensley replied, with a directness for which he was to become reknowned. Superintendent Dodd murmured something to the effect that *he* was in charge of the division, and a few days later Wensley left his beat forever when he joined the CID. He was to become its most glittering ornament, achieving the rank of chief constable CID – the first *policeman* to do so since Williamson. From the criminals he was to earn the nickname, 'the Weasel'.

Wensley appreciated that his new colleagues may have appeared a little rough and uncultivated to some but found they had 'a wonderful knowledge' of criminals and a great enthusiasm for their work. He, too, adored being a detective, finding the work varied and fascinating and quickly learned the tricks of his trade.

'Do not misunderstand me,' he wrote later. 'I could not then, and cannot now, miraculously deduce the author of a crime from a piece of burnt matchstick, but I could at least say, often with reasonable certainty, who was the probable author of a crime by the circumstances in which it was carried out.' (He may merely have been referring to the methods of Sherlock Holmes, although there had been two 'burnt match' references in contemporary writing. Major Arthur Griffiths refers to a real-life murder solved 'by the simple discovery of a few half-burnt matches' which the murderer had left behind when lighting candles in the victim's room to foster the illusion that he was still alive'. And a 'spent match', left in an unlikely place deliberately to mislead the Scotland Yard detective – which it does – is seen for what it was by Martin Hewitt, Investigator, in 'The Lenton Croft Robberies' published in the *Strand Magazine*, in 1894.)

More importantly, Wensley learned how to gather evidence and catch the criminal. Pure reasoning was all very well, he pointed out, 'but the blood and bones of all practical detective work is information'. The simplest way to get information, he soon discovered, was in the age-old way – through informants – and, to this end, he made a small personal sacrifice. He had always been strictly teetotal but quickly realized that asking for a lemonade in an East End pub made him stand out like a very sore thumb, so he took to ordering a beer or a whisky – but made each drink last a long time.

As well as the East End gangs who picked pockets and those engaged in robbery with violence and protection, there were others who banded together to commit house-breaking and burglary. In 1901, Wensley was instrumental in breaking up one of the most successful. It was twelve strong and headed by Berthe Weiner, a German woman 'with a genius for generalship'. Berthe's planning was immaculate, from the conception of the crime to the disposal of the goods, and her gang left few clues. Their targets were houses standing in their own grounds in well-to-do suburbs of North London. The jobs were carried out mob-handed – in groups of four or five – which, while it increased the likelihood of being discovered, certainly decreased the likelihood of being challenged. Some lone policemen who did so, were injured, sometimes seriously, whereas others, Wensley was convinced, turned a blind, self-preserving eye – and he didn't blame them.

One day, it struck the (by now) Detective Sergeant Wensley that a group of Germans, often seen hanging around in Shadwell, appeared not only to have an adequate supply of leisure but also of money, and he began to wonder how that came about. He and his colleagues did some 'shadowing' and eventually discovered that most of these Germans lived in a house in Albert Street, down by the docks. Frau Berthe Weiner was not only a frequent visitor but also paid the rent. Acquiring further information proved difficult as the gang members spoke little English and were as wary as they were clannish.

Eventually, Wensley managed to weasel his way into the confidence of an acquaintance of theirs who revealed Berthe's king-pin (or, perhaps, queen-pin) status and the scope of the gang's operations. A raid on the Albert Street premises and those of Berthe and some relatives uncovered sufficient stolen property to link them to thirty-six burglaries. Further searches were aided, and hints about their intended defence strategy in court gained, by the fact that, while in custody the men talked loudly and

uninhibitedly in their own tongue – quite oblivious of the fact that
one of the policemen present was 'a man with a very complete
acquaintance with the German language'. After receiving their
(quite severe) sentences, the gang – according to Wensley's new
boss, Local Inspector Tom Divall – foamed at the mouth like mad
dogs and uttered the most terrible threats towards Wensley and
him.

Obviously, Divall felt very differently about Wensley (who was
by now a *first class* sergeant and thus Divall's right-hand man) than
had his original local inspector, and in his memoirs consistently,
and rather endearingly, refers to him as 'my pal Wensley'.

Divall, too, had gained his experience in a rough-tough area,
dockland Deptford on the south side of the Thames. One of the
biggest police problems there had been aliens from the New World
– big and brawny Americans – cattle-boat men, 'chiefly of the
scum of New York, Chicago, etc.' who, while waiting around for
two or three weeks to get a return boat, would get 'mad drunk' and
attack the police.

In 1905, a new aliens bill was introduced into Parliament and,
this time, was passed, despite strong opposition. Most aliens were
now forbidden to enter unless they had arranged accommodation
and employment. Those already here, Italians in particular, began
sponsoring members of their own families to come over to help
with their businesses, and this 'chain immigration' made for more
settled communities. As Detective Inspector Sweeney had
noticed, it was not from among the normal family men and women
of the working-class alien that most criminals sprang, but from
among the unattached. 'The former are well conducted, and, as a
whole, more sober than the English, it is the unattached who are
the undesirables.' Italian families also began to venture out of
crowded London to places as far afield as Wales and Scotland,
while Jewish and other organizations encouraged their immigrants
to disperse to less-populated areas – or not to come at all.

In 1905, an event took place which could not have happened in
early or mid-Victorian times – an ex-detective was sued for libel by
an immigrant for statements he had made in his memoirs. It could
not have happened earlier as detectives only started to have their
memoirs published during the last decade of the nineteenth
century. Then, quite suddenly, there was a rush into print.
Newspapers published stories of the adventures of retiring
detectives, *Police Review* featured profiles of policemen they

thought worthy of notice – and these were by no means only chief constables – and the volumes of memoirs followed. If nothing else, these were at least an antidote to the endless, self-satisfied, barrister's eye views of crime seen from the safety of the courtroom.

As well as being the first into print Moser's memoirs were the most critical of authority, but then he did not have a pension to worry about because, in fact, his service had been quite short – only ten years.

All these literary outpourings were making Scotland Yard and the Home Office most uneasy. Indeed, one of the reasons Abberline gave for not entering the memoir lists was clearly set out in one of his occasional handwritten asides in his recently-surfaced scrapbook of newspaper cuttings. Like the other notes, this sounds like a public statement rather than a personal jotting:

> At the time I retired from the service the authorities were very much opposed to retired Officers writing anything for the press as previously some retired Officers had from time to time been very indiscreet in what they had caused to be published and to my knowledge had been called upon to explain their conduct and in fact they had been threatened with actions for libel.
>
> Apart from that there is no doubt the fact that in describing what you did in detecting certain crimes you are putting the Criminal Classes on their guard and in some cases you may be absolutely telling them how to commit crime. As an example in the Finger Print detection you find now the expert thief wears gloves. [Sic]

What he did *not* comment on, and what so many would be agog to hear, were his opinions on the search for Jack the Ripper. (Similarly, Greenham says nothing about the abortive Brussels White Slave enquiry, but plenty about his time guarding Queen Victoria, while she travelled abroad.)

In their memoirs, Lansdowne and Greenham were anxious to inform a public fed on a diet of detectives who wore false moustaches that, in reality, disguise was rarely used by the police. Lansdowne quoted a newspaper article from the time of the Ripper which suggested that detectives must have a vast wardrobe of clothes, wigs, beards, imperials (a tuft of hair below the lower lip), and moustaches – and even hinted that they sometimes dressed as women.

'Now all this is fudge,' wrote Lansdowne. 'During the

Whitechapel business a zealous stripling certainly did put on women's attire one night, but he was not commended for his detective instinct in so doing.'

He could only recall two other instances of the use of disguise. The first was the detective who stood on a plinth and covered himself with a baize cloth to resemble a statue in order to catch a workman thief at the Great Exhibition in 1851 (in fact, it was at the Great Exhibition of 1862). The second was when an Inspector G— dressed himself as a clergyman in order to catch a shopkeeper selling indecent prints. 'It was scarcely a credit to the cloth that a clergyman's attire was considered the best disguise; but it was.' The 'Inspector G—' was probably Greenham, for he quotes such a case as the only time *he* donned disguise.

By contrast, Littlechild claimed that a curate's apparel was a favourite with detectives – because it was easy to adopt and disarmed suspicion. While admitting that some of his colleagues at the Yard disapproved, he defended the practice of using disguise. Such 'make-up' was very valuable to a detective, he declared, 'especially in his younger days'. He himself had pretended to be a surveyor and a sanitary inspector, and also disguised himself as a cabman – done up in a long coat, 'a horse-cloth on my arm, carrying a whip and badge well displayed'. He agreed that false moustaches and beards were silly, but pointed out that one could change 'the natural hair upon one's face'. (There tended to be a great deal in those days, worn in a variety of designs and combinations.) Like Inspector Field before him, Littlechild clearly enjoyed the whole pantomime. He even admits that (to fool a publican friend who had bet that he could see through any disguise) he had once remained 'in the black', after a Metropolitan Police Minstrel Show, and entered the pub, strumming his banjo! He was promptly ejected – and won his bet.

Although Lansdowne neither approved of the use of handcuffs or of disguise, he did think police rewards were a good thing. The subject was always a contentious one to outsiders, and rightly so, but ex-Detective Inspector Lansdowne did not shrink from giving his wholehearted approval of the system. It had always been his experience, he declared, that the prospect of a good reward on the completion of a case, 'is a wonderful stimulus to exertion, and will keep a man at work until any hour of the day or night, when, if he chose to be less active, he might, with perfect honesty, be quietly resting at home in the bosom of his family'. (Mr Coathupe, who served with the branch back in the mid sixties, was less convinced of the value of rewards. He told the 1878 committee on detectives that the men used to hang around the office for days to get a case which would pay them well and never dream of arresting a thief on the street.)

John Sweeney was mute on the question of disguise, although there is a story of him tailing an anarchist who, thinking he must be a beggar, offered him a piece of bread. He did, however, reveal quite a lot about the dreary occupation of 'shadowing', taking pains to describe just how wide the Special Branch were spreading their net and how fat were the files at the Yard on politically motivated suspects. This was quite a development – earlier in their history, such revelations about the Metropolitan Police would have caused an outcry, but then people had been frightened by the bombs. Nevertheless, it was indiscreet of him, as were one or two personal remarks about those he guarded, but it was none of these which was to get him dragged into court.

Sweeney's memoirs followed the common pattern – relating, step by step, his career from early days. He began as a constable at Hammersmith where his keenness caught the eye of the local inspector and earned him the chance to become an acting sergeant before he was out of his teens. This meant that men old enough to be his father had to take orders from a young man 'fresh from the wilds of Kerry'. His subsequent comments on this are somewhat unpleasant: 'But there are men who can never rise higher than the rank of constable, cannot hope for anything better than standing in the streets controlling traffic, and instructing pedestrians to take the first turning on the right and the second on the left. They are dull fellows with no touch of acuteness.'

It was the fact that he *was* from Kerry which was to lift him out of the rut and propel him into the Special Branch. After becoming a sergeant, he was *en route* to service in Brixton in 1884 when he was diverted to the Yard – as one of the posse of extra men drafted in to cope with the Fenian threat. A genuine Irish accent and background was invaluable for this duty and he recalls how, on one occasion, he evaded discovery and danger at a Clan-na-Gael (an offshoot of the Fenians) meeting by reading out a pamphlet in the Gaelic tongue.

Following a long stint of shadowing suspects and port duty at Hull, he was one of two officers kept on at the Yard when things quietened down. There followed several Royalty protection duty postings at Balmoral and Osborne; the guarding of visiting dignitaries and foreign royals, and finally some anarchist watching. It was his comments on a combination of these last two which got him into trouble.

He may have become just a little too accustomed to saying what he liked. (According to John Quail, in his book on British Anarchists, *The Slow Burning Fuse*, after an attempt to adjust his evidence at the Walsall Anarchists Trial, Sweeney was referred to regularly in later anarchist papers as 'Sweeney Todd the Perjurer'.) Certainly he seems to have been somewhat reckless in his book when he claimed that, not only was the prominent Italian art dealer, Luigi Parmeggiani, a notorious anarchist and thus not a fit person to become a British subject, but also that his collection of antiques and 'curios of all sorts' was largely a result of the receiving of stolen goods. The remarks were an aside to his descriptions of his guarding of the visiting Empress Frederick of Germany (the eldest daughter of Queen Victoria), and how amused he had been that he had to escort her to examine Parmeggiani's antique collection. The monarchy were, of course, prime targets for the anarchists, and one would have thought that, given that the Empress of Austria had been assassinated only the previous year by an Italian anarchist, concern, rather than amusement, might have been in order.

In court, Sweeney stuck by his anarchist claim, and brought several witnesses, police and civilian, to prove it. So effective was this that the jury sent a note to say they were convinced Parmeggiani was an anarchist and didn't need to hear any more. (Parmeggiani had claimed that much of the evidence against him referred to his elder brother who (oddly) was also named Luigi). But Sweeney had to admit that he could not sustain his other allegation about the Italian being a fence, and was duly found guilty on that count. His defence counsel, Mr Shearman KC, asked the jury to consider very carefully before they took the savings of Mr Sweeney – who had spent a life time protecting the public against anarchists – and gave them to – a proved anarchist. They duly considered – and awarded Parmeggiani damages of one farthing.

Another ex-detective involved in a libel case a couple of years earlier had not come off so well. Ex-Inspector Meiklejohn, now out of prison, sued Major Arthur Griffiths for his remarks about him in his report of the Turf Fraud trial in his book *Mysteries of*

Police and Crime – but the jury found for the defendant without retiring.

In his book Griffiths also remarks on the shrinkage of the world, due to the increase in ease of travel, and how the contraction of neutral ground (presumably due to the increase in extradition treaties) militated against the criminal – as did modern inventions. 'Electricity is his worst and bitterest foe, and next to it rank the post and the press. Flight is checked by the wire, the first mail carries full particulars everywhere, both to the general public and the ubiquitous international police, brimful of camaraderie and willing to help each other.'

Of course, it could be argued that some of the inventions were of almost as much use to the criminal, certainly it had long been held that the immediate publication in the press of all the details known about a crime, police movements and evidence available, was often unhelpful to the cause of law and order. A number of coroners, magistrates and judges had remarked upon this.

Like Dickens before him, Griffiths thought that, 'if he can be persuaded to talk', there was no better company than a good detective. He had met them in all sorts of places, in railway trains, on steamboats and at glittering soirées where they were 'certainly not the least gentlemanlike of the guests assembled'. He also gives a picture of Mr Macnaghten, second in command of the CID. Macnaghten, thought Griffiths, was essentially a man of action.

> ... a man of presence is Mr Macnaghten – tall, well-built, with a military air, although his antecedents are those of a public school, of Indian planter life, than of the army. His room, like his chiefs, is hung with speaking tubes, his table is deep with reports and papers, but the walls are bright with photographs of officials, personal friends and notorious criminals.

15 Anarchy

Despite the new aliens act there remained many desperate foreigners at large in London and, as the first decade of the twentieth century was drawing to a close, the behaviour of some of them became extreme. The first incident occurred, not in the East End, but in Tottenham, in North London. Two Latvians, Paul Hefeld and Jacob Lepidus, set in train The Tottenham Outrage which, as it developed, had the air of a Keystone Cops chase – except that the outcome was tragic rather than comic.

It began at 10.30 a.m. on a Saturday morning in January, 1909, when, as was the custom, Albert Keyworth, a 17-year-old clerk, brought the wages from the bank to Schnurmann's rubber factory near Tottenham High Street. Lepidus and Hefeld, both armed, were lying in wait and, as the boy alighted from a car, they went to snatch the money. The boy put up a fight, as did the driver who was shot at several times. Miraculously, he escaped injury – possiby due to his enveloping, ankle-length, motoring coat. Not so, a burly gas stoker who came to their aid. He was shot at four times and received injuries (but, again miraculously, these proved relatively minor) giving the thieves the opportunity to grab the money and run.

What was particularly stupid about this attack was that, not only was the factory within view of a police station, but also, the victims had a car at their disposal with which to pursue the robbers. On hearing the shots, two policemen, PCs Newman and Tyler, ran out of the station and set off in pursuit, Tyler jumping on board the victim's car. They quickly caught up with the fugitives, who fired on the vehicle, putting it out of action – at the same time, mortally wounding a 10-year-old boy. The pursuers continued the chase on foot, despite Hefeld turning around every now and then to fire at them. PC Tyler was shot down with a bullet wound in the head. He died soon after reaching hospital.

The chase covered four or five miles, Lepidus and Hefeld crossing footbridges over the River Lea and the Great Eastern Railway and, in turn, commandeering a tram, a milk cart and a van. Police also commandeered motor cars in an effort to keep up, and erected road blocks. Eventually, the robbers came to a dead end and were faced with climbing a fence alongside the little River Ching. This was too much for the exhausted Hefeld, who was shorter than Lepidus, and, as his pursuers closed in, he shot himself. His wound was not instantly fatal, but he died in hospital three weeks later. By now, the crowd of pursuers included two armed policemen and duckshooters from the Tottenham Marshes. Lepidus crossed some fields and burst into a workman's cottage where he ran upstairs to the bedroom. As police closed in, firing, he, too, shot himself.

There is a divergence of opinion as to whether the Tottenham Outrage was politically linked or was simply criminal. Special Branch thought it was the former, one of a series organized by a notorious Russian revolutionary, Christian Salnish.

Two years later Salnish was possibly involved in the organization of a further appalling incident – a crime, and the event that followed, which would eclipse even the horror of the Tottenham Outrage – and of which Wensley was later to remark: 'Until I read of it afterwards I confess I did not know how thrilling the siege of Sidney Street had been ... Melodrama may be all very well for the spectator, but it is sometimes very tiring work for those called upon to play a principal part ...'

The story is well-known. One City of London policeman was shot dead and three wounded, two of them mortally, when members of a gang of Russian and Lettish revolutionaries came out firing, after having been disturbed while robbing a jewellers in Houndsditch. Wensley, who never believed they were anything but common criminals, became involved because his division, on which he was now local inspector, abutted the City, close to the scene of the crime, and the perpetrators escaped on to his patch.

The day after the murders police found the body of one of the gang, accidentally shot by his fellows, and, during the next few days, arrested several suspects. An informer told police that two more of the gang were in hiding on the upper floors of 100 Sidney Street. The famous siege followed, in which periods of waiting by City of London and Metropolitan Police officers alternated with sudden activity and a great deal of confusion. Rather quaintly, when the police wanted to notify the surrounded men that their position was hopeless, they knocked on the downstairs door and, on getting no response, threw a handful of gravel at the upper windows. This gesture was answered by a fusillade of shots – one of which struck 40-year-old Detective Sergeant Benjamin Leeson who staggered towards Wensley, crying, 'I am shot!'

He was removed to some shelter where he murmured, 'Mr Wensley, I am dying. They have shot me through the heart. Give my love to my children. Bury me in Putney.' In fact, he wasn't and they didn't, but moving him to hospital required that he be manhandled on a stretcher over a shed roof – right under the eyes of the fugitives. As the bullets whizzed past them, the not surprisingly agitated Leeson cried, 'You are taking me into the line of fire again!' He managed to roll the rest of the way to safety, but Wensley was left pinned down in the shed gutter. He became frozen, not only by the water and ice in the gutter, but also by the fact that if he moved at all he drew fire. Half an hour passed before the gunmen were sufficiently distracted for him to move. During that time, rumours that he had been shot not only spread rapidly, but were published by some newspapers.

Some of the police managed to arm themselves with bulldog revolvers and shotguns and rifles borrowed from a miniature shooting range but it became obvious more fire power might be needed so the army were called in, in the shape of a detachment of Scots Guards from the Tower of London. The whole drama came to an end when the house caught fire. Two bodies were found in the ashes, one of which had a bullet through the head, thought to have been caused by incoming fire. Leeson, who had been shot in the chest, made a good recovery and, as Paul Begg remarks in his *Scotland Yard Files*, 'lived to write a highly colourful account of his career'.

Wensley admits to coming out of the affair 'with perhaps greater credit than I honestly earned'. The enquiry was in the hands of the City detectives 'of whom I was only the ally'. He was an ally, too, in another concurrent case which may or may not have been connected with the siege of Sidney Street and may or may not have been politically motivated.

The day before the siege began, the body of a middle-aged man was found on Clapham Common. The victim had suffered severe wounds to the head and there were cuts across his face. Local Inspector Alfred Ward, told Wensley he thought the victim might be one of 'your Yiddish friends'. It transpired that Wensley was indeed able to identify him quite quickly as Leon Beron, 'a quaint little Jew of Russian parentage', who had been a 'rather noticeable character' in Whitechapel. Beron was a property owner (and possibly also a pimp and receiver) who liked the ladies and often carried large sums of money. He had last been seen in the company of another striking-looking man, the tall and handsome Steini Morrison, who had a criminal record. Morrison was duly arrested and charged with murder. Found guilty and sentenced to death he was later reprieved but always protested his innocence and died in prison in 1921.

There has been much speculation about whether Steini Morrison was guilty, and much discussion as to the possible motives for the murder. Among the ideas mooted is that the murder was ritualistic and possibly committed in revenge; that Beron could have been an informer on revolutionaries, and that the slashes on his cheeks were crude esses which possibly stood for 'spy' – or were a secret society sign. Wensley pooh-poohed these notions, as he did the proposition that Steini was innocent. He even went so far as to say that, being the only person living who knew all the circumstances, 'after twenty years I am still convinced that Steini Morrison was convicted justly as any murderer I have ever known'.

He does concede that police suspected and, in fact, almost charged another man as an accomplice, but Detective Inspector Ward had felt this would only confuse the issue for the jury and could result in both men escaping justice. Some commentators read something sinister into the fact that police did not reveal that Beron himself may have been an unsavoury character but, if anything, it should be up to the defence to bring this out. In any case, it would have the same effect – that of confusing the jury. Their task was difficult enough, given that many witnesses did not speak or understand English and probably had divided loyalties or were even hostile. Indeed, the prosecution of those arrested for the cold-blooded murders of policemen at Houndsditch failed, partly for those reasons, although now there is no doubt of their guilt.

Down the years, Scotland Yard detectives had continued to be called in by certain provincial forces, some of whom had no detectives of their own. But, too often, the call for help arrived too late, after the trail had grown cold and the unskilled local men had muddied or even unwittingly destroyed much of the evidence. In addition, the Yard detectives continued to face hostility and sometimes even deliberate obstruction from resentful provincial policemen whose local knowledge could have helped solve the crime.

In 1907, the Home Secretary, Herbert Gladstone, decided to do something about this. What was needed, he decided, was an ever-ready pool of experienced detectives which the chief constables would be encouraged to utilize immediately upon the discovery of a serious crime – of a nature that suggested an effective investigation might well be beyond local expertise and resources. The first team consisted of five men; Detective Chief Inspectors Fox, Dew, Kane and Arrow, and the man who selected and led them, Frank Froest, now a superintendent.

Chief Inspector Fox had handled the Stratton murder case, the first in which fingerprint evidence had played a major role. John Kane was the man who had always been of the opinion that Beck and Smith were being confused and, when Beck was arrested again in 1904, made the first police moves to sort the whole thing out. As a result Beck was granted a free pardon and £5,000 compensation.

Charles Arrow was now almost due to retire and did so shortly after joining the team, to take on the strange task of setting up a special branch in Spain to assist in combating the numerous bomb outrages. (The relative sparsity of anarchist/nihilist/revolutionary bombings in the United Kingdom, as compared to the rest of Europe, was probably due to the fact that, on the whole, our regime was less repressive than most. Police efficiency may also have played a part and, as the revolutionaries did most of their plotting and bomb-making here, the more sensible among them preferred not to over-antagonize their hosts.)

Evidently the Spanish felt our police had something to teach them but, unfortunately for Arrow, there was nothing secret about his lucrative three-year contract (with liberal insurance cover). Protests against it began even before his arrival in Spain and continued throughout his stay. The press and huge crowds were awaiting him at Barcelona where he was to be based. He gave them the slip and thus gained some brownie points for demonstrating one of his many disguises. But the weather was hot, mosquitos were plentiful, police guards under his window kept him awake at night and, not only was his social life curtailed due to the constraints imposed by his guards, but he found his company was actually avoided as being too dangerous. He ploughed on with the setting up of his force, struggled with the setbacks caused by the never-ending red tape and, eventually, put his special branch into operation.

Nothing, however, could halt the impetus of the simmering revolution. The people wanted a republic. At the end of his second year, an insurrection in Barcelona was crushed in what became known as 'The Bloody Week'. Francisco Ferrer, a leading socialist, was executed for his part, although Arrow did admit that the man had done a great deal to promote education for all. He also admitted that whilst the bombers were ruthless, so too were the Spanish authorities. Attacks against Arrow continued in the press and at public meetings, so it was no surprise to him when he was paid off a few months before his term was completed.

The fourth chief inspector in what was to be dubbed The Murder Squad, was 44-year-old Walter Dew. He was destined to become the most famous of them all as the man who caught Crippen – although wags have suggested that he should have been called the man who let Crippen go. Born in Northampton, he had first worked as a clerk in a solicitor's office, then in a seed merchants, being sacked from the latter because he dallied to watch a fire at the Central Criminal Court. Among his early experiences in the Metropolitan Police was dealing with sheep stealers in Harrow. Not lone rustlers of the odd ewe, but organized gangs who caught and slaughtered whole flocks and carried off their carcasses in horse-drawn vans.

Dew's first experience as a member of the fledgling squad was not a happy one. He had been called in quickly enough – just three and a half hours after the finding of the body – but it was what the Salisbury Police (in Wiltshire) had allowed to happen at the scene in the intervening hours which made his heart sink. The victim was a one-legged, 12-year-old boy, Teddy Haskell, who had been found dead in bed with his throat cut. By the time Dew arrived, the boy's body had been thoroughly washed, the bedclothes rearranged and the house cleaned of all traces of blood. The boy had been saving up to buy himself a cork leg but half of the £8 accrued so far was missing. The lock had been wrenched from the drawer in which he kept his money.

Mrs Haskell, the boy's mother, told Dew that while she had been sitting in her kitchen at about 10.20 p.m. the previous evening, she had heard a noise. As she went into the passage to find out what was going on, a man had run past, throwing a knife down, which had spattered her sleeve with blood. A nephew, who had arrived at that time, said he had not seen any man, despite having run out when she called out, 'Stop that man.' The intruder, Mrs Haskell told the police, was about forty years old, five feet five inches in height and wore a suit, but no collar and tie. Police brought out bloodhounds to help search the surrounding area and set up road blocks but without success.

The murder weapon, a recently sharpened kitchen knife, proved to have come from Mrs Haskell's scullery and eight sovereigns were found in her possession. Dew was also curious about some freshly laundered men's clothes in her bedroom. They belonged to a Mr Mold, she told him, a steward on the liner *Adriatic*, who lodged with her when on leave. Suspecting that Mrs Haskell may have murdered her son because he stood in the way of her marriage to Mr Mold, Dew set off in search of him – in a tender from Plymouth which caught up with the *Adriatic* at Cherbourg. But having interviewed the man he found him genuinely fond of the boy and saddened by his death. Despite this, Drew was convinced that Mrs Haskell had killed her own son. He arrested her and charged her with murder. The inquest jury brought in a verdict against her but the trial jury was unable to agree. The judge, Mr Justice Ridley, horrified that the police had allowed the bloodstains to be removed, said he could not imagine a greater act of folly. (By then, (1908), a German scientist had found a means of distinguishing between animal and human blood, and this discovery had been instrumental in convicting a killer as far back as 1898. There had, as yet, been no test cases in the United Kingdom but, in the Haskell case, the source of blood was not in dispute, it was the proof of its whereabouts which could have been significant.)

At the second trial, the judge's summing up favoured a guilty verdict, but the jury found Mrs Haskell not guilty and their decision was greeted with cheers – possibly, as in the case of Constance Kent, a demonstration of local solidarity against outsiders such as Dew. The case did, however, bring about fresh instructions from the Home Office to constabularies that they must do everything possible to preserve the scenes of crime.

Reading about the Crippen case sometimes makes one feel like setting up a Cora Crippen Defence Society. For some strange reason, much of the sympathy in this case had gone to the murderer, Hawley Harvey Crippen. Some writers appear to believe everything he said about Cora despite the fact that he was shown to have lied so effortlessly about everything else. Possibly, the apologist tone of editor Filson Young's introduction to *The Trial of Hawley Harvey Crippen* helped sustain this picture of Cora, drawn by (invariably male) writers, as the vain and silly slut who pushed the mild and patient doctor over the edge. Cora had plenty of faults, but she did have friends who cared enough about her to get the enquiry going, whereas Crippen had none.

Chief Inspector Dew and Sergeant Mitchell had gone to see the American doctor after being alerted by them becuse they were unhappy about his assertion that Cora had died in California after going there to visit a sick relative. They had been made more suspicious by the fact that his little secretary, Ethel Le Neve, who he had been sleeping with for three years, had jumped into her shoes almost immediately, even wearing Cora's jewellery and furs. When challenged by Chief Inspector Dew, Doctor Crippen immediately changed his story – Cora had left him, probably for another man, and he had merely spread the tale to save face. Dew and Mitchell looked around Crippen's house and found some items packed up. Crippen told him they were about to 'remove' – which they did, the following day, without leaving a forwarding address.

The rest is police history: the finding of some of Cora's remains in the cellar, the identification of the fugitives who were travelling as father and son on the Atlantic steamer, *Montrose*, and the epoch-making wireless message to the police in London from the man who really caught Crippen – Captain Kendall. The rest was a replay of the transatlantic chase after the railway murderer Muller, forty-six years earlier. Dew and Mitchell caught a faster ship, the ss *Laurentic*, and formed a welcoming party for Crippen and Le Neve on the other side.

Meanwhile, it had been discovered that this man, whose patience was claimed by excusers to have suddenly snapped, had put in his order for the poison (hyoscine), thought to have killed Cora, several weeks before, and since her disappearance, had been pawning her jewellery because he was in financial trouble. Crippen was convicted of the murder and hanged. Le Neve was found not guilty of being an accessory.

Not everyone went along with the subsequent near-canonization of the doctor (whose career, incidentally, was curiously like that of Neill Cream). As Colin Wilson and Patricia Pitman pointed out in the *Encyclopaedia of Murder*: '... criminologist William Le Queux, who claimed to have met Crippen in 1908 (the doctor was seeking information on untraceable poisons for a novel he proposed to write), held a less charitable view: "Hawley Harvey Crippen was certainly one of the most dangerous criminals of his century".'

16 War

It was a Zeppelin which finally got Wensley to Scotland Yard. Like Abberline before him he had been happy to stay in Whitechapel where his local knowledge was of most use and, despite promotion to chief inspector, was allowed to do so. But, in the autumn of 1916 his old friend, Chief Inspector Alfred Ward, was killed by a bomb dropped on to his house by a Zeppelin. Wensley automatically became the senior detective chief inspector and, as such, lost 'his peculiarly detached position'.

Ward's death was not the first loss he had suffered in this terrible war. In August 1915, his eldest son, 21-year-old Frederick Martin Wensley, had been killed by a shell in a trench in France. By the time Wensley arrived at the Yard his younger son, 18-year-old Harold, was serving at the front.

It was to be another air raid, a year after that which had killed Ward, that brought about the Regent Square Murder. The mystery began at 8.30 a.m. on 2 November 1917, when Thomas George Henry, a resident of Regent Square in Bloomsbury, was setting off for work. His eye was drawn to a bulky sackcloth parcel lying on the grass, just inside the square's railings. He put his hand through, felt around the parcel – and came to the conclusion that it must contain half a sheep.

'The sheep' took some getting at. Once the string was cut there were two layers of wrapping to remove, one of sacking, the other of sheeting – before a woman's torso was revealed. Rather unnervingly, it was clad, as Wensley put it, 'in delicate underclothes of lace and blue ribbon'. After Mr Henry had recovered from the initial shock, he blew the whistle which he just happened to have on him. This attracted the attention of many of the other residents of the square. One would imagine that he would have had enough by then but, while he was awaiting the arrival of police, he examined a smaller parcel – lying about a yard away. It contained a pair of legs. Fortunately, none of the remains were bloody, in fact they were surprisingly dry.

Further inspection by the experts revealed that the remains were those of a woman about thirty years of age, approximately five foot tall, who had given birth at some time, had been healthy and well nourished, was of clean personal habits and, judging by 'the superior quality of her underclothing' had been in fairly comfortable circumstances. On a piece of brown paper underneath her superior quality vest lay a note, on which was written in angular writing 'of a distinctly foreign appearance', the words, 'BLODIE BELGIUM'.

By now, local inspectors were known as divisional inspectors and the one in charge of the CID on E division, where the body was found, was John Ashley. Apart from the 'foreign' writing, his only clue was a laundry mark on the corner of the sheet. With this, his men managed to trace ownership of the sheet as belonging to a Frenchwoman, Madame Gerard, the wife of a chef serving in the allied armies. She had not been seen in her Munster Square flat (some fifteen minutes walk from Regent Square) since the night of 31 October, when there had been a particularly bad air raid – one of the worst London had suffered thus far.

Inside her flat were found a photograph of a man (not her husband) and an IOU for £50 from a Belgian butcher by the name of Louis Voisin – who conveniently turned out to be the man in the photograph. He lived in Charlotte Street, also no more than fifteen minutes walk from Regent Square. For a time, Mme Gerard had been employed by Voisin as his housekeeper.

Wensley was later extremely tactful in describing his arrival on the scene. Since the venue of death had not been established the enquiries might lead anywhere out of the division or even the force area, he declared. The division was a busy one, 'and it would have been scarcely fair to have expected him to carry on a special case demanding close attention and probably heavy work outside the limits of his district'. He went to Bow Street where he found that Ashley and his men 'had been energetically at work and had accumulated a considerable amount of very valuable information. He was obviously pleased when I told him I had come to co-operate'. Obviously, the man couldn't keep away from an interesting case.

The Belgian butcher and Madame Berthe Roche, the woman who lived with him, were invited along to the station, as were twenty or thirty others. Most of these were foreign refugees acquainted with Madame Gerard but Voisin and Roche were interviewed first. Voisin was a short, thickset man possessed of an 'exceedingly powerful frame'. He faced Wensley 'with a sort of aggressive determination. His line was a profession of ignorance'. According to Voisin the missing woman was not dead but had left for France to see her husband, in company with a woman friend. She had told him she was going and had asked him to feed her cat while she was away – which he had done.

Rumours that raised women's voices were heard coming from Voisin's rooms on the night of the heavy air raid added fuel to police suspicions but, as yet, the torso and legs had not been identified so police were temporarily blocked. They had found blood in Voisin's kitchen – but then, he was a butcher, and claimed that he had brought home a calf's head to be cut up. Tests to establish whether the stains were human or animal would take time. Meanwhile, Wensley asked the man to write out the words 'Bloody Belgium', several times. Each time it came out 'Blodie Belgium' in a hand somewhat similar to that found on the brown paper. They searched Voisin and among his keys found one for his cellar. Alfred Collins, the young detective sergeant who conducted the search, left no cask unturned – not even the one which was full of sawdust. Inside, he found the head and hands of the murdered woman – Madame Gerard. As well as a positive identification of the victim, they provided police with some indication as to how she had died – by the wounds to her head and defensive marks on her hands. (They also realized why the hands had been removed – they were easily identifiable from old burn scars.)

The blood in Voisin's kitchen proved to be human, which knocked his calf story literally on the head. He and Roche were arrested. The woman was thunderstruck, Wensley reports, and seemed to think that Voisin had betrayed her. She screamed at him in French, calling him a deceiver and a wicked man. He was phlegmatic and merely shrugged, murmuring, 'It is unfortunate.' He did not deserve her scorn, however, for when he came up with a story to fit the facts he thought police had so far discovered, he was adamant that Roche had no knowledge of any murder.

What he now claimed had happened was that he had gone to Madame Gerard's flat to feed her cat as requested, and had found it covered in blood – and her head and hands wrapped in a flannel jacket. Thinking it was a trap set for him he did not know what to do – so he cleaned the place up (thereby getting bloodstains on his clothes) and took away the head and hands. 'The rest of the body was not there.'

Meanwhile, police and forensic scientist, Bernard Spilsbury, were piecing together the most likely course of events. They came to the conclusion that Madame Gerard had first gone to an underground station to shelter from the air raid. Afterwards, since further attacks were possible, she had decided to take refuge with her lover, Voisin, who lived nearby – only to find Berthe Roche there. 'Conceive the situation,' Wensley remarks, 'as the two half-hysterical Frenchwomen unexpectedly confronted each other, with their lover asleep in one of the other rooms.' (Roche sat up, unable to sleep, because she was frightened of air raids.) Because some of the blows were thought to be too light for a man of Voisin's strength, they guessed that Roche had attacked Madame Gerard and, seeing she had gone too far, Voisin had finished her off.

Wensley expected to be attacked at the trial for getting the suspect to write 'Blodie Belgium' before being cautioned. And so it proved, but the judge held that the evidence was admissable nonetheless – Voisin had merely been asked to assist the police, and had done so.

As there was little direct evidence against Roche she was acquitted of the main charge by direction of the judge, but was later found guilty of being an accessory after the fact. She was sentenced to seven years penal servitude, during which time she became insane. Voisin was found guilty and, unusually, the judge passed the death sentence in French. After a delay to allow him to give evidence for Roche, he was hanged.

It was the swiftness of the action at the outset which had ensured the success of the case, Wensley points out in *Detective Days*, before the Belgian butcher had the opportunity to get rid of the head and hands. 'As it was, the body was discovered on Friday. Thanks to Ashley's activities its likely identity had been established by Saturday. On that day, Voisin and Roche were detained and by Monday the case against them was practically established.'

Many criminals were away at the front but, nonetheless, there was still plenty of work: enforcing DORA (Defence of the Realm Act) regulations such as evasion of war service and other offences which surfaced due to wartime conditions. The shortage of gold and silver, for example, led normally quite law-abiding citizens to indulge in melting down currency for its precious metal content which was worth considerably more than the face value of the coins.

There was also the continuing, ever-eager search for spies. Scotland Yard was inundated with anonymous letters about suspect activities. 'If I had believed everything I heard in those days,' says Wensley, 'I should have had half the foreigners I met – whether Germans or not – put under arrest as spies.' As Basil Thomson, who had replaced Melville Macnaghten as assistant commissioner CID, remarked in *Queer People*, 'The spy mania was a godsend to the adolescent liar' – and many others besides.

Given the stamp of some of the real spies who were captured, it all seemed rather unnecessary. Rather than fade into the background as a good spy should, most of them seemed to stand out like beacons. One was hugely fat, another, a South American negro half-caste. Many had weird and wonderful accents and they invariably purported to be commercial travellers. While this gave them a convincing reason for getting about so as to inspect our military installations, it was a cover quickly blown as so few of them knew anything about the goods they purported to be selling.

Head of the CID, Basil Thomson, through whose hands most of them passed, divided spies into patriotics and hirelings. The latter, he thought 'should be treated like the vermin he is and nailed to the barn-door as a warning to others.'

One of the 'hireling' spies was a Peruvian with a Scandinavian father and his name alone, Ludovico Hurwitz-y-Zender, would have made a saint suspicious. He knew so little about the sardines he was supposed to be selling that he sent a huge order to Norway outside the canning season. Several 'cigar salesmen' ordered vast quantities of cigars for naval bases such as Portsmouth, when everyone knew sailors did not smoke Havanas. (Like the sardine orders, these were coded messages. For 10,000 Cabanas, 4,000 Rothschilds and 3,000 Coronas read ten destroyers, four cruisers and three battleships.) Another travelling salesman had been a gentleman of leisure given to violin playing, and was obviously too well dressed and elegant for his calling. He was allowed to play his violin in the Tower right up to the time of his execution. Then there was the Uruguayan-German who would carefully explain that he was in poor health and Loch Lomond (where torpedo tests just happened to be in progress) had been recommended to him as a health resort.

Unlike later spies, what these unprofessionals lacked was a swift means of communication (such as radio) which did not have to pass through British hands. Letters and, occasionally, telegrams seemed to be their only means, but such was the fear of spies that the authorities had the censors busy well before the war began. The credit for most of the captures was largely due to them, although Basil Thomson, the trumpeted spy catcher, tends to be a little low key about their vital role. Various methods to avoid the censors' eye were tried, such as the use of 'secret writing' and invisible ink, while one spy even attempted to indicate vital military statistics by the number of stamps he used.

Once arrested many of their fake passports were found to have been written in the same distinguished and scholarly hand, as though to help the police along, which was soon to become familiar to their captors. What added a certain pathos to their tales was that much of the information they tried to send could have been culled from *The Times*, which was sent across the Channel daily.

'The first serious spy to be arrested,' reports Thomson, 'was Lody.' Lody had lived in the US where he acquired 'what he believed to be fluent English with an American accent'. He made a bad start by sending a telegram from Edinburgh to his contact in Stockholm which the censors thought suspicious enough to check further. He then hired a bicycle and explored the neighbourhood, including Rosyth Harbour 'asking too many questions for an ordinary sightseer'. In London, he gave the anti-aircraft defences the once-over followed by an inspection of the Liverpool docks before leaving for Ireland, where he was arrested and held for the Yard men to collect. Lody had held a commission in the Germany navy and was a reserve officer. He was tried at the Westminster Guildhall at the end of October 1914, and made no defence other than that he was doing his duty. He was found guilty and executed at the Tower of London. His demeanour and bravery impressed all those with whom he came in contact and he left a letter thanking them for their kind treatment. As Thomson said, 'He never flinched, he never cringed, but he died as one would wish all Englishmen to die – quietly and undramatically, supported in his courage by the proud consciousness of having done his duty.'

Anton Kuppferle was the next in line to sit in Thomson's inquisitorial chair – which, he discovered, seemed to have a psychological effect on suspects who, when asked a particularly disconcerting question would instinctively try to raise themselves by the arms to reply. Later, it was demonstrated that this was simply because it was lower than his which led him to the conclusion that witness boxes should be lower not higher than those of examining counsel. 'Primitive races have found this out, for their chiefs stand erect while their inferiors squat on the ground when they are being questioned.'

Kuppferle was no less brave than Lody, 'but grotesque in his inefficiency, and forbidding in his personal appearance' (in fact, from his photograph he looks almost comically Prussian). He was also lower class. As Thomson explains, he was 'a typical German non-commissioned officer, stiff, abrupt, and uncouth'. Kuppferle, who pretended to be a Dutch salesman of woollen goods, wrote 'probably the first letter that contained writing using invisible ink'. In it, he described war vessels he had observed while crossing the Atlantic from America to Liverpool. Despite his inferior status Kuppferle beat his captors in one sense – by committing suicide after the first day of his trial. He left a long, farewell letter on a slate in his Brixton cell saying, among other things, that he had not wished to be hanged – but shot like a soldier.

The anti-German feeling which abounded also affected the lives of some police officers with German antecedents. One police constable, Joseph Schoenfelder, who had completed two successful years as a winter patrol at Albany Street, was at last appointed a permanent Patrol at Finchley in March, 1916. (Uniformed men were employed in plain clothes during the winter months to assist in catching burglars. If successful, they would be taken into the department on probation as a patrol – later, 'aide to CID'.) A few months later he changed his name to 'Smith'.

Among the more mundane problems caused by the war was an epidemic of pickpockets. For long a London problem, it had developed into a much bigger one in the packed city during wartime – particularly on the underground, where trains had been reduced to a minimum. The resultant overcrowding, both in the carriages and on the platforms, was a haven for the lightfingered. One young detective sent out to catch them was Detective Constable Peter Rosie from Wick. He disguised himself as a railway porter, a ruse he found most successful, though tricky at times when determined passengers demanded answers to their questions about services. Some of his quarry operated in the classic manner – in small gangs – others worked strictly solo and some also adopted simple disguises. One old-timer posed as a clergyman – that easily-popped-on dog collar again – and another, who was smartly dressed and of military bearing, played the retired colonel to perfection. His impressive appearance did act as something of a handicap, however, inasmuch that he was highly visible in a crowd.

At last this long and bitter war drew to a close and husbands, fathers and sons began to come home. Wensley's younger son was not among them. He contracted influenza on Armistice Day and died four days later. Small wonder that in his later photographs, Wensley wears a somewhat melancholy air. He dedicated his book to his lost boys (as did Dew in his memoirs, to his fallen son) and wrote a short sketch of each including, touchingly, the comments made about them by their colleagues and commanding officers.

One defect in the CID system which had become increasingly obvious over the years, was that each division, and even the Yard itself, continued to act as separate units. What was needed to combat the growing mobility of the criminal was more co-operation and movement between them. When asked by Thomson, in 1916, for ideas to correct this, Wensley had suggested that a senior detective should have overall control of the CID in several divisions, and he would act in co-operation with his equivalent colleagues. Additionally, a roving body of detectives should be created so that they could be sent in wherever a special need arose.

When the war ended these suggestions were put into operation. The Metropolitan Police district was split into four, with one CID superintendent covering each quarter. The men appointed to these posts were Albert Hawkins, Arthur Neil, Francis Carlin – and Frederick Wensley. They were immediately dubbed – The Big Four.

The suggested mobile group of detectives was also established, and the fact that these men had two police tenders at their disposal, with which to chase suspects, added greatly to their public image. They became The Flying Squad.

By now, detectives were being given six weeks training which included lectures on criminal law and procedure and practical training with the aid of 'the magic lantern'. Some detective training had already begun by the time Thomson had become Assistant Commissioner CID in 1913 and, while he found that, as a result, the men were efficient on legal matters, record keeping, and the handling of the public, he found them wanting in matters practical. When it came to keeping observation of a suspect or searching premises, they lacked imagination, and their descriptions of persons wanted, he found 'colourless'. Such vital points as peculiarities of gait and speech were omitted. (This was certainly not the case, for example, in the Crippen murder in 1910. The 'Wanted' police notice describes the doctor as somewhat slovenly, given to wearing his hat on the back of his head and throwing his feet outwards as he walked. His manner was 'very plausible' and he was quietly spoken and 'remarkably cool and collected'. The 'nice-looking' Ethel dressed 'well, but quietly' and 'looked intently when in conversation'. All peculiarities well-noted there but, of course, they may have emanated from Cora's artistic friends.)

Thomson informed the 1919 Desborough Committee on the Police Service of England, Wales and Scotland, that provincial forces were now sending officers to the detective training courses – which helped breakdown barriers between them and the Met. He also revealed that the rewards system was still in operation (for some time they had been issued only from a central police pool) but these were now very small. They remained, however, allotted according to rank. 'It generally is five shillings for a constable, seven shillings for a sergeant, ten shillings for an inspector and 15 shillings for a chief inspector.' To those who have, shall be given.

Gentlemen detectives had been tried and found wanting, he told the committee, who were back on the old track of if we pay more maybe we could attract public schoolboys and educated men. Thomson assured them if he wanted something done which was beyond the capabilities of his present men, he could bring someone in on a temporary basis, 'Just in the same way as if I have work that entails employment of a woman, I can always get a policeman's wife or somebody to do the work quite efficiently, and therefore I am not very much in favour of female detectives.'

At the end of the Great War, as at the end of most wars, a large number of people were footloose and restless. Many were back from the front, glad to be alive and, often as not, unlikely to return to their old, humdrum occupations – if the jobs still existed. It was inevitable that many turned to crime. Quite a number, including the old 'professional' crooks, were often armed with weapons picked up during their war service, and some were mobile –

whereas the police were neither. Even if a criminal had no car he found it simple enough to steal one, commit the crime and drive off – with police in pursuit – on foot. 'The police', wrote Walter Hambrook who had earlier been astonished by the lack of telephones, 'had not a single motor car.' (Not *quite* true. In 1903, the commissioner and receiver had been issued with cars and there were one or two stores and despatch vans.)

The crime wave grew, with gangs speeding around, smashing and grabbing with impunity – and quite prepared to show violence towards any who resisted them. When police did buy a few cars they were assigned to divisional superintendents to replace the old dog carts used to tour their outer stations. After a while, a few detective inspectors were given motor cycles but this did little to help combat the new scourge, 'the motor bandit'. Small wonder that when the new mobile squad, with its two old army lorries, was launched in 1920, it was deemed an instant success – it could scarcely have failed.

The Flying Squad – so dubbed by the aptly named crime journalist, G.T. Crook, just a few days after its birth, was eighteen strong. Each van contained a driver, four constables, two sergeants and two inspectors. The senior inspector and the man in charge, was Walter Hambrook. The team sat on two wooden benches along the inside of the vehicle and kept observation through a small window in the back and, later, through holes bored in the van sides. For their first sortie they decided to take on one of the gangs which had been thumbing their noses at police. It operated either from Camden Town or the Elephant and Castle so the vans went on 'a skirmishing expedition' in both directions.

'On the second evening out', reports Hambrook, 'we saw a man we all knew to be a desperate gangster jump into a half-ton covered van which was standing in the Old Kent Road.' It headed for the Elephant and Castle and, *en route*, picked up six more men three of whom were notorious criminals. In Tooting High Street some of them got out and surveyed the shops and flats but did nothing. However, the team managed to keep them in sight on the run back to their garage. 'This was in itself a very important point gained. We were now hot on the scent.'

Both vans kept watch on the garage, turn and turn about. Their vigil lasted about thirty-one hours, 'then came our reward'. At 4 a.m. that day, five of the gang arrived, carrying objects wrapped in newspaper. One of these was long and thin – like a jemmy. The metallic clang heard by the squad team when the parcels were thrown into the back of the suspect van confirmed their suspicions that they contained house-breaking implements.

In Parliament Square, three more men were added to the gang's team. The Squad and the gang were now evenly matched in numbers but not, Hambrook suspected, in weapons. He began to wonder what luck they would have armed only with their truncheons 'against desperados who I knew would use lethal weapons as soon as we challenged them'. But he comforted himself with the thought that he had brought along his heavy walking stick.

A silversmith's shop in Victoria Street was given the once over by the gang and rejected, but the van stopped outside another shop in the Pimlico Road, where two or three of the men got out. One of them carrying a jemmy. Hambrook began 'deploying his men' whereupon the villains instantly took fright, rushed back to their van and took off at high speed. The Flying Squad gave chase in their old army lorry and 'got athwart the van' causing it to stop. Both vehicles emptied of their human cargo – the villains coming out armed with 'knuckle-dusters, loaded life-preservers and daggers' – and at that moment a thunderstorm broke out around them.

Hambrook used his stick 'to great advantage' but was laid low by a life preserver. Nevertheless, the police won the battle, the van was found to be laden with 'burglarious implements' and the suspects were charged with being in possession of these by night, with intent to break and enter premises. Three were identified as men who had struck down a PC with a jemmy a few nights before. 'These were the first arrests made by the new mobile force.' Hambrook's injuries, although not serious, prevented him from attending court that day, '... but it was a merry experience, and one I am proud to have had'. (He comes over as a bit of a gung-ho character, but his heart was in the right place. For example, he deplored the way some French and German police treated extradited prisoners when he handed them over, showing scant regard for their dignity or comfort).

Of course, the word quickly spread about these new, mobile police so the tenders went into disguise, with an assortment of number plates and advertising posters on the van sides. It was soon realized that just being mobile was not enough. What would be ideal was that long-sought-after combination of mobility and communication. Many experiments were going on with the idea of providing police with wireless links but operating them from a moving base proved particularly difficult. Large buildings and bridges screened the radio waves, there was heavy interference from the dynamos and magnetos of passing cars and similar problems from the electric trams. The earliest aerial blew the squad's cover good and proper, with its poles protruding from the roof of the van gaining it the nickname 'the bedstead'. The limits of technology at the time had shown wireless telephony to be impractical and it was replaced by wireless telegraphy which required an operator to sit in the van, tapping out Morse code. 'Then the day came when the Flying Squad turned out in brand new, private motors cars each provided with a wireless telegraph apparatus with no visible aerial, and the officers were delighted to exchange the darkness and discomfort of a covered van for the upholstered luxury of a fast private motor car.'

Other mushrooming post-war problems concerned the increasing in illegal gambling clubs, the use of cocaine, and the influx of wealthy visitors, eager to spend and see the sights so long denied them. In the wake of the rich and fashionable came hoards of confidence tricksters. Such was the problem that Detective Inspector Charles Leach was instructed to form a squad to combat them. He describes entering a cafe, famous at that time, and seeing twenty to thirty con men sitting at various tables around the room. (This was the lad who kept observation out in the cold, waiting to be fed when forgotten by his policeman father. Now he moved in elevated circles where silk top hat and tails were often part of his uniform.) Like many police officers, Leach seems to have become fascinated by con men whom he considered 'the aristocrats of crime'.

Few of them were Englishmen, he reveals, most being Australians or Americans, with a few Frenchmen and the odd Spaniard mixed in. All were well-travelled, elegant but not ostentatious, 'and fellows of infinite resource'. Had they not managed to ingratiate themselves with 'a mark' on the liner or train *en route*, they would haunt London sights and the lounges of the best hotels. Favourite guises were stockbroker, racehorse owner, retired cattle farmer or gold miner – or simply, gentlemen of leisure. Among themselves they were known only by apt nicknames such as Dictionary Harry, Dave the Liar, Cyclone Jarvis, The Indiana Wonder and Chicago Solly. Most of the deceptions centred around can't-lose bets, sure-thing investments and rigged card games, and one of the greatest difficulties for police was to get 'the mark' to charge once the offender had been caught. However outraged initially, most of those conned felt too embarrassed to let the world know how easily they had been duped.

While under the spell of the con man the victims could be so excited by the prospect of easy money that it was often difficult or even impossible to save them from themselves. One of Leach's team was Detective Inspector Percy J. Smith, who was later to write a book about the subject called, simply, *Con Men* in which he describes such a failure.

After seeing one of his American guests in company with a known 'trickster' called Davidson, a hotel manager alerted the local police who sent over two detectives. The con man was not present, only a quiet friend, when they had a chat with the American, warning him of the dangers of associating with Davidson. But their advice was far from welcome. The recipient resented the intrusion in his personal affairs and insisted he had not entered into any business deal with Davidson, nor had he drawn out any large sums of money recently.

What the detectives did not know was that, despite the fact that the American had vouched for the integrity of his companion, the quiet friend had only been acquired on the journey across the Atlantic and he, too, was a con man. Neither was it true that no withdrawals had been made. Five thousand pounds in notes were sitting in the pocket of the dupe while the detectives were talking to him. It was for investment in 'a sure thing' but discretion was vital. Some infinite resource came immediately into play when the quiet friend jumped to his feet, saying he thought 'the tecs' were impostors, most likely a gang trying to relieve them of their cash. He was going to make sure his was in a place of safety.

The pair hurriedly took a cab to Selfridges where the friend told the American to hold the taxi while he put his £10,000 into his safety deposit box. The now frightened dupe exclaimed, 'Here, put mine in as well.' The quiet friend went in the front door of Selfridges and straight out of the back. It was 'a sad and chastened man' who told Inspector Smith the story.

By the end of 1922, there were rumours that women might be brought into the CID. 'As can be imagined,' reports William Rawlings, who was then a detective constable, having managed to get into the CID in the record time, seven months, three weeks, 'there was a good deal of debate on the subject, most of us men ranging ourselves pretty solidly against the invasion of what we thought of as a purely masculine preserve. It didn't make any difference, naturally. The women of those days, full of the pioneering spirit, were determined and to oppose them at all was merely to fight a rearguard action' (*A Case for the Yard*).

An irritatingly glib statement of the type to which women have become accustomed. In the event, Lilian Wyles, the first woman detective in the Metropolitan Police, got into the branch by default and it was to be a very long time before she, or any woman, was allowed anything like equal status in the department.

After the Geddes cost-cutting axe fell in 1922, in addition to reducing the number of dogs and horses, the Metropolitan Police attempted to disband the small force of uniformed women admitted three years earlier – but not sworn in or given power of arrest and, thus easily deemed unsuccessful. But the women fought back. Lady Astor, one of the two new women MPs backed them, there was in-fighting too complex to describe here, and a scandal ensued. Finally, twenty women were kept, plus one to be attached to the CID, to take indecency statements. (Rawlings actually credits Louisa Pelling, who joined the Special Branch at this time, with being the first woman in the CID because Wyles had no detective duties as such.)

Lilian Wyles achieved her position partly at the expense of her woman colleagues, but her way was not to be easy. She had to put up with a great deal of rudeness and disdain before working her way into favour. A somewhat waspish woman, not free with her praises, she has nothing but good to say of Wensley, 'a diamond of the roughest kind ... with a heart of pure gold'. He had, she noticed, never really got over the loss of his beloved sons.

Wyles first came into contact with Wensley in 1923 when he sent a motor cycle to collect her and take her to Ilford Police Station. When she arrived, Wensley drew her to one side. 'I want you,' he said, 'to go to the room where Mrs Thompson is, for a short time. Listen to what she says. Don't say much yourself; keep to "yes" and "no".' He patted her arm and she crossed to the room where Mrs Thompson was waiting. A couple of nights earlier her husband had been stabbed to death in the street while walking home with her.

In her memoirs, *A Woman at Scotland Yard*, Lilian Wyles describes the state of Mrs Thompson:

She was agitated and excited, keeping on pacing the room and gazing from the window. She wanted to know why she must stay in that room, and in the station; why could she not go home? As she looked from the window which overlooked the station yard she had a clear view of the side door of the station, and the door of the CID office ... Then she turned impatiently from the window, so did not see issuing from the station a group of men, the D.D.I., two sergeants, and another young man who was a stranger to me. They walked slowly by the window where Mrs Thompson had been standing. Later, she was to get a glimpse of that young man. Then her hand flew to her mouth, there was a slight scream, and Mrs Thompson moaned: 'Not that, not that! No! No! Why did he do it? Oh, God!'

The strange young man was Bywaters and her outburst would help to hang them both.

Later in that decade, policemen began to see the wisdom of having more women officers around – for their own protection against allegations of intimidation, or worse, when handling female witnesses and defendants.

Things had come to a head with the Savidge Affair – and Wyles' involvement in it. Chief Inspector Collins, a brilliant detective but very much of the old school, had been sent to collect Miss Savidge for questioning about an alleged indecency offence with a man of some substance. Under instructions from Wensley he was obliged to take Lilian Wyles along with him, but treated her with his customary arrogance. During the questioning which followed he had turfed her out of the interview room, and later tried to browbeat her into making a statement at his dictation exonerating him of patronizing and bullying Miss Savidge. But Wyles turned on him – and he crumbled. In the event, she not only saved him by telling lies but was called upon to nurse him through the enquiry. After that, not only was Wyles accepted by CID officers but never again would Collins (or most other male officers) attempt to question a woman suspect without a woman police officer being present.

It would be nice to say that the place of women in the CID was then assured but, in reality, it was only in this role of protecting the male officer and dealing with female offences the men did not fancy handling. A few more women filtered into the branch during the next decade (three women detective constables joined C division CID in 1932) but even by 1945, Wyles had only sixteen woman detectives under her control, each new appointment 'a struggle to achieve'. Of course, just how hard she fought is difficult to say, she does give the impression of being a bit of a Queen Bee, enjoying her role of sole confidante and mother confessor to male officers.

By the 1930s it was obvious that the CID were again failing to keep up with the times, and there were worries about corruption and a lack of co-operation with the uniform branch. Obviously, what was needed, yet again, was a committee. It was convened in 1933, sat for five years, and produced a five volume, 500-page report. This was, as police historian T.A. Critchley pointed out, 'of the greatest value, scrapping most of that which had gone before and laying the foundations of all that followed.

Principal Sources

Public Record Office
Case records, administrative and miscellaneous files and personnel
registers in the Metropolitan Police and Home Office series

Metropolitan Police Museum and Metropolitan Police Library
Police Orders, Commissioners Annual Reports, Parliamentary,
Home Office Committee Reports, *Police Gazette*, Personnel
Registers, Miscellaneous material

British Newspaper Library
Numerous national and local newspapers and magazines
Police Review and Parade Gossip
Police Guardian

Select Bibliography

Abberline, Frederick, *Annotated Press Cuttings Book* (unpublished, Metropolitan Police Museum)

Anderson, Sir Robert, *The Lighter Side of My Official Life* (Hodder, 1910)

Arrow, Charles, *Rogues and Others* (Duckworth, 1926)

Begg, Paul, and Skinner, Keith, *The Scotland Yard Files: 150 Years of the CID* (Headline, 1992)

Brown, Bernard, *History of Metropolitan Police Divisions: The Job* (Metropolitan Police Newspaper, 1987–8)

Browne, Douglas G., *The Rise of Scotland Yard* (Harrap, 1956)

Bunker, John, *From Rattle to Radio* (K A F Brewin Books, 1988)

Carlin, Francis, *Reminiscences of an Ex-Detective*, 3rd ed. (Hutchinson)

Caron, Henri Le, *Twenty-Five Years in the Secret Service* (William Heinemann, 1893)

Cavanagh, T.A., *Scotland Yard Past and Present Experiences of Thirty-Seven Years by Ex-Chief Inspector Cavanagh* (Chatto & Windus, 1893)

Cherrill, Fred, *Cherill of the Yard* (The Popular Book Club, 1955)

Cobb, Belton, *Critical Years at the Yard: The Career of Frederick Williamson of the Detective Department and the CID* (Faber, 1956)

Critchley, T.A., *A History of Police in England and Wales* (Constable, 1979)

Dew, Walter, *I Caught Crippen, Memoirs of Ex-Chief Inspector Walter Dew CID Scotland Yard* (Blackie, 1938)

Dilnot, George, *The Trial of the Detectives* (Geoffrey Bles, 1928)

Divall, Tom, *Scoundrels and Scallywags (And Some Honest Men)* (Benn, 1929)

Drahms, August, *The Criminal* (Macmillan, 1900)

Elliott, Douglas J., *Policing Shropshire 1836-1967* (K.A.F. Brewin Books, 1984)

Fanning, Arthur S.P.S., 'Training the Metropolitan Policeman: A Historical Survey from 1829–1910' (The Metropolitan Police Training School Magazine, 1963)

Gaute J.H.H. & Odell, Robin, Murder Whereabouts (Harrap, 1986)

Greenham, G.H., Scotland Yard Experiences from The Diary of G H Greenham, Late Chief Inspector, Criminal Investigation Department, Scotland Yard (George Routledge, 1904)

Griffiths, Major Arthur, Mysteries of Police and Crime (Cassell, 1898)

Hambrook, Walter, Hambrook of the Yard (Robert Hale, 1937)

Heyes S.H., (concluded by F.D. How), The Life of Sir Howard Vincent (George Allen, 1912)

Kingston, Charles, The Bench and the Dock (Stanley Paul, 1925)

Lambourne, Gerald, The Fingerprint Story (Harrap, 1984)

Lansdowne, Andrew, A Life's Reminiscences of Scotland Yard, Detective-Inspector Late of the Criminal Investigation Department, Metropolitan Police. In One-and-Twenty Docket (Leadenhall Press, 1890)

Leach, Charles E, On Top of the Underworld, The Personal Reminiscences of Ex Divisional Detective Inspector Charles E Leach, Late of New Scotland Yard (Sampson Lowe, Marston, 1933)

Littlechild, John George, Reminiscences of Chief Inspector Littlechild, (Leadenhall Press, 1894)

Lock, Joan, Blue Murder (Robert Hale, 1986)

—— Dreadful Deeds and Awful Murders: Scotland Yard's First Detectives 1829–1878 (Barn Owl Books, 1990)

—— Marlborough Street: The Story of a London Court (Robert Hale, 1980)

—— Tales from Bow Street (Hale, 1982)

—— The British Policewoman: Her Story (Hale, 1979)

Mayhew, Henry, Mayhew's London, Being Selections from 'London Labour and the London Poor', 1861 (Abridged edition, edited by Peter Quennell) (Hamlyn, 1969)

Macnaghten, Melville L., Days of My Years (Edward Arnold, 1915)

Moore-Anderson, A.P. The Life of Sir Robert Anderson KCB LL D and Lady Agnes Anderson (Marshall, Morgan and Scott, 1947)

Moser, Maurice, Stories from Scotland Yard, told by Inspector

Moser, Late of the Criminal Investigation Department, Whitehall and recorded by Charles F. Rideal (George Routledge, 1890)

Petrie, Glen, *A Singular Iniquity: The Campaigns of Josephine Butler*, (Macmillan, 1971)

Quail, John, *The Slow Burning Fuse: The Lost History of the British Anarchists* (Granada, 1978)

Rawlings, William, *A Case for the Yard, Ex-Deputy Commander William Rawlings OBE MC* (John Long, 1961)

Rosie, Ex-Chief Inspector, '*I Watched the Underworld*' (*People's Journal*, 1938–39)

Smith, Henry, *From Constable to Commissioner, The Story of Sixty Years Most of them Misspent by Lieut-Col. Sir Henry Smith KCB* (Chatto & Windus, 1910)

Smith, Percy J., *Con Man. The Personal Reminiscences of Ex-Detective Inspector Percy J. Smith (Late of Scotland Yard)* (Herbert Jenkins, 1938)

Sweeney, John, *At Scotland Yard, Being the Experiences during Twenty-Seven Years' Service of John Sweeney Late Detective Inspector, Criminal Investigation Department, New Scotland Yard* (Grant Edwards, 1904)

Thomson, Basil, *Queer People* (Hodder & Stoughton, 1922)

Wensley, Frederick Porter, *Detective Days, The Record of Forty-Two Years' Service in the Criminal Investigation Department* (Cassell, 1931)

Wilson, Colin, & Pitman, Patricia, *Encyclopaedia of Murder* (Pan, 1984)

Wyles, Lillian, *A Woman at Scotland Yard* (Faber, 1951)

Young, Filson Ed., *The Trial of Hawley Harvey Crippen* (William Hodge, 1920)

Index

Abberline, Insp. Frederick G., 116–19, 121–4, 127, 133, 176, 194
Abrahams, Mr, 76
Alexander II, Tsar, 72
Alfred, Prince, 72
Allday, Sgt., 87
Alt, Henry, 123–5
Andrews, Insp. Walter, 133
Andrews, Sgt., 74
Anderson, Sir Robert, 43, 134, 160, 167
Anthropometrics, 147–51, 168–9, 170
Annual Register, 91
Armstrong, Eliza, 131
Arnold, Supt. Thomas, 122
Arrow, Ch. Insp. Charles, 151–2, 189–90
Arrow, Mrs Charles, 152
Ashley, Insp. John, 195, 197
Astor, Lady, 207

Baby Farming, 53–9, 71
Backhouse, Mr R.O., 29–31
Balcombe Tunnel Murder, 100–6
Balfour, Jabez, 155–6, 160–3
Barker, William, 26
Bartlett, Adelaide, 138
Bastendorff, Mr Severin, 96–7
Beach, Thomas Billis, *see* Caron, Henri Le
Beck, Adolph, 164, 189
Beer, Mr & Mrs, 58
Beer, Jessie, 58–9
Begg, Paul, 187
Benson, Harry, 72, 75–6

Bernard, Dr, 60
Beron, Leon, 188
Bertillon, Alphonse, 148, 150
Besley, Mr E.E.T., 166
Bleak House, 69
Bond, Ch. Cons. Major, 74
Booth, Bramwell, 131
Bouillon, Mme, 64
Bradshaw, John William, 44–5
Bramwell, Judge Baron, 50
Branagan, Michael, 165–6
Bravo, Charles, 72–5, 80
Bravo, Florence, 73–5
Brett, Detective, 165
Brewer, Mr, 102–3
Brown, Ann, 44, 68
Brown, Hannah, 146
Brown, Mary, 44
Brown, Mr, 58
Browne, Douglas, 142
Bucket, Insp., 69, 127
Buckle, Revd, 164
Bulow, Baron, 80
Burdett, Charles, 118
Burke, Capt., 35
Burke, Thomas, 110
Burton (Fenian), 123
Buswell, Harriet, 79
Butcher, Sgt., 63, 66
Butcher, Insp., 165
Butler, Josephine, 129–30
Bywaters, Frederick, 208

Carlin, Supt., Francis, 201
Caron, Henri Le, (Thomas Billis Beach), 110, 134
Casey, 35

217